History in Times of Unprecedented Change

Also Published by Bloomsbury

Published

Historical Teleologies in the Modern World (2015), Edited by Henning Trüper, Dipesh Chakrabarty and Sanjay Subrahmanyam

Philosophy of History After Hayden White (2015), Robert Doran

R. G. Collingwood: A Research Companion (2016), James Connelly, Peter Johnson and Stephen Leach

Full History: On the Meaningfulness of Shared Action (2016), Steven G. Smith

The Concept of History (2017), Dmitri Nikulin

A Short History of Western Ideology (2018), Rolf Petri

Debating New Approaches to History (2018), Edited by Marek Tamm and Peter Burke

Theories of History: History Read across the Humanities (2018), Edited by Michael J. Kelly, Arthur Rose

Forthcoming

Rethinking Historical Time, Edited by Marek Tamm and Laurent Olivier

Historicism: A Travelling Concept, Edited by Hermann Paul and Adriaan van Veldhuizen

History in Times of Unprecedented Change

A Theory for the 21st Century

Zoltán Boldizsár Simon

BLOOMSBURY ACADEMIC
LONDON • NEW YORK • OXFORD • NEW DELHI • SYDNEY

BLOOMSBURY ACADEMIC
Bloomsbury Publishing Plc
50 Bedford Square, London, WC1B 3DP, UK
1385 Broadway, New York, NY 10018, USA

BLOOMSBURY, BLOOMSBURY ACADEMIC and the Diana logo
are trademarks of Bloomsbury Publishing Plc

First published in Great Britain 2019
This paperback edition published in 2021

Copyright © Zoltán Boldizsár Simon, 2019

Zoltán Boldizsár Simon has asserted his right under the Copyright,
Designs and Patents Act, 1988, to be identified as Author of this work.

For legal purposes the Acknowledgements on p. xii constitute
an extension of this copyright page.

Cover image: Atomic bomb symbolic montage.
(© H. Armstrong Roberts/ClassicStock/Getty Images)

All rights reserved. No part of this publication may be reproduced or transmitted
in any form or by any means, electronic or mechanical, including photocopying,
recording, or any information storage or retrieval system, without prior
permission in writing from the publishers.

Bloomsbury Publishing Plc does not have any control over, or responsibility for,
any third-party websites referred to or in this book. All internet addresses given
in this book were correct at the time of going to press. The author and publisher
regret any inconvenience caused if addresses have changed or sites have ceased
to exist, but can accept no responsibility for any such changes.

A catalogue record for this book is available from the British Library.

A catalog record for this book is available from the Library of Congress.

ISBN: HB: 978-1-3500-9505-2
PB: 978-1-3501-9272-0
ePDF: 978-1-3500-9506-9
eBook: 978-1-3500-9507-6

Typeset by Integra Software Services Pvt. Ltd.

To find out more about our authors and books visit www.bloomsbury.com
and sign up for our newsletters.

Contents

Preface: On Novelty	vii
Acknowledgements	xii
Living in Times of Unprecedented Change: A Prologue	1
Postwar historical sensibility	1
The prospect of unprecedented change	7
The unprecedented in retrospect: A dissociative relation to the past	11
The inadequacy of narrative philosophy of history	16
(No more) narrative domestication of the new	20
What about narrative in times of the unprecedented?	23
The outline of the book	27
Part One On Historical Change	33
1 A Quasi-Substantive Philosophy of History	39
Talking quasi	39
Substantive days and quasi-times	41
History moves again	46
The return of the future	50
History as a disrupted singular	55
The lingering threat of substantive thinking	57
2 The Dissociated Past	61
Whose past?	61
Neither the practical nor the historical past	63
Not even the presence of the past	69
Our apophatic past	74
Essentially contested historical knowledge	76
3 The Unprecedented Future	79
History and the future	79
The triad of cataclysm	80
Utopian thought	88
Posthistorical dystopia and negative utopia	93

Posthistorical dystopia and eschatology	97
The temporality of the singular event	101

Part Two On Historiographical Change — 105

4 The Expression of Historical Experience — 109
- Blasphemous rumours — 109
- The unnameable expression — 112
- Our everyday notion of expression — 114
- Naming experience as the expressed — 115
- The expression of historical experience — 119
- How the trick is done — 123

5 Encountering the World — 127
- What about truth and falsity? — 127
- A phenomenology of historical studies — 132
- Encountering the world, encountering the past — 134
- (Realist irrealism, irrealist realism) — 138
- Doesn't look like anything to me — 139
- The aesthetic moment — 143
- From non-sense to sense — 146

6 The Step toward Historical Sense-Making — 151
- On the difference between experience and experientiality — 151
- The approval of a demand — 159
- The present approval of a demand of the future about the past — 161
- Making sense of non-sense historically — 164
- Historical and historiographical change — 167
- A summary — 169

The Unprecedented and the Crisis of the Political: An Epilogue — 173
- An evental historical sensibility — 173
- The emancipation dilemma and political change — 175
- The unprecedented and the crisis of the political — 179
- The future of the political — 183
- Is this still history? — 188

Bibliography — 191
Index — 203

Preface: On Novelty

Contrary to common belief, history is not concerned with the past. It is all about novelty. History's primary concern is not what is considered to be old but that which looms on the horizon and which, in the present, is conceived of as new and different from whatever has been before. This also means that history is not only a matter of a perceived difference between past and present, a theme Zachary Schiffman meticulously explored in *The Birth of the Past* (2011). Above all, history is a matter of an anticipated difference between present and past on the one hand, and whatever the state of affairs may be in the future on the other. The sheer existence of history – both as a wider sensibility and as a discipline – is due to this openness to future change, to the prospect of difference, because it is only insofar as the future appears as open to change that the past can look different and, thus, 'historical' in the first place.

But the prospect of difference is not without further complications. The possibility of change taking place in the future entails a sense of unfamiliarity with the perceived novelty that is coming, a novelty that has to be made sense of and has to be familiarized. Therein lies the all-important function of history as we know it: the modern Western historical sensibility renders expected future (and experienced present) novelty familiar by telling you that whatever appears as novelty is actually old, in the sense that it is only the latest stage of a longer process. The modern Western concept of history tells you that the yet unknown is just a newer version of something we already know, that the new is nothing other than a more timely and developed shape of a past potential. In other words, although history as we know it certainly entails looking at the past and at whatever is perceived as old, this happens in order to cope with the future and whatever is perceived as new.

The immediate reaction to this claim – not only from the majority of professional historians but from everyone invoking the modern historical sensibility as described above – of course, would be to point out that even this is nothing new. A prompt and automatic riposte to confronting the claim that history is a conceptual strategy to cope with newness would be that neither the question of novelty nor the question of modern history's engagement with newness and the future is new. As to the former one concerning the novelty of novelty, Michael North argues that newness is not simply not new but, in fact, is practically as old as human concerns can be. In writing a history of novelty,

North ends up claiming that 'perhaps the most basic conclusion to be drawn from a history of the new is that it has had a history at all – that novelty is not just a modern concern but a timeless problem' (2013: 203).

Then, as to the question of the novelty of asserting history's concern for newness and the future, a quick invocation of Karl Löwith would, again, result in downplaying its newness. In the middle of the last century, in mapping the characteristics of the enterprise of philosophy of history, Löwith was already making the rather strong claim that 'the future is the "true" focus of history' (1957: 18). By this claim, however, Löwith did not intend to depict the modern notion of history as I do. He did not think of history as a kind of intellectual tool Western modernity put to use in order to cope with novelty. Löwith was more concerned with the future as the focus of history in the sense of history 'determined by an eschatological motivation', more concerned with a 'vision of an ultimate end, as both *finis* and *telos*', which 'provides a scheme of progressive order and meaning' with an 'eschatological compass' that 'gives orientation in time' (18).

Although Löwith's claim about the future as the focus of history works in a completely different register, it brings to light a crucial aspect concerning the way in which novelty, the future and the modern notion of history are interrelated. The crucial aspect in question is that of *orientation in time in terms of directionality*. The directional orientation of the modern idea of history may not necessarily be eschatological (as Löwith's much debated thesis holds) but it is necessarily a directionality toward the *future*. What's more, as soon as such directionality binds the past and the future together in a temporal continuum, the future appears as the necessary extension and expansion of the past, which opens up the possibility of actively working toward the postulated future. Yet this directional orientation toward the future and the postulated future itself can appear as desirable only insofar as the novelty it promises is already seen in a familiar light. Being smoothed into a historical process, tamed novelty appears as the future that the past has already pointed towards.

What this means is that such orientation toward the future has been possible in the modern period precisely because of history's simultaneous efforts to familiarize the very novelty in question. The two operations, I think, constitute two sides of the same coin regarding history's engagement with novelty. To define this engagement as the central contention of the further investigations of this book, I wish to offer the following description: *the modern idea of history is an intellectual tool Western modernity put into use to appropriate and thereby also to enable perceived novelty, on the one hand, and to work toward the achievement of this very novelty which – once being appropriated – could appear as a desired future state of human affairs, on the other.*

This idea of history, which I intend to examine in this book, is a Western invention. To avoid any misunderstandings, I would like to make clear from the outset that whenever I mention 'history' I mean a Western product of the late Enlightenment, both as a concept that encompasses past, present and future into a temporal whole as a course of human affairs, and as the institutionalized and professionalized practice of historiography. Most of the time, however, I will use the phrase 'historical sensibility'. By this I mean the way in which, since the invention of the modern notion of history, we conceive of ourselves and the world as 'historical'. By this, in turn, I mean the way we conceive of ourselves and the world as changing over time, the way we render such change over time familiar and meaningful by putting past, present and future states of affairs in relation to each other, and also the way we integrate singular events and occurrences into this larger and meaningful temporal unit.

This being clarified, I also need to say a few words about the recurring question of the 'we' invoked here. Because 'we' is still probably the only way to conveniently address questions that may concern more than the first person singular, throughout this book I will use 'we' whenever I mean more people than myself. The limits of the extension of this 'we' that I would consider to be apt are rather obviously marked by the aforementioned understanding of 'history' as a Western invention. All other qualifications will appear when necessary during the more detailed discussions in the relevant chapters.

What these qualifications indicate is that the 'history' that interests me has existed ever since the future was conceived of as the promise of novelty. Not just any novelty, though, but *novelty as a possibility in the realm of human affairs in the mundane world*. This is precisely the innovation that was introduced by the modern notion of history, overlooked by Löwith's interpretation of (philosophy of) history as secularized eschatology. The modern notion of history enables change over time in human affairs that does not come as a matter and result of a supernatural intervention. Accordingly, instead of granting altered conditions in a promised otherworldly setting, historical change appears as a matter and result of human efforts (unintended or deliberate) in the earthly human world. This view of modern history is, I believe, in accordance with Reinhart Koselleck's semantic approach to historical concepts (with a focus on the German context). Koselleck, in touching upon the question of novelty, said that around the second half of the eighteenth century 'the divide between previous experience and coming expectation opened up, and the difference between past and present increased, so that lived time was experienced as a rupture, as a period of transition, in which the new and unexpected continually happened' (2004: 246). It is since then that the continuous occurrence of perceived newness has been familiarized and appropriated by the freshly invented conceptual tool 'history' on the one hand, and it is since then that it is possible to act upon the promised future of the very same 'history' on the other.

In light of all this, perhaps it does not seem preposterous to claim that making the new appear as a constituent and integral part of a larger trajectory – as part of a historical process – could very well be the most significant invention of modernity. Or, in a more modest version of this claim, history can be considered at least as one of the most significant of such conceptual inventions. In either versions, the claim is very close to the view Hannah Arendt advocated more than half a century ago, namely, that 'the modern concept of process pervading history and nature alike separates the modern age from the past more profoundly than any other single idea' (1961: 63). But the birth of this modern concept of history seems to have occurred earlier for Arendt than for Koselleck. Whereas Koselleck (2004) traces a monumental shift of heavily interrelated conceptual changes between 1750 and 1850, in Arendt's view the modern concept of history 'arose in the same sixteenth and seventeenth centuries which ushered in the gigantic development of the natural sciences' (1961: 53). Nevertheless, the chronological disagreement between Koselleck and Arendt is resolved by Arendt's remark concerning the time when such a modern processual historical sensibility came into effect. As it stands, Arendt eventually makes clear that 'the great impact of the notion of history upon the consciousness of the modern age came relatively late, not before the last third of the eighteenth century' (68).

The chronology implied by Arendt and Koselleck, as well as the emphasis on the radical innovative potential they both assign to the modern concept of history, form the background of the work I wish to carry out in this book. However, it is only its background, and not its focus, since the modern historical sensibility is not where my genuine interest lies. What interests me most, rather, is the question of how we make sense of novelty today, which I believe is fundamentally different from how the modern notion of history operates. The modern notion is the background against which I wish to conceptualize whatever we mean by 'history' today. Accordingly, the questions I attempt to answer are the following: *What does it mean to conceive of ourselves and the world 'historically' at the beginning of the twenty-first century?* How do we conceive of historical change today? And how does the changing conception of historical change relate to the way we conceive of change in historiography (the scholarly practice that accounts for historical change)?

The central theme of the coming pages is that today, since at least the middle of the last century, the Western world entertains future scenarios, configures change over time, and conceives of novelty in various domains of human life in a way that is itself new. Inquiring into such novel conception of novelty amounts to inquiring into whatever we mean by history and whatever historical sensibility we may have today, as the previous pages attest. Whatever we mean by 'history' is itself prone to change. If the way we perceive novelty and change in human affairs changes, it means that our historical sensibility, the way we conceive of ourselves and the world as changing over time, itself changes. I can only agree with Eelco Runia that 'it is about time to focus on how, in history as well as in historiography [...] the new comes about' (2014: xiii). As the coming chapters will show, I may not fully agree with Runia on the question of how to conceptualize the coming about of the new but I most certainly think that exploring the question of novelty, and especially an emerging sense of novelty, is the primary task today.

To foreshadow the contours of this novel sense of novelty, history and 'historical sensibility' as opposed to the modern one, I would again like to cite Koselleck on how, in the late eighteenth century, 'the divide between previous experience and coming expectation opened up, and the difference between past and present increased, so that lived time was experienced as a rupture, as a period of transition, in which the new and unexpected continually happened' (2004: 246). As accurate as this description may be concerning the late eighteenth and the nineteenth centuries, much has changed since then. The lived time as a rupture that Koselleck talks about and the increasing difference between past and present gave way to a novel sense of novelty in certain domains of life in Western societies. The past no longer looks merely different from the present and the future; past and future look now increasingly *disconnected*. Lived time does not merely appear as a rupture that could be familiarized by the operation of the modern concept of history. Lived time, I think, appears today as the time of the unprecedented, the recognized rupture that can no longer be smoothed into a deep continuity. Present-day Western societies, I believe, live in times of unprecedented change. This book is an effort to come to terms with such a novel configuration of lived time as unprecedented change by conceptualizing it as an emerging historical sensibility.

Acknowledgements

Diverse exchanges contributed in various ways to the endeavour that resulted in this book. My gratitude is multifarious, and I wish it was possible to express it accordingly by crediting everyone who inspired, influenced and shaped this undertaking in one way or another – sometimes without even knowing it. Among those that I can mention, I would like to thank István M. Szijártó for his long-standing support, without which I may have never pursued any academic project in the first place. I am especially thankful to Johannes Grave and Kalle Pihlainen for their sustained engagement with and constant support for this book, which they supervised in an earlier version as my PhD project.

Since the beginning of this project, I had the opportunity to present and discuss its core ideas at many conferences and workshops with numerous colleagues, regularly turning formal events into occasions of informal discussions that always prove to be more profound. For such informal conversations over the last few years that shaped my endeavour I am indebted to Jouni-Matti Kuukkanen, Eugen Zelenak, María Inés La Greca, Valdei Araujo, Andre de Lemos Freixo, Delia Popa, Marek Tamm, Chris Lorenz and Keith Jenkins. For their formal and informal co-operation – culminating in two workshops held in Bielefeld (2015 and 2017) and in my three-month stay at Ghent University (2016) – and for the continuing exchange of ideas I thank the team of the International Network for Theory of History, especially Anton Froeyman, Berber Bevernage, Katie Digan, Egon Bauwelinck, Kenan Van De Mieroop and Broos Delanote.

I am greatly indebted to many of my wonderful colleagues temporarily or permanently residing in Bielefeld at different stages of their career. I thank Dorothee Wilm, Thomas Welskopp, Lili Zhu, Natalia Zakharchenko, Marius Meinhof, Rodrigo Marttie, Jana Hoffmann, Oleksandra Tarkhanova, Stefan Laffin, Frank Leitenberger, Martina Kessel, Mahshid Mayar, Cleovi Mosuela, Christian Vogel, Lars Deile and Cosmin Minnea.

Finally, I am grateful for the most engaged work of Beatriz Lopez at Bloomsbury with the manuscript and the entire book project, and to Dan Hutchins who took over the project at the production stage. My gratitude is of course extended to the reviewers of the initial book proposal and the final manuscript for their comments concerning the potential ways in which the arguments of this book could be strengthened. I also thank the journals

Rethinking History and *History and Theory* for granting permission to reprint the following articles. Paragraphs and sections of Chapter 1 and Chapter 2 appeared earlier in 'We Are History: The Outlines of a Quasi-Substantive Philosophy of History,' *Rethinking History* 20 (2) (2016): 269–279. Chapter 4 was published in a close to identical version as 'The Expression of Historical Experience,' *History and Theory*, 54 (2) (May 2015): 178–194. Copyright © 2015 Wesleyan University. Reprinted with permission.

Living in Times of Unprecedented Change: A Prologue

Postwar historical sensibility

The premise of this book is embarrassingly simple. It states that the modern historical sensibility – the one that makes sense of the world and human beings in terms of developmental processes – has been radically challenged by another one that has increasingly come to prominence since the early postwar years. Yet this emerging postwar historical sensibility has not been explicitly addressed, explicated and conceptualized as such in a coherent theoretical manner. Accordingly, the challenge that I wish to respond to seems just as embarrassingly simple as the premise of this book: to gain an understanding of the altered historical condition of Western societies by articulating and conceptualizing it in the shape of a more or less comprehensive theoretical account.

Recently, theories of presentism have come nearest to such an endeavour. Together with philosophies of history, they are the closest associates of this book. The idea of presentism was developed by François Hartog (2015, first published in French in 2003) and advocated shortly afterwards by Aleida Assmann (2013) and Hans Ulrich Gumbrecht (2014). What these theories understand as presentism, nevertheless, is not what most historians mean when referring to the term. Whereas the common understanding of presentism is the interpretation of the past in light of the values of the present, the idea of Hartog (2015) is a neologism that concerns a specific way the past, the present and the future are conceived of as hanging together. Hartog coins the analytical category 'regimes of historicity' in order to examine the various ways the internal relation of past, present and future are configured. Or, to phrase it differently, the category is designed to enable the investigation of the potential organizational structures imposed on experiences of time. In Hartog's view, one of the triad of past, present and future tends to dominate the other two in different arrangements. In a wonderfully original and strong thesis – which I believe is the heart of theoretical work regardless of questions of agreement and disagreement – Hartog claims that a future-oriented regime of historicity of the modern world has been giving way to one that focuses on the present. Assmann and Gumbrecht share this view inasmuch as they claim with Hartog that the present point of view became, so to speak, omnipresent after the Cold War, when the future ceased to structure historical time.

Theories of presentism attest to a shared sense that something is going on with the way Western societies conceive of themselves historically. Gumbrecht even claims that 'the ways the horizons of the future and the past are experienced and connect with an ever broader present give form to the as yet unnamed chronotope within which globalized life in the early twenty-first century occurs' (2014: 73). Talking about such a new chronotope, as well as talking about a new 'regime of historicity', most certainly connects with the aforementioned task I wish to carry out. At the same time, as much as I admire the originality and the intellectual scope of the scholarship behind theories of presentism, the cultural criticism according to which Western societies witness the extension of the present – its terms and concerns – over the past and the future, and thus lose track of expecting change in the future, is fundamentally at odds with the main contentions of this book.

I will address disagreements in more detail shortly. At this point it seems more fundamental to introduce the second close associate, having been around much longer than theories of presentism and making the undertaking of the coming pages look just as suspicious as simple. For conceptualizing an emerging historical condition and a novel historical sensibility may resemble the work of modern philosophies of history of the Enlightenment and the nineteenth century. In attempting to understand their own times, these philosophies of history invented the modern notion of history as a conceptual tool to gain such an understanding. It might sound like I am attempting to do something similar with respect to a broadly construed postwar period, stretching from the mid-1940s to today.

But has the entire enterprise of the philosophy of history (history understood as the course of affairs) not been abandoned precisely during this period? Yes, it certainly has. Has it not been abandoned for good reasons? Yes, it has been abandoned for excellent reasons. Nevertheless, the reasons for continuing to theorize or philosophize about history are just as good, and nothing compels anyone to do so in the same way modern philosophies of history do. This would even contradict the task of conceptualizing an emerging postwar historical sensibility. Simply returning to the abandoned enterprise of modern philosophy of history with its conceptual tools and resources would only mean a return to the modern historical sensibility invented by those very conceptual tools and resources.

The task requires a theory and philosophy of history with qualities other than those of the modern one. Yet, however differently such an endeavour may proceed, it cannot but define itself in relation to that which it wishes to supersede. Hence the exposition of what constitutes the core and significance of this book must begin by sketching how it relates to the modern philosophy of history. This significance, I think, has already become visible as the price Western societies had to pay for the abandonment of those philosophies of history. Unfortunately, it is hardly ever mentioned that this abandonment left Western societies without a concept of history, that is, without a theoretical-conceptual account regarding change and novelty in human affairs. Furthermore, the abandonment did not merely leave Western societies without a feasible account about how change in human affairs takes place; it also left these societies without the possibility of change.

The reason for this lies in the operative function of abandoned philosophies of history, mentioned earlier, namely, the conceptualization of change over time in human affairs by seeing the past, the present and the future together *as* history. As they opened up the future, as they postulated a future different from the past and present and, nevertheless, saw that different future together with the past and the present as constituting a *course*, philosophies of history created the possibility of change in the human world that is supposed to take place within and as history. Given that the modern concept of history, the possibility of change and a vision of the future (different from the actual and past state of affairs) are closely tied to each other in this way, abandoning the concept of history might easily mean abandoning too much. As a necessary (and deeply unrecognized) entailment, it means abandoning the possibility of change and the idea of a better future too.

It is not just an accident that the postwar abandonment of the idea of history resulted in the emergence of two main intellectual themes, both intended to describe our 'historical' conduct since the fall of the Berlin Wall and the collapse of the Soviet Union. The first is the idea of 'the end of history' as the arrival of the idea of liberal democracy. Francis Fukuyama's *The End of History* (1992), in arguing that the idea of liberal democracy cannot be improved upon, abandons history by fully engaging with it and claiming that it has already come to its ultimate fulfilment. As a potential fulfilment, however, it means nothing other than the denial of the possibility of further change. Because if we actually were at the end of history, it would mean that no further change can take place. Fukuyama claims precisely this, although with the important qualification that this does not mean that no minor change whatsoever will even happen, but the 'ideal of liberal democracy could not be improved on' (1992: ix). In other words, Fukuyama's thesis concerns large-scale historical change as a developmental improvement on the human condition, and it relies on the very idea of history to which it claims to put an end.

The second main theme is the idea that our age is best described as presentist. As mentioned earlier, theories of presentism also represent one of the two closest connections of this book's endeavour in mapping the changing configurations of past, present and future. Yet, all affiliation aside concerning the nature of the inquiry, the idea that the currently reigning regime of historicity is a presentist one seems questionable to a crucial extent. To begin with, it shares with Fukuyama's 'end of history' theme the deep conviction that future change as large-scale historical change can no longer take place. Not because the modern idea of history is finally fulfilled, as in Fukuyama, but because it is no longer in effect. Hartog claims that the modern future-oriented idea of history has been overtaken by another regime of historicity characterized by a 'crisis of the future', which 'unsettled the idea of progress and produced a sense of foreboding that cast a shadow over our present' (2015: 196). Although Hartog's main focus lies in the altered relationship to the past in terms of an emerging memory culture and reigning discourses of heritage and debts to the past, the 'foreboding' he refers to concerns visions of the future. Hartog claims these visions are structured around a 'precautionary principle' that produces another sense of indebtedness (not to the past but to the future) to regulate and mitigate threatening environmental and technological risks (198). Accordingly, presentism rules due to a dual indebtedness that merely extends the present both to the past and to the future.

The problematic aspect of such a diagnosis is its sole focus on the sociopolitical domain. I believe that the cultural diagnosis of presentism does not do justice to the visions of the future in the technological and ecological domains (in artificial intelligence, transhumanism, biotechnology, human-induced environmental change, biodiversity loss, the Anthropocene debate, and so on) as future expectations. It does not engage with them as visions of the future in their own right but only as correlates of the sociopolitical domain that demand precautions. In doing so, theories of presentism conceive of such visions in terms of the very agenda set by the modern future-oriented concept of history that aimed at sociopolitical betterment of the human condition. Contrary to this, my approach in this book is designed to make sense of the historical sensibility – of the vision of change over time – that underlies the technological and ecological domains, and it attempts to investigate their relationship to the sociopolitical domain not merely in light of the agendas of the latter. What we need to understand today is the emerging historical sensibility in those domains, and *what we need to conceptualize is the way in which those domains, in their own right, conceive of change over time.*

We can attempt to raise the most crucial sociopolitical concerns and their transformation only when such an understanding is achieved, only when the underlying historical sensibility of the technological and the ecological domains is conceptualized as a rival historical sensibility (and that is, as you will see, anything but presentist). This is what I wish to do in the coming six chapters and the Epilogue.

But let me dwell on the issue of presentism a bit more by asking the question: what sort of 'historicity' would not entail change? It is not hard to see how the question hints at an unintelligible situation. For if we were truly presentist, we could not even have a future postulated as different from the present. And if we did not expect such a future to take place in one way or another (as the technological and ecological domains pretty much do expect those changes), and if we were truly living in a 'world so enslaved to the present that no other viewpoint is considered admissible' (Hartog 2015: xiii), then change over time in human affairs would be impossible. And not having a sense of such change would mean precisely that we had no sense of 'historicity' and no historical sensibility at all. If we were truly presentist, what we would have would be a 'regime of ahistoricity', a time regime of eternal changelessness (much like Fukuyama's 'end of history' as fulfilment).

Yet, just because the idea of a presentist 'regime of historicity' is terminologically questionable, it does not mean that the cultural analysis of presentism is not right to one extent or another. Thus the question to ask is whether this really is the case. Do we really lack visions of the future we consider *plausible*? Are we really presentist, are we at the end of history, are we left without any sort of historical sensibility both in visions of the future and in relation to the past? Have we really ceased to conceive of ourselves and the world as 'historical' in terms of changing over time on a large scale? Well, I don't think so. We have undeniably grown sceptical about a *certain* historical sensibility. In many respects, we no longer deem a *certain* concept of history, a *certain* notion of change and a *certain* vision of the future feasible: to a large extent we have lost the concept of history that configures the course of affairs as the development of one single subject (freedom, reason or humanity), we have lost the notion of change as the stages of the development of this subject and we have lost the vision of the future as the potential fulfilment of this development.

As indicated in the brief discussion of Hartog's idea of presentism, this *certain* concept of history is at its core a distinctly sociopolitical concept. I agree with Hartog that it is of diminishing significance, but I do not think that what has challenged the modern concept of history is a presentist regime of historicity. The idea of presentism seems to work in the very same political register as the modern concept of history it claims to supersede. In order to understand our recent condition, in order to comprehend an entire historical sensibility in its emergence in the technological and ecological domains, we need to significantly broaden our scope. I will shortly come to what this exactly means.

As to the question of a politically focused historical sensibility of diminishing significance, I will refer to this in various ways throughout this book. Whenever I happen to mention modern, processual or developmental historical sensibility, or whenever I talk about the Enlightenment invention of history, I mean or imply this one. It more or less covers what Hartog means by the modern regime of historicity. It is not really news, however, that Western intellectuals became sceptical about the modern idea of history. Accordingly, the fact that the Western world lost this peculiar historical sensibility does not actually mean a *loss*. There is, in fact, a long tradition of criticism of the modern idea of history running parallel to the very idea itself, the latter, nevertheless, appearing as the dominant one throughout the nineteenth century. Hence the question to answer goes as follows: from what time is it plausible to talk about *the dominance of a sceptical attitude* toward history and other related ideas?

Raymond Aron's *Introduction to the Philosophy of History*, originally published in 1938 in French, opens with the following sentence: 'The title of this book runs the risk of misleading the reader who might identify the philosophy of history with the great systems of the beginning of the nineteenth century, so discredited today' ([1938] 1961: 9). But even if 'the great systems' of philosophy of history already occurred to Aron and many others as largely discredited before the Second World War, it does not mean that by then the entire modern historical sensibility had become questioned. As Chapter 1 and Chapter 3 will argue, the dominance of a sceptical attitude towards the modern idea of history – a general sceptical attitude that includes not only philosophy of history but ideologies, utopian thought and any kinds of metanarratives in postmodern thought – took root only in postwar times.

Leaving behind a certain kind of historical sensibility, however, does not equal the disappearance of any sense of considering the world and ourselves as 'historical' in other terms. I believe what is happening instead is that Western societies are shifting from an appeal to the developmental modern idea of history to an appeal to a non-developmental one. The traces of this ongoing shift, the traces of an emerging new historical sensibility, are unmistakably present in current sociocultural practices of everyday life as well as in academic practices: *on the one hand, our postwar future vision – in the technological and ecological domains – is increasingly taking the shape of what I call unprecedented change; on the other, the way we relate to the past is shifting from an associative approach to a dissociative one.*

All in all, the claim I wish to argue for is that Western societies are not presentist but are living in times of unprecedented change, meaning that present relations to both the past and the future are increasingly *conceived of* in terms of such unprecedented changes. In order to bring clarity and concreteness to the issue, on the coming pages first I introduce future prospects of the unprecedented, then present a few sociocultural practices that imply the same disconnection with respect to the past. These concrete instances attest to the significance of the overall endeavour of the book: to provide a conceptual understanding of such phenomena within the frame of an emerging historical sensibility. Finally, I will also briefly discuss the more technical issue of how such theoretical work relates to the formerly dominant approach of narrativism in the theory and philosophy of history.

The prospect of unprecedented change

Over the last couple of years, I have argued in a series of essays that postwar Western societies gave birth to a vision of the future that characteristically differs from the vision of the future of the Enlightenment (Simon 2015a, 2017, 2018a). Whereas the Enlightenment vision of the innate perfectibility of human beings and human societies made sense against the backdrop of the coeval invention of history as the continuous developmental process of the expected fulfilment, postwar visions of the future do not promise to fulfil anything like an already assumed past potential. Instead, in the shape of nuclear warfare, anthropogenic climate change and technological visions of artificial intelligence, bioengineering, transhumanism and radical enhancement, the postwar Western world increasingly conceives of its future as changes that do not develop from previous states of affairs but bring about something unprecedented.

But what exactly does it mean to subsume such visions of the future under the category of unprecedented change? In what sense do postwar visions of nuclear warfare, anthropogenic climate change, and artificial intelligence qualify as unprecedented changes? At the most general level, *all these prospects revolve around the possibility of the radical alteration, and even the extinction, of the human being as we know it*. All these visions of the future share the ultimate potential of pushing humanity, by virtue of its own activity, beyond a point of no return. This point of no return is the anticipated singular event, after which human beings are assumed to lose control over engineering their own condition. The most apparent anticipated singular events are a quick and devastating global nuclear war (the most familiar catastrophic prospect after the Second World War); a climate apocalypse (Oreskes and Conway 2014) as a result of passing critical 'tipping points' (Lenton et al. 2008; Nuttall 2012) after which nature takes over anthropogenic climate change; and a technological singularity (Vinge 1993; Chalmers 2010; Shanahan 2015) followed by an 'intelligence explosion' – that is, the point when a greater-than-human intelligence becomes able to upgrade itself and design even greater intelligence in a supposedly quickly accelerating fashion.

Whether any of this will actually take place is not a question that matters for my argument about an emerging postwar historical sensibility. What matters is that all these prospects are considered as possible and appear as feasible visions of the future in postwar Western societies. Similarly, in the late Enlightenment and throughout the nineteenth century, what mattered for conceptualizing change in human affairs as history was simply the assumption that human beings and human societies are perfectible, and not the question whether it can plausibly be claimed that societal and human perfection have really been played out over time. Utopian socialists, for example, most certainly acted upon their belief that such perfectibility can be carried out over the course of history, even though in retrospect the actual purposeful achievements in the desired 'perfection' can be questioned. On this ground, what matters for an explorative work on contemporary Western historical sensibility is simply the question of the existence and dominance of a *vision* of the future that is widely considered to be feasible, and not the question of its actual realization.

What sets novel visions of the future apart from those typical of Western modernity is that postwar prospects of existential catastrophes and dystopian visions are hardly conceived of as desired future outcomes of a developmental process. Unless you are building your private Death Star and planning to destroy Earth, there is a strong chance you do not consider human extinction as a prospective *achievement*. You probably do not consider human extinction as a *fulfilment* of a process within which humanity itself stages its own disappearance, and you do not take action to facilitate such an outcome. Unlike the future visions of the modern historical sensibility, postwar dystopian prospects are not *desired* outcomes. Or, for that matter, they are not even *outcomes* in the sense that such prospects are not imagined as end results of processes.

Chapter 3 will elaborate on all this in much more detail. At this point the important aspect to flesh out is that instead of appearing as utopian promises to live up to, postwar visions of the unprecedented are conceived of as threats that call for action in order to *avoid* the worst prospects of human extinction. But even if human extinction can be avoided, the complete alteration of the human condition as we know it remains a dominant prospect. In fact, even Hartog is perfectly aware of technological visions and postwar catastrophic future prospects. However, instead of conceding that visions of climate and nuclear catastrophe and visions of runaway technological change contradict the overall cultural diagnosis of 'presentism', instead of considering these prospects as structural changes in expectations of the future, Hartog accommodates them into his theory of presentism by claiming that calls for precaution in case of catastrophic prospects only extend the present into the future (2015: 193–204).

This compels me to briefly consider whether such accommodation of technological and ecological prospects into a theory of presentism is a plausible intellectual operation. To begin with, it seems to me that Hartog takes for granted two things: first, that all future prospects are catastrophic and, second, that avoiding future catastrophe equals changelessness and means only the preservation of what there already is in the present. Both are, I believe, false assumptions. Colonizing Mars and making humanity a 'multi-planetary species', as recently envisioned by Elon Musk (2017), or being able to cure presently incurable diseases by genome editing and genetic engineering (Gordijn and Chadwick 2008), likely do not come out as overwhelmingly catastrophic prospects. The case is rather that the *potential* of technology is deeply ambiguous in appearing both as the greatest promise and the most critical existential threat to humanity, as best illustrated by the recent discussions on artificial intelligence, especially following Nick Bostrom's book *Superintelligence* (2014). Thus, although it is true that the momentous changes technology promises might result in a catastrophe for what we consider today as human lifeforms, profound changes are expected to take place in the human condition even when existential catastrophe is avoided.

Inasmuch as such prospects are conceived of as unprecedented changes – say, the creation of greater-than-human intelligence that, in principle, remains inaccessible to the human mind – they cannot really appear as extensions of the present simply because by definition they are perceived as having no precedent in the present and the past. Accordingly, conceptualizing visions of the future as unprecedented change is of the complete opposite effect than of Hartog's presentism. Instead of emptying prospective threats and taming the future in general as the notion of presentism does, the notion of unprecedented change fosters the recognition of novelty without downplaying it. It aims at coming to terms with such prospects *as* visions that even alter the way we think 'historically'.

Now, all this leaves us with unprecedented change as the expectation of an epochal transformation. Yet, even 'epochal transformation' may be a misnomer inasmuch as it hints at being just another stage in the gradual development of human affairs. This could not be farther away from expectations of unprecedented change. Instead, either as worst-case scenarios of human extinction or as complete alterations of the human condition as we know it, *future prospects of the unprecedented revolve around a vision of the birth of posthuman beings and a vision of an upcoming posthumanity.*

But what exactly does unprecedented change mean as the prospect of a posthuman future? Perhaps in a surprising way, it has little to do with 'posthuman' and 'posthumanism', notions by now quite commonly used within the humanities and social sciences, in the shape of a critical posthumanism (Wolfe 2010; Braidotti 2013b). Critical posthumanism has grown out of a philosophical criticism of humanism and humanist assumptions about knowledge and the self, challenging what it perceives as human exceptionalism and anthropocentrism in humanities scholarship. Typically it intends to do away with the division between nature and culture, or renegotiate the boundaries between human and non-human animals (Haraway 2008), although it oftentimes considers the technological non-human (Hayles 1999; Braidotti 2013b). However, its primary concern is to establish a new knowledge regime of 'posthuman humanities' (Braidotti 2013a), or of a closely related 'ecological humanities' (Domanska 2015b). What this means is that critical posthumanism stays within the confines of envisioning a future as a next step in human development, where human beings extend their intraspecies sensitivities into an overall inter-species sensitivity that transforms human knowledge.

Contrary to this, what I mean by posthuman is a potential newborn subject of history that is no longer or never has been human. It is a subject that is expected to outperform the human subject and may replace or supersede the human as the subject of a postulated historical transformation (Simon 2018c). Accordingly, by posthumanity I mean *the prospect of* a condition that is no longer or has never been a human condition. Such an understanding of the posthuman as a non-human being that is about to be created reflects the sense in which posthumanity appears in debates on technology. Debating the prospects, merits, shortcomings and threats of human enhancement (Agar 2010; Cabrera 2015; Clarke et al. 2016), bioengineering and biotechnology (Fukuyama 2002; Sharon 2014), transhumanism (Bostrom 2008b; Hauskeller 2016), artificial intelligence (Bostrom 2014) and related technological prospects (Chalmers 2010; Coeckelbergh 2013; Shanahan 2015) is nothing other than debating the very question of whether technology inevitably leads to the bringing about of sentient non-human beings, and whether the prospective beings still can be considered human.

To avoid misunderstandings, this is not to say that critical posthumanism and the prospect of a technological posthumanity are completely unrelated. They are, in fact, intertwined and overlap in multiple ways that simply lie outside the scope of this book, because the difference in their defining characteristics seems more pertinent: whereas humanist posthumanism debates the latest human condition, ecological and technological posthumanity discusses the prospect of a condition that has never been or is no longer human. And again, this is not to say that there is widespread agreement that the coming posthumanity as a condition escapes the confines of what we have previously called the human condition. This is only to say that the potential and the possibility of the prospect of posthumanity is at the core of (debates on) visions of the future, and that the prospect of the unprecedented ultimately boils down to the prospect of such posthumanity.

The unprecedented in retrospect: A dissociative relation to the past

Perceived unprecedentedness is not merely the question of postwar future prospects. The same temporality and the same configuration of change over time underlies the way Western societies began to relate to the past in the last half-century. Whereas visions of the unprecedented take the shape of singular events, in certain retrospective cultural practices it can be recognized as dissociative relations to the past in terms of identity. Whenever you claim an identity-dissociation from the past, you disconnect your present condition or the present state of affairs from past conditions or past states of affairs. What you claim by such a disconnection is not merely a radical temporal break but also a radical change that has already taken place, separating what you think you may be from what you think people have been in the past. Differently put, in an identity-dissociation from the past you conceive of the past in terms of an unprecedented change that has already happened, that is, an unprecedented change that brought about what you think you may be now, disconnecting you from the times before.

The retrospective conception of change as unprecedented provides further explanation for a crucial aspect that is an integral element of the prospect of the unprecedented too: the question of the subject of change. Who and what exactly is the subject of a change that is unprecedented? Unlike processual and developmental change, unprecedented change does not mean change *in the condition* of a subject; instead, it means a change *of* the subject. Whereas developmental change is conceived of as a change that an otherwise definite and identifiable subject goes through, unprecedented change displaces the subject itself. As a future prospect, it entails either extinction prospects or the replacement and supersession of the human by the posthuman, while the unprecedented in retrospect is about a replacement and supersession in terms of dissociated identities in the human world.

As my first example, the sense of being disconnected from the past – that is, being after an unprecedented change – is precisely what underlies the recent phenomenon that Anton Froeyman called *moral anachronisms* in a few conference talks I witnessed. Unfortunately, Froeyman has not turned these talks into papers. With his verbal consent, however, I would like to hijack the term and reinterpret it as follows. Briefly put, moral anachronisms are remnants of the past – institutions, customs and habits, objects, practices, traditions – with continuing existence in the present, despite the fact that the moral values they were once erected upon are no longer held. Whereas Froeyman, being inspired by Derrida (1994), considered moral anachronisms as remnants of the past that 'haunt' the present and do not want to go away, I think that they are objects (institutions, traditions, habits and so forth) on which present communities exercise dissociative measures. For moral anachronisms are not held dear or celebrated deliberately by a certain community; they are targets of heavy societal critique and social protest, directed *against* the survival of the past in the present.

Consider the examples of the Rhodes Must Fall protests to bring down the statue of Sir Cecil Rhodes in university campuses in South Africa and Oxford, or – as one of Froeyman's original examples – the efforts to ban the comic book *Tintin in the Congo* in Belgium (Vrielink 2012). Underlying the many possible interpretative grids that can be applied to these phenomena (mostly in terms of identity politics), there is, I think, a shared sense of a dissociation from the past. Although dissociation may concern only one single aspect of the *Tintin* comics and the 'historical' figure of Rhodes, and although there may be a hundred other aspects in which an associative relation to them may still be effective, that single dissociative measure overpowers any possible associative measures and eventually results in an overall dissociation and the demand of complete erasure. Therein lies the novelty of the situation: not in the fact of claiming dissociation from the past but in the fact of the immediate and harsh *overall dissociation* that emerges out of the breakdown of *a single aspect* that previously has been one among the many aspects of association. The sheer act of demanding removal and the sheer act of demanding the ban tacitly implies a sense that 'we', in the present, are no longer those people who could reasonably erect a statue to Rhodes and write or read a comic book like *Tintin in the Congo*. Such moral anachronisms could have been introduced at a certain time by certain people, but they could not have been introduced today by 'us'. And this 'us' is an identity that denies association with people of the past who actually erected statues to Rhodes and wrote or read *Tintin in the Congo*.

Exercising dissociative measures on the past in the shape of moral anachronisms is paralleled by an intellectual inability to positively define associative and affirmative patterns. The present appears today simply as *post-past*, which is the second major example that I would like to mention. Western societies were under the postmodern condition, structuralism was displaced by poststructuralism, whereas post-truth politics seem to rule today when posthumanity looms on the horizon as a vision of the future (or, according to some, as already present). To be clear, I am not exempt from giving in to the tendency to define new phenomena as simply post-past phenomena. The earlier discussion of posthumanity already testified to this, and Chapter 3 will testify it again. What I wish to point out is that the inability to define novel sociocultural phenomena in any other way than defining it as post-past phenomena attests to the fact that the present appears in the most elementary manner. It simply appears as anything but the past. Whatever post-times we live in and whatever post-activity we are engaged in, its primary meaning is nothing other than a sheer dissociation from whatever has been before. At the most general level, if there is a condition of Western societies, it is neither postmodern nor post-truth or, for that matter, posthuman, but the common denominator of all postism: it is a post-past condition, a condition of an overall dissociation from the past, a condition of which the only thing to be certain of is that it is something other than any past condition that has ever been.

Jörn Rüsen (2016) has also remarked on postism recently. It seems important to point out that even though Rüsen has a keen eye for observing the tendency, his poignant understanding of postism as a cultural phenomenon is far from my interpretive framework. Rüsen thinks that postism means 'losing the ground of history' and attests to the emptiness of the future. Contrary to this, in my understanding the post-past condition is not the loss of a meaningful relationship between past, present and future. Rather, it is one of the most apparent sociocultural indicators of an emerging new configuration between past, present and future as unprecedented change.

If you wonder how all these general societal tendencies boil down to historiography, think of Samuel Moyn's book *The Last Utopia: Human Rights in History* (2010), which is my third example. The entire book is devoted to the justification of why human rights are an invention of the 1970s, despite any appearance that would point to a longer 'history'. Moyn's central thesis is that human rights came to prominence at the time when utopian thought collapsed, offering an alternative to already discredited grandiose political visions as 'the last utopia'. To prove the thesis, Moyn challenges what he calls church history in the following way:

> Historians of human rights approach their subject, in spite of its novelty, the way church historians once approached theirs. They regard the basic cause – much as the church historian treated the Christian religion – as saving

truth, discovered rather than made in history. If a historical phenomenon can be made to seem like an anticipation of human rights, it is interpreted as leading to them in much the way church history famously treated Judaism for so long, as a proto-Christian movement simply confused about its true destiny. (2010: 5–6)

What Moyn here calls church history is of course nothing other than the modern historical sensibility put to work, looking for origins of present-day phenomena in the deep past and sketching its process of development. And what Moyn offers as an alternative is an entire book on what a particular present-day phenomena – human rights – is not. Each chapter of *The Last Utopia* is an exercise in proving how anything before the 1970s is not a preceding, underdeveloped state of what later became known as human rights: human universalism in ancient Greek philosophy, in Christianity or in the Enlightenment, or anticolonialism. To Moyn, none of these appear as predecessors of what today we understand as human rights. As a result, as odd as it may sound, Moyn devotes an entire book to argue for the thesis that human rights emerged as an alternative to collapsed utopian visions without actually arguing *for* the functional supersession of utopia by human rights. *The Last Utopia* has little to say about modern utopian thought and the ways human rights may relate to utopianism by replacing it. What it does have a lot to say about is how human rights do not relate to anything else.

Moyn's operation might not be as exceptional as it first appears. The takeaway message of the closing pages of *The Last Utopia* sounds at least strikingly familiar: 'instead of turning to history to monumentalize human rights by rooting them in the deep past, it is much better to acknowledge how recent and contingent they really are' (225). The reason why this may sound strikingly familiar is that Moyn's contention echoes the basic general contention of social constructionism as applied to the particular case of human rights. If you can disregard Moyn's phrasing about the contingency of human rights as if it was 'really' the case, what this contention shows is that the occurrence of human rights, as a historical subject, is anything but inevitable. It did not arise out of a processual improvement on previously available conceptual schemes but came to exist as a product of a certain sociocultural and political environment at a certain time, and might vanish at another time as well.

As Ian Hacking's wonderful analysis of constructionist thought demonstrates, considering something to be a social (cultural, linguistic) construction claims precisely that the thing in question is not inevitable (1999: esp. 1–34). This core constructionist claim is the next example I would like to mention as a present-day sociocultural phenomenon that already exhibits a dissociative relation to the past. On the one hand, the constructionist claim of non-inevitability relies on an evocation of 'history' that is supposed to testify that the socially (culturally, linguistically) constructed subject has no essence or nature. On the other, what the constructionist claim means by this 'history' is not the past (and assumed future) development of a subject that retains its self-identity amidst all changes but the creation of a new subject that comes into being by replacing an old subject it does not associate with.

Social constructionism is, I believe, an alternative view of history and an alternative historical sensibility – an alternative historicity, if you like – that we have not yet understood and recognized conceptually. The almost exclusively epistemological focus of the discussion of the last decades around constructionism veiled the deeper structure of an emerging sense of historicity that the much debated epistemological claim of constructionism rests upon. In other words, the constructionist appeal to history was mistaken for an appeal to history as we know it, history as business as usual. Even Hacking's analysis regards history as something unproblematic when it describes the most basic, 'historical' grade of constructionism: 'someone presents a history of X and argues that X has been constructed in the course of social processes. Far from being inevitable, X is the contingent upshot of historical events' (1999: 19). However, by relying on the modern historical sensibility, presenting the history of X amounts to nothing other than presenting how X developed into what it is today. History in the modern condition would sketch a historical trajectory of X, which is far from being a means of showing up the contingency of X. Because the sketched trajectory is an associative measure applied to X that binds the present understanding of X to its past and thereby determines the present of X by the past of X. Contrary to this, the historical sensibility underlying constructionism turns to the past in order to testify how X did not develop from it, much like Moyn did in the case of human rights.

The question of constructionism is not how X got here and become what it is now, but when X (which, according to the modern historical sensibility, is usually considered as being around for quite some time in different shapes) was invented. This is why the historical sensibility of social constructionism is occupied with 'inventions' and 'births'. The archetypical constructivist book or academic article title – if it is not the most conventional one announcing *The construction of X* – features *The Birth of X* or *Inventing X*. Whatever is presented to be born in all these cases comes into existence as a subject that does not appear as the result of a process of unfolding from the deep past; instead, it is presented as coming into existence due to human efforts under certain conditions that make it possible to construct that subject in that very shape. When those conditions disappear, the constructed subjects disappear with them and get superseded under new conditions by new subjects, which have no ties of association to the past subjects they supersede.

Considerably in line with the core constructionist claim, Michel Foucault (1984) even explicitly attempted to theorize a novel sense of historicity that he called 'genealogy', which is my last example. Foucault's genealogy is of course not what we commonly understand as tracing the lineage of a present-day family to its supposedly still effective roots. This would only be an instance of the developmental continuity of modern historical thinking. Instead, Foucault refers to 'the genealogist' as a synonym for 'the new historian' and claims that one of the uses of genealogy as a novel history is 'the systematic dissociation of identity' (93–94). What's more, Foucault calls this history 'effective history', which 'differs from traditional history in being without constants', as 'nothing in man – not even his body – is sufficiently stable to serve as the basis for self-recognition' (87). The way change over time may take place without constants, the kind of historical change that lacks a self-identical subject of change that can be identified as the very same subject before and after the change, is an instance of what I wish to conceptualize as unprecedented change. This is not to say that Foucault intended to design a theory of unprecedented change in his genealogy or in his account on shifts in the *episteme* – loosely speaking, in conditions of possibility of knowledge regimes – in *The Order of Things* (2002). Nor is it to say that Foucault wished to sketch an overall philosophy of history. This is only to say that Foucault's historical endeavour is one of the most powerful deliberately offered alternatives to the modern historical sensibility. It is not something that I would like to elaborate on but something that interests me as the most explicit of those sociocultural practices of the postwar period that already attests to an emerging historical sensibility that I try to conceptualize.

All the above cultural practices, including that of Foucault's intellectual enterprise, are instances of a dissociative relationship to the past. Together with the earlier discussed prospects as instances of the unprecedented future, they form the background of the endeavour of understanding a distinctly postwar historical sensibility. So far so good. There is, however, a rather obvious question that follows from this self-assigned task: how exactly should the work be done? Would the narrativist mainstream of theoretical work on history be helpful in coping with unprecedented change? This is the question I would like to discuss in the remaining pages of this chapter.

The inadequacy of narrative philosophy of history

Understanding an emerging postwar historical sensibility is not confined to the question of a novel conception of historical change. It also entails the exploration of how historical writing operates under the altered conditions. To the extent that history as a conceptualization of change in the course of human affairs is reconceptualized, historical writing as the study of change in the course of human affairs needs to be reconceptualized too. Accordingly, attempting to understand an emerging postwar historical sensibility implies the challenge of bringing together the two main senses of the word history again: the course of human affairs and historiography.

As odd as it may sound, the biggest obstacle to meet this challenge is the mainstream orientation of the theory and philosophy of history in the postwar period: narrativism. The reason for this is easily guessed by anyone keeping an eye on theoretical debates concerning history. With the demise of classical philosophies of history, postwar theorizing about history has been reduced to an almost exclusive focus on historical writing. Following the heyday of analytical philosophy of history in the 1950s and 1960s (where the question of narrative in history received theoretical attention first), the publication of Hayden White's *Metahistory* (1973) opened an era of theorizing history as historical writing in terms of historical narratives as literary artifacts – just to allude to another famous essay of White (1978: 81–100). Whereas historians remained suspicious about Whitean narrativism to a large extent, the approach quickly achieved an all-too-dominant position within the theoretical field, mixed with various insights of phenomenology, deconstruction, poststructuralism, literary theory and so forth.

Having said this, I must be clear that I do not wish to run an argument against particular narrativist insights. Nor do I wish to claim that Whitean narrativism in general was a failure. It was not. In fact, for decades it explored the most pressing questions and themes in the theory and philosophy of history in the most excellent way. Not to mention that the potential of White's work for future research is still a divisive issue (Rigney 2013; Kuukkanen 2015; Simon and Kuukkanen 2015; Pihlainen 2017). What I wish to claim is only that although narrativism was well suited for certain purposes and greatly enhanced our understanding of how modern Western historical writing functions, it rather seems to me that the entire narrativist framework is incapable of coming to terms with the newly emerging felt concerns of postwar Western societies. This claim, I reckon, may sound bizarre, considering that in the previous paragraph I have just talked about the all-too-dominant position of narrativism exactly in the postwar period. How can it be, then, that narrativism appears as both incapable of attaching to such felt concerns and nevertheless manoeuvres itself into a dominant position?

The answer I would like to give is that narrativism became dominant not as a comprehension or a recognition, but as a counterweight of the felt concerns of postwar Western societies. Note the qualification 'newly emerging'. Narrativism was still perfectly attuned to older emancipatory concerns in the political domain, which gained a new life in the shape of the social liberation movements of the 1960s. As an experiential horizon, this accounts for the extent to which narrativism has been attuned to societal concerns by providing stories of empowerment. But this is only one side of the coin, to which I will return in a short while. The other, and much less known, side is what I am more interested in and what I wish to emphasize, namely, that, at the same time, narrativism has intervened and downplayed novel concerns of the unprecedented that have arisen from the increased human capacity to alter the human condition beyond recognition or simply erase it.

But again, what exactly does it mean that narrativism became dominant as the counterweight of such concerns? And, more importantly, how could this happen? As a point of departure in trying to outline an answer, it seems reasonable to begin by considering the question of the specificity of history. Whitean narrativism recast what had been thought previously about the operations of historiography on the premise that history writing is no more than a subcategory of the wider category of literary writing. By subsuming history writing into such a wide category, Whitean narrativism sacrificed any specificity-claim of history writing to literary meaning-making, which, in turn, was associated with the linguistic meaning-making practices of Western culture. Oddly enough, associating history writing with literary writing did not come together with the appreciation of the literary qualities of historical studies. On the contrary, White argued in an essay entitled 'The Burden of History' that unlike literature, historical studies lost contact with the wider audience (1978: 27–50). He claimed that the public status of the discipline is considerably lower because the literary meaning-constitution of academic histories failed to keep up with the culturally relevant literary meaning-constitution of novels of their own time. Accordingly, the remedy that White offered looked like this: professional history writing may become relevant for our contemporary life only insofar as it properly lives up to contemporary ways of literary meaning-making.

It is necessary to point out that White's overall argument is more nuanced inasmuch as it claims the same about the relation between historical studies and scientific practices of their own time. According to White, history writing is stuck with late nineteenth-century conceptions of science and mid-nineteenth century art, and thus it necessarily remains bad art and bad science by contemporary standards. Nevertheless, science plays a minor role in 'The Burden of History' and hardly any in White's general understanding of historiography over the following decades. Moreover, the role science plays in the argument of 'The Burden of History' concerns only the extent to which historians claim to be engaged in an activity that is both artistic and scientific and not the intention to elevate historical studies into being good science. In light of all this, it seems safe to claim that what White and

White-inspired historical theory advocates generally is turning historical writing into good literature.

This narrativist recommendation was, needless to say, devastating to the question of the specificity of historiography. Recommending more literary orientation for the sake of wider societal relevance on the basis of being a subgenre entails that the more relevant history wishes to be, the more literature-like it has to be, and thus the less autonomy and specificity can be attributed to it. Within the narrativist framework, what makes history relevant is not what it can claim on its own. Or, to phrase this in a more thesis-like fashion: narrativism simply could not elevate historical writing to prominence on the ground that it is 'historical' writing; instead, it had the contrary effect of rendering the 'historical' of historical studies insignificant.

As a consequence of the over-reliance on what historical writing shares with other kinds or all kinds of 'writings', narrativism *inadvertently* even rendered insignificant the question of what makes historical writing 'historical' in the first place. Under the spell of narrativism, even theories of history typically reflected on history inasmuch as it appeared as something other than what is specific to history. Strictly speaking, history was the most interesting for narrativist research and narrativist theories to the extent that it was *not history*. Ultimately, all this attests to the inability of Whitean narrativism to explain why anybody would bother specifically with 'historical' writing. No wonder that Keith Jenkins, inspired heavily by Whitean narrativism and postmodernism, came to the conclusion that we better just forget history (both as historical writing and as the course of human affairs) once and for all (2009: 54–63).

Although narrativism is of limited use in identifying the specificity of history, it can still account for what makes historical studies specific *within* the wider category of literary writing (cf. Pihlainen 2017). But it is simply badly suited to address the question of the specificity of history as a distinct way of making sense of the world and ourselves. To repeat my earlier point, this is not to say that narrativism is a failed project of uninteresting insights. This is only to say that certain questions cannot be answered within a narrativist framework, and in order to answer them it is necessary to step out of it.

Stepping out of the narrativist framework, however, must not come as a militant opposition or as a full-blown refutation of decades of theoretical work on historical narratives. Nothing prevents the possibility of integrating many narrativist insights into another, much wider framework (even if this probably entails the reconceptualization of those insights in a way that narrativists themselves may find overly inappropriate) or the possibility of establishing another framework as a supplement to the narrativist orientation. What both these otherwise not irreconcilable scenarios call into question is only *the dominance and integrative force* of narrativism within the theory and philosophy of history. They call narrativism into question not by a deep engagement with narrativist arguments and not by giving different answers to the same questions, but simply by asking other questions that appear as the most demanding in our current sociocultural environment – questions that, by a strong chance, cannot even be posed by a narrativist approach.

(No more) narrative domestication of the new

I believe that the most urgent and demanding questions concerning history stem from the manifold phenomena introduced in the previous sections. Current concerns of Western societies revolve around what I conceptualize as perceived unprecedented changes, in the shape of both future expectations and dissociations from the past. In both cases, the unprecedented is conceived of as a change that brings about *a disconnection between the past, the present and the future*.

This situation poses many questions that beg answers. To begin with, would it even be possible to make sense of the unprecedented in its very unprecedentedness – especially when it takes the shape of a vision of the future – if, by definition, it disconnects from everything prior to it, that is, everything we may know (whatever we mean by knowing)? If you turn to the modern historical sensibility, it will tell you that obviously there is no such thing as radical novelty anyway. Since its invention and institutionalization, the function of history (both in the sense of the course of affairs and historical writing) was to make sense of the new. Whenever the modern Western world encountered something new, history intervened and integrated the freshly encountered novelty into a long-term developmental pattern, thereby creating the sense that whatever appears as radically new is actually nothing *substantially* new. History showed how the freshly encountered new was already present in the past in an altered, undeveloped form. It showed how the new has its origins in the old and how a current state of affairs grew out of a previous state of affairs, in which the potential of what seems to be current has already been traceable. It did not deny novelty as such but tamed the profundity and radicality of any newness, by conceiving of it as part of a deeper continuity, by conceiving of it as the latest development of an old and already known phenomenon.

Of course, this fundamental operation is not merely the defining characteristic of academic historical studies but concerns the entire modern historical sensibility. Various instances of it can be found both within and outside the narrower disciplinary confines. As a paradigmatic example, you can think about Max Weber's ([1930] 2001) thesis on how capitalism (the current state of affairs for Weber) grew out of a protestant work ethic (the previous state of affairs). Or, as an example closer to the theme of this book, Karl Löwith's secularization thesis may be just as illustrative. What Löwith (1957) claims in the end is that classical philosophy of history (the newer phenomenon) is nothing other than a more current secularized version of Christian eschatology (the older phenomenon). Finally, by the very same logic, the latest aspirations of transhumanism concerning the possibility to enter a posthuman condition are prone to sense-making by the invocation of the modern historical sensibility. Hence the claim of the opening sentence of the essay by Shelia Jasanoff on posthuman imaginaries, that 'religious or secular, humanity's dreams of the future have always been posthuman' (2016: 73); and the claim of the opening sentence of the historical sketch of transhumanism by Nick Bostrom, that 'the human desire to acquire new capacities is as ancient as our species itself' (2005: 1).

To a large extent, the operation is well known. In making the case for his investigations into discontinuity, Eelco Runia notes that 'historians are amazingly smart, and brilliantly creative, in chasing monstrous discontinuity away and establishing continuity' (2014: xiii). Although such characterization of historical work is a recurring theme in Runia's book, the deepest exploration into exactly how and why historical writing functions like this has been carried out by Hayden White in an essay on the politics of historical interpretation. In the essay, White talks about the 'domestication of history' and the 'domestication of historical thinking' in the context of the aesthetic categories of the 'beautiful' and the 'sublime' (1987: 58–82). Whereas subsuming human affairs under the category of the sublime would be the recognition of chaos, meaninglessness and formlessness, White argues that historical studies have been established on the premise of relegating the realm of human affairs into the category of the beautiful, which he associates with the domain of 'sense'. In White's view, historical studies give shape, sense and meaning to the human world by de-sublimation, by beautifying the sublime meaninglessness and disorder of history understood as the course of human affairs.

Runia and White touch upon something crucial here, although White's account of historical sense-making requires an equally crucial modification, for the domestication in question cannot be the 'domestication of *history*' or the 'domestication of *historical thinking*'. White simply cannot consistently hold the following two claims together: first, the explicit contention that modern history was born under the aegis of the domesticating function of de-sublimation; and second, the implied claim that it somehow existed out there before and became de-sublimated and domesticated in Western modernity. The only consistent claim is that history itself (again, understood both as a concept that unites the world of human affairs in a postulated course and professional historical studies) performs the work of domestication, and what history domesticates is the perception of radical novelty in the human world. The only consistent claim, and also the claim I wish to advance, is that *the modern concept of history is nothing other than a way of making sense of the world and ourselves through the operation of domesticating experienced novelty, and the domestication itself means the incorporation of the new into a pattern of deep temporal continuity, thereby configuring novelty as developing out of the old.*

This, I believe, is how Western modernity transformed human existence and things of the world into 'being historical': by creating a trajectory of constantly changing but essentially self-identical subjects. Since the invention of the concept of history and the institutionalization of the discipline of history, the operation of domesticating the new can be carried out on practically every particular subject. What's more, the work of domesticating the new has been carried out precisely by the means and in the form of historical narratives that White studied. If White is right that modern historical writing is essentially a narrative exercise, and if it is also the vehicle of the domestication of the new, then it follows that narrative itself is the vehicle of the domestication of the new. Moreover, to connect all this to the contention of the previous section, if (1) White is correct regarding the domesticating function of historical writing, (2) historical writing is essentially a narrative exercise, and (3) the domesticating function of historical writing is today an obstacle to making sense of current societal concerns, then it follows that White's conception of history as essentially a narrative exercise is the biggest obstacle to theorizing another notion of history that could be able to recognize unprecedented novelty.

But to be clear, domesticating experienced novelty by crafting historical narratives has been a feasible and instructive enterprise in times when visions of the future concerned only perfections of that which has been conceived as imperfect but already existent in the present and the past. When philosophies of history explicated the gradual betterment of human societies and human beings, when emancipatory visions dominated the political domain, when nation states were yet to be built, the gradual development of the new from the old was extended both into the past and into the future. The perceived and desired new (be it nation state, human freedom or anything else) that was made to be already present in the past as an assumed potential in an altered and undeveloped form, was considered as the very same subject that was supposed to develop further in the future.

All in all, the narrative domestication of the new was a perfectly legitimate and instructive operation in times when the concerns of the Western world took the shape of developmental visions of the future, deep continuities and associative measures. But it no longer seems adequate in times when these concerns take the shape of unprecedented change. In times when present communities conceive of those who erected statues to Cecil Rhodes as people 'we' have never been, and in times when beings created by enhancement or artificial intelligence research are regarded as beings who we expect to be anybody but 'us', the modern historical sensibility of domesticating the new – the modern historical sensibility of narrativism – no longer seems to be able to comprehend current sociocultural phenomena. This is the sense in which narrativism appears today as a counterweight of the newly emerging concerns of postwar Western societies.

What about narrative in times of the unprecedented?

Two clusters of vital questions arise out of the above picture. First of all, anybody may ask, is all this actually a bad thing? Should we not celebrate counterweighing felt concerns as a much needed moment of critique? Should we not welcome this as an intervention that tames all the crazy tech-enthusiasm, extinction-talk and catastrophism that have pervaded public discussions recently? And if, in times of unprecedented change, narrative domestication still comes out as an obstacle to overcome, then the second question is as follows: would this entail the end of narrative? Would this mean that we no longer need historical narratives to make sense of ourselves and the world? Would this mean that we no longer need historical narratives in White's terms, that is, to impose meaning upon reality 'in the form of well-made stories, with central subjects, proper beginnings, middles, and ends, and a coherence that permits us to see "the end" in every beginning'? (1987: 24).

To begin with the first question about the evaluation of the function of historical narratives in times of unprecedented change, it is of course possible to regard narrative domestication as a critique of felt concerns. However, if counterweighing felt concerns qualifies as a good thing, then regaining historiography's status of public prominence must qualify as a bad thing. For achieving public prominence in wider society requires not a counterweighing of but an attunement to whatever that wider society deems to be of great significance.

As discussed earlier, the public prominence and relevance of historical studies in the nineteenth century was due to such an attunement to the sociocultural concerns of contemporary life in the shape of nation-building processes and emancipatory thinking. On the one hand, it is true that the discipline of history was institutionalized as claiming to be a 'scientific' practice; but, on the other, as Chris Lorenz (2008) argues, it could not cease to serve practical purposes all along. If the postwar decades witnessed White-like complaints about the loss of the public relevance of historical studies and if more recently we have witnessed calls for its re-establishment both in academic publications targeting the profession (Guldi and Armitage 2014) and magazine entries addressing policy-makers (Allison and Ferguson 2016), this is precisely because historical studies ceased to be attuned to the societal concerns *of their own times*. Whereas the most urgent felt concerns of the Western world have changed and taken the shape of unprecedented change, historical studies in general continued to be engaged in the operation of narrative domestication, *tacitly* approved and supported by Whitean narrativism in the theoretical field.

Nevertheless, when – in the 'The Burden of History' – White took notice of the loss of the public status of historical studies and recommended keeping up with contemporary ways of literary meaning-making, he touched upon something important. I believe that White was right in detecting that the ties of historical writing to contemporary life had been loosened. Yet, he was wrong in assuming that the reason behind loosened ties was that professionalized historiography got stuck with nineteenth-century modes of literary meaning-making. Rather, it seems to me that what made historical writing lose its prominent public status was the diminishing societal relevance of the meaningful temporal pattern of developmental continuity that history kept on offering even in times of unprecedented change. What became more and more irrelevant in the postwar period was not history as a literary artifact still engaged in outdated modes of *literary* meaning-making, but a specifically modern 'historical' way of *temporal* meaning-making. Historical writing kept on offering a scenario of change over time in human affairs that resonated less and less in Western societies. While relations to both the past and the future had begun to convey a sense of disconnection, historiography insisted on finding connections. It kept on offering its service of narrative domestication even when societal concerns began to demand a recognition of *untamed novelty*.

But to return to the main question about critique, would being attuned to felt concerns necessarily entail the lack of history's critical function? No, of course it would not. Critique is instrumental in targeting long-held inherited attitudes and taken-for-granted conceptual schemes wherever it detects them. Yet, automatically applying such critique to newly emerging concerns before even attempting to understand them by developing novel conceptualizations may be more damaging than beneficial (which is precisely what is currently happening to the notion of the Anthropocene, as humanities criticism rather habitually started to project its long-established categories over a novel category emerging from a natural scientific discourse). A more fortunate critical function can be performed under the condition of being attuned to societal concerns. In fact, this is what modern history has been standing for since its invention. In making sense of the world and ourselves in terms of processes, the modern historical sensibility challenged inherited attitudes and taken-for-granted conceptual schemes of an eternal and changeless constitution of the mundane world of human affairs. It enabled and supported collective human endeavours to achieve a future that has been conceived of as 'better' by being attuned to felt concerns of emancipation. Besides, the affirmation of developmental emancipatory concerns was a critique of inherited ideas like that of a constant human nature, challenged by the idea of the perfectibility of human beings and human societies over the course of history.

All in all, in Western modernity, crafting historical narratives of changing states of affairs and domesticating new sociocultural phenomena appeared both as an affirmation of sociocultural concerns and a critique of inherited schemes. Today, I think that it is still necessary to fulfil this dual function. It is just that the modern concept of history is no longer capable of doing that, because what has changed since the invention of history is precisely that the modern historical sensibility became the inherited pattern of thought that is out of touch with newer sociocultural concerns: *today one could not find a more taken-for-granted conceptual scheme that could be subjected to critique than history and historical thinking*. With historical narratives of temporal domestication becoming unable to cope with the challenge of making sense of what Western societies came to perceive as unprecedented changes, the modern historical sensibility is no longer a solution to current problems but itself is a problem. Instead of asking over and over again how our modern understanding of history can contribute to the solution of current sociocultural problems, it is time to face the task of approving what those problems demand from historical thinking.

This contention leads right up to the second question about the possible end of narrative. Would the recognition of societal concerns of unprecedented change entail the utter insignificance of historical narratives that domesticate the new? Well, the answer is yes and no. It certainly entails that historical narratives are of little or no use in grappling with unprecedentedness. Yet this does not mean that historical narratives (and scholarly research on them) have already vanished. Nor do I advocate that they should vanish in the near future. It must be clear that I do not wish to argue that the modern historical sensibility and its operation of domestication by historical narratives are completely over, have already disappeared without a trace, or have entirely been superseded by a postwar historical sensibility.

What I wish to argue for is that there is a postwar historical sensibility that we do not yet understand, and that the chief task of the theory and philosophy of history today is to come to terms with this. The characteristically postwar sociocultural endeavours of the Anthropocene, nuclear weaponry or technologies of human enhancement and artificial intelligence research demand us to conceptualize a novel way of conceiving of ourselves and the world as historical, attuned to these endeavours and able to make sense of them. At the same time, certain contemporary sociocultural undertakings, like that of emancipatory politics (which, in each of its forms, requires continuity as gradual empowerment), are still made sense of and supported by a persisting modern historical sensibility. Which is fine and necessary.

What I think has truly gone is the *dominance* of the modern historical sensibility in the Western world. Today, historicizing present-day phenomena of perceived unprecedentedness by narrative domestication (making sense of the new by integrating it into a trajectory of deep developmental and processual continuity) does more harm than the good it may achieve. However, projecting a postwar historical sensibility of disconnection onto concerns that emerged at earlier times may be just as damaging. Subsuming (ongoing) emancipatory projects that were launched a long time ago under the perception of unprecedented changes may have the undesirable consequence of resulting in the sense that Western societies are done with empowerment and emancipation. Despite the most obvious persistence of discrimination and wrongdoing, it may reinforce an already existing tendency to conceive of the Western world as the one that is done with evils of past committed by people other than 'us' (Bevernage 2015; Van De Mieroop 2016).

Both possibilities are equally undesirable, while the present coexistence of two historical sensibilities that convey the sense of two different temporalities is a source of serious inconveniences, troubles and misuse. Separately, neither the modern nor the postwar historical sensibility can comprehend the concerns the other is attuned to, while their domains may all too easily be conflated. Yet, the way we perceive sociocultural concerns is our own choice, and therein lies the importance of attempting to conceptualize the emerging postwar historical sensibility (and recognizing it as such is already a step in that conceptualization). Whereas the modern historical sensibility and the modern concept of history is and has been a subject of discussion for at least two hundred years, the temporality that informs postwar concerns of unprecedented change is yet to be explored and understood as historical in its own way. Having an insight into how they intersect must be preceded by the exploration and preliminary conceptual understanding of the latter. It is only in achieving a preliminary conceptual understanding of *both* historical sensibilities that it becomes possible to discuss questions of how they relate to each other.

Once the postwar historical sensibility is explored, it becomes possible to discuss whether the temporality of the technological domain as the most powerful instance of the unprecedented necessarily intrudes into the sociopolitical domain by introducing newer forms of inequalities, whether this constitutes a threat to emancipatory endeavours, or whether the technological and the political domain can peacefully coexist, both minding their own business. Then it would be possible to pose the question of which, if any, domains of human life we would still keep as being of an emancipatory temporality (that narrative domestication captures the best) among domains of the unprecedented.

Finally, I am aware of how all this may appear as monumentalizing otherwise diverse ideas on history. But I think that this is a necessary feature of any theoretical-conceptual understanding worthy of its name. Such an understanding aims at the general that binds together particularities, which can be considered as a shortcoming only by assuming that a perfect and full account of anything is possible, compared to which the lack of certain aspects can be noted. Every research has its limits, and the limits of this research includes an inattentiveness to particular varieties and nuances. Yet, just because a theoretical understanding is a genre on its own and just because this book talks about two apparently monumental historical sensibilities, it does not mean that it is incompatible with research interested in exploring non-Western 'historical' temporalities (Meinhof 2017). Nor is it incompatible with investigations into the multiple temporalities in different domains of human life and endeavours in Western societies (Jordheim 2014). What this book wishes to explore is a deeper level of shared configurations of change over time that underlie a plurality of historical time, regardless of the varieties concerning the tempo or pace of change in multiple temporalities.

The outline of the book

All that said, I would like to offer the following summary of the above introductory thoughts and considerations. At the gravitational centre of the coming pages, there will be the question that I think enquires into the fundaments of the constitution of Western societies today: how can we conceive of the world and ourselves as 'historical' in times when both future prospects and past affairs are perceived in terms of unprecedented change? Unlike the central tenets of narrativism, this question is not reduced to an understanding of history as historical writing. Furthermore, the question is not about what history – in all its possible senses – shares with anything else; the question is not about what history is as something other than itself. The question of the book is about what history is unlike anything else, about what can be considered as specific to history.

The autonomy of history lies in the necessary connection between history understood as the course of affairs (and thus philosophy of history as the enterprise that conceptualizes such a course of affairs) and history understood as historical writing, both being integral parts of the very same conceptual invention of the period between 1750 and 1850 that Koselleck (2004) calls *Sattelzeit*. It is the overall conceptualization of history that exhibits a specific temporal organizational structure – that is, a specific configuration of change over time in human affairs – as a specifically historical way of sense-making. This temporal organizational structure, however, is not immune to change. If today we still conceive of the world and ourselves as 'historical', then the chief task is to explore the change in the way Western societies configure change in human affairs as history. Then the main challenge is to conceptualize history today, to conceptualize history in times of unprecedented change.

I attempt to meet this challenge in the shape of six chapters and an epilogue. The chapters are distributed into two parts: the first three chapters of the first part conceptualize history understood as the course of affairs, while the chapters of the second part supplement this with a theory of history with respect to history understood as historical writing. Although the two parts have their respective focus, discussing history as the course of human affairs is hardly possible without any reference to history as historical writing. In a similar vein, sketching a theory of historical writing requires occasional recourses to history understood as the course of affairs. Even though these casual gateways already establish a connection between the two parts of the book, the task of pulling the threads together on a tighter basis will be the task of Chapter 6.

Chapter 1 opens the conceptualization of history as the course of affairs by paying dues to the already effective intellectual resources of the enterprise of rehabilitating philosophy of history – in an appreciative tone but also in a critical manner. This rehabilitation, despite recent tendencies, can in no event constitute a return to already discredited conceptual schemes and old patterns of thought about history. Accordingly, if postwar criticism of the idea of history and bitter denunciations of philosophy of history are of value, then the question is whether (philosophy of) history is possible under the condition of taking its postwar criticism seriously. By outlining a *quasi-substantive philosophy of history* that postulates movement and conceptualizes change over time in the course of human affairs without invoking ideas of directionality, teleology, substance and overall meaning, Chapter 1 gives an affirmative answer to this question. The notion of history emerging out of the investigations is *history as a disrupted singular*. Whereas the notion of history invented by classical philosophies of history configure change in human affairs as the development of a single subject along a temporal continuum, history as a disrupted singular configures change in human affairs as the supersession of ever new subjects.

The next two chapters elaborate on the enterprise of a quasi-substantive philosophy of history and on the notion of history as a disruptive singular. In sketching the conceptual consequences, Chapter 2 focuses on the question of the relation to the past, while Chapter 3 investigates the role of the future in a quasi-substantive philosophy of history. Proceeding on the basis of the issues addressed in this prologue as features of living in times of unprecedented change, these chapters address, respectively, the issue of a dissociated past and the issue of a catastrophic future as integral parts of a comprehensive theoretical undertaking.

With respect to the relation to the past, Chapter 2 argues that even when the past is conceived of in terms of identity-dissociations, studying it is inevitable and has a constitutive role in making sense of ourselves and the world. True enough, this constitutive role no longer means the possibility of positively rooting identities in the deep continuity of a historical trajectory. Rather, it means that in times when the past is dissociated and positive answers to identity questions are impossible, studying a dissociated past is the best tool we have to negatively indicate who and what we no longer are. I argue that under these conditions historical writing functions as a provider of *essentially contested knowledge of the past*, tightroping between what I will call an *apophatic past* and a present past.

As to the role of the future in a quasi-substantive philosophy of history, Chapter 3 tracks a change in the structure of Western future-orientation. It turns to the past to investigate the utopian visions of the future of Western modernity in order to make sense of a characteristically dystopian vision of the future of postwar times. Whereas utopianism was the necessary entailment of a processual and developmental historical sensibility directed toward a future fulfilment, postwar dystopianism comes as the expectation of the unprecedented, transformative singular event. The historical investigations into Western future-orientation provide the basis of characterizing the emerging historical sensibility as *evental* and exploring 'the temporality of the event' or an 'evental temporality' as opposed to the processual and developmental temporality of the modern period. Keeping that in mind, Chapter 3 closes the first part on history understood as the course of affairs.

The three chapters of the second part sketch a theory of history in the sense of historical writing. What links this second part about historical writing to the first part about history as the course of affairs is the common theme of change and novelty. Whereas the first part of the book investigates how Western societies configure change in the course of human affairs as history, the second part accounts for historiographical change. The two changes are heavily interrelated, and the main objective of the second part of the book is to bind them together. In this spirit, Chapter 6 – the last chapter – attempts to re-establish the connection between history in the sense of the course of affairs and history in the sense of historical writing, by sketching how change in history understood as the course of human affairs and change in history understood as historical writing inform each other. In the final analysis, the three chapters of the second part outline a theory of historiographical change that reflects how Western societies conceive of change in human affairs in times of unprecedented change.

Chapter 4 takes its point of departure in a dilemma that paralyses recent theoretical approaches to historiography. The dilemma stems from the rather exclusive linguistic focus of postwar theoretical work on history, which reduced the understanding of philosophy of history to be solely a philosophy of historical writing. The dilemma concerns the relationship between experience and language, and claims that either you have one or the other, but you cannot have both. It claims that you either have an immediate experience that is doomed to remain mute and ineffable, or you have language, linguistic conceptualization and narrativization without an experiential basis.

Although this dilemma has recently become a dogma, I believe that it is a false one. Separating the domains of the linguistic and the non-linguistic and claiming their mutual hostility and exclusivity is neither a very illuminating idea nor a particularly useful one. Insofar as you maintain the separation of the linguistic and non-linguistic, you remain unable to account for the occurrence of new insights and change in historiography. Accordingly, in order to be able to account for historiographical change, Chapter 4 tries to put language and (historical) experience into a productive interaction by bringing the notion of expression into the equation. In conceptualizing a process of sense-formation and meaning-constitution in historical writing, the chapter condenses a theory of historiographical change into a struck-though 'of' as the expression of historical experience.

Chapter 5 digs deeper into the question of novelty and change in historical writing by focusing on an initial moment of experience, that is, an initial moment of an encounter with the world. This moment of a sudden encounter with something non-linguistic (experience), something that makes no sense, something that resists conceptualization and something before which pre-existing conceptual schemes break down, is the moment that renders possible the entire process of grappling with language and looking for ways of expression. Conceptualizing this moment as an encounter-event with (a remnant of) the past and the external world results in a position that is neither full-blown realist nor full-blown irrealist. The encounter-event attests to the existence of an external reality but does not claim epistemological access to it. Instead, Chapter 5 interprets the encounter in aesthetic terms, as a moment of non-sense, as a moment that cannot be subsumed even under the aesthetic category of the sublime, because that would already imply a certain sense attributed to the encounter. At best, the encounter-event qualifies as less than sublime, that is, as proto-sublime.

Encountering with the world, however, does not necessarily lead toward expression. Inasmuch as nothing arises out of the encounter, it does not even qualify as an event and remains insignificant. Many times we are content with having experiences that do not make sense even for ourselves and we just leave things like that. There has to be yet another step, a moment of impulse that pushes us towards expression, a moment that pushes us from non-sense toward sense-making. Chapter 6 investigates this moment as an ethical demand. The main contention of the chapter is that the ethical impulse to take the step towards expression in historical writing stems from our vision of the future – the vision that informs our notion of history understood as the course of affairs. Hence, historiographical novelty is ultimately linked with the prospect of novelty in the course of affairs, and historiographical change is tied to historical change.

Finally, the Epilogue offers some concluding remarks on the emerging evental historical sensibility in two respects. First, it elaborates on the scope of the possibility to configure change over time as unprecedented in different domains of human life and human endeavours, with special attention paid to the political domain; and second, it asks the question whether the emerging evental historical sensibility can – in a reasonable manner – still be called 'historical' in the first place.

Part One

On Historical Change

Philosophy of history, in its classical modern sense, accounts for change over time in human affairs. This probably does not come as a shocking revelation. It is especially not shocking when measured against the work of professional historical studies, which pretty much seems to do exactly the same: accounting for change over time in human affairs. (Or, to be more precise, historical studies account for change in the condition of practically any and every subject insofar as the subject in question is perceived as having a relation to human affairs – a relation from which the 'historical' significance of even non-human subjects are derived.)

Unlike historical studies, however, philosophy of history is more than an account of change over time in the condition of a particular subject. True enough, in philosophy of history there is a subject that goes through changes, which is typically the largest possible subject of the human world: humanity itself. But what distinguishes it most significantly from historical studies – among quite some other things that are not relevant for the present purposes – is something other: philosophy of history is, so to speak, *the* account of change over time in human (and human-related) affairs. In other words, it not simply one possible account on change in the condition of the largest possible subject; it is the account of a *kind* of change that the modern Western world came to call 'historical'. It is the account of a *type* or a *configuration* of change over time that every particular approach within historical studies aligns with, deliberately invokes or tacitly implies when dealing with any particular subject. Whereas particular approaches of historical studies came to investigate change in the condition of particular subjects, philosophy of history – in the first place – configured change as 'history' with respect to the largest possible subject: humanity as the history of the entire course of human affairs. In fact, the very modern idea of history, as it has been elaborated by classical philosophies of history since the late Enlightenment, was nothing other than the conceptualization of such change that created the possibility of 'historicizing' every particular subject.

When, by the middle of the last century, the entire enterprise of philosophy of history became largely unfeasible, its account of historical change became of ill repute too. Yet the general idea of accounting for 'historical change' seems to be of ill repute only as a result of the bad name of the particular idea that historical change takes the shape of a directional unfolding that also offers a meaningful explanation of all events instead of offering only a theory of historical change. Abandoning a general idea because of a deep dissatisfaction with a particular form in which it has been formulated was, I believe, one of the most momentous intellectual mistakes of the last century. This is the message that the following chapters intend to deliver.

As of today, such an enterprise may still be of ill repute. But the situation looks far less unanimous than it was in the second half of the last century. As an indication of the fundamental disagreement over the question of the feasibility of philosophy of history, consider the two extreme poles. On one side, you find *The SAGE Handbook of Historical Theory*, representing the institutionalized common view on theoretical work regarding history, limited to questions about historical knowledge as produced by historical writing. In its introduction, Nancy Partner, the co-editor of the volume, expresses her contempt for the enterprise of philosophy of history, as well as for any effort to outline 'a theory of history' associated with 'some unified system explaining or predicting the course of world events in the manner of older styles of philosophy of history' (2013: 3). On the other side, you find more enthusiasm about the prospect, for example in the prediction of David Christian (2010) about the revival of universal history. As a founder of the 'big history' approach (loosely speaking, the intention to provide an overall historical interpretation of practically everything following the Big Bang), Christian's prediction is obviously motivated by the need to ground his own approach in a more general tendency. This, however, does not diminish the significance of the fact that in Christian's approach theorizing about history as the course of affairs does not necessarily mean 'older styles of philosophy of history', as Partner states. What Christian predicts is the revival of the enterprise in line with contemporary 'scientific' standards and concerns.

Big history, of course, already wants to be a practice that meets those newer scientific standards. Yet, those who are not its practitioners see it more as an endeavour that relies on the very familiar presuppositions of old philosophies of history (Hesketh 2014; Megill 2015). In its ambivalent perception, I think that the case of big history perfectly captures the current overall climate in Western historiography: on the one hand, long-term historical thinking is definitely back; on the other, one cannot escape the feeling that it suspiciously resembles the developmental directionality of the modern concept of history that classical philosophies of history devised.

As to the renewed engagement of the discipline of history in long-term interpretations, the most powerful call for opening a wider discussion is probably *The History Manifesto* (Guldi and Armitage 2014). However, the book itself appeared at a time when such a renewed engagement had already been apparent, and not only in the shape of big history. The long-term perspective also deeply pervades the invention of deep history (Smail 2008; Shyorck and Smail 2011); it is evident in the Big Data approach to history with the ambition of 'creating and analyzing a global dataset on human societal activities', that is, a 'world-historical dataset', in order to 'portray long-term, global change in human society' (Manning 2013: 2); and, most importantly, within the professional discipline of historiography it is manifested clearly in the spectacular rise of global history.

As a sign of the times, probably the most suggestive aspect is neither the recent flood of global history handbooks nor the rapidly growing number of scholarly works on 'the global history of' practically anything. The most symptomatic aspect of the current historiographical climate is the fact that once-pioneering historiographical approaches of the past decades that intended to examine the small, the micro and the local in a bottom-up manner are now measured against global history. For example, microhistory – building on the premise that, despite its focus on the micro and the local, it actually always wished to answer big questions by examining the small – has recently been searching for methods of affiliation and compatibility with the dominating approach of the global (Trivellato 2011; Epple 2012). At the same time, as seen from the rising global history, microhistory's efforts might be welcomed. At least they find implicit approval in the very first introductory sentence of Jürgen Osterhammel's *The Transformation of the World* (one of the most celebrated works in global history as of today), claiming that 'all history inclines toward being world history' (Osterhammel 2014: xv).

By attributing such a universal inclination to the entire discipline – an inclination that is supposedly equally present in every possible historical approach, school and methodology – Osterhammel implies a very specific role for global history, namely, being the master discourse of 'all history'. This point leads straight to the other defining feature of the current historiographical climate: the disciplinary gesture toward the global seems to make use of both the ambitions and the conceptual toolkit of long-discredited 'older styles of philosophy of history' (as Nancy Partner called them). For it must be clear that the inclination Osterhammel attributes to all histories suspiciously resembles the inclination of all histories toward the ultimate unitary story of history itself as told by classical philosophies of history. The general account of philosophy of history of change over time in human affairs, the conceptualization of history itself as a directional and developmental unfolding, was supposed to enable, bring together and also house all histories as their general framework. Global history is very much prone to function the same way today. True enough, Osterhammel's version of global history, with its frank admittance, is only one among many brands of global history. Others might be less explicit than Osterhammel about an intention to return to 'grand narratives' (2014: xix), but regardless of whether they disclose it or not, even the most conventional brands of global history – which define their approach by the shared interest in interconnections, entanglements, exchanges and transfers – tend to presume a general framework of reference that inadvertently relies on conceptual schemes inherited from Enlightenment historiography and philosophy of history (cf. Fillafer 2017).

And there is nothing particularly startling or puzzling about this, because there simply is no bigger, deeper and more global history than what the enterprise of philosophy of history has been. Thus, the fact that long-term historical approaches make use of the most familiar conceptual toolkit available to them cannot come as a surprise. On the other hand, the fact that there are no surprises here does not mean that everything is right with reviving discredited conceptual tools. It is not just coincidence that philosophies of histories became of ill repute; but it is not just coincidence either that Western societies cannot let long-term historical thinking go.

I believe that this situation demands an endeavour that satisfies both tendencies. It means nothing other than the possibility of long-term historical thinking that, nevertheless, does not revive long-abandoned conceptualizations. The question of the hour is: how can we arrive at this? As to the answer, I think that if current historiographical approaches to long-term change do not wish to fall back to a dependence on the conceptual toolkit of 'older styles of philosophy of history', they cannot but look for an opportunity to join forces with efforts that wish to theorize historical change on the most general conceptual level by creating a new vocabulary and a new conceptual toolkit. The inherited conceptual schemes of 'older styles of philosophy of history' may best be abandoned by the emergence of newer styles of philosophy of history. Accordingly, it is for the benefit of historiographical practice to keep an eye on historical theory. But this is only one side of the coin. In fact, it is for the *mutual benefit* of both historiographical approaches to the long-term and theoretical or philosophical considerations of history as the course of affairs to keep an eye on each other. As discussed above, philosophy of history in the sense of being a philosophy of the course of affairs still has the reputation of being an intellectual blind alley. Whereas the discipline of history is already on the long-term track, theories and philosophies of history still hesitate to make the move from a study of historiography to a study of both historiography and history as the course of affairs.

With the next three chapters, I wish to make the move, so to speak. In what follows, I attempt to sketch a conceptualization of historical change. Or, in other words, I attempt to sketch a general account on how change over time in human (?) affairs is conceived of. Not as a meaningful interpretation of human history as modern philosophies of history did but as an account on a novel kind of historical change.

The chapters explain why such an enterprise is still necessary and how it can be carried out in the first decades of the twenty-first century, in the context of contemporary concerns. However, this context implies other kinds of modifications too. The most important of them is that historical change, the shared interest of long-term historical approaches and philosophical takes on history, should be regarded today neither as a directional and teleological unfolding nor as an objective property of the course of affairs itself. Nothing compels us to stick with such views. It seems to me more beneficial and feasible to regard history in a more pragmatic (and maybe even pragmatist) fashion, as a conceptual tool in our hands that we make use of, relative to our purposes and sense-making efforts. This is how the following chapters approach the task of trying to sketch a feasible philosophy of history today as a conceptualization of historical change in times of the unprecedented.

1

A Quasi-Substantive Philosophy of History

Talking quasi

I would like to begin by easing a possible anxiety that the title of this chapter might produce: I do not wish to deliberately propose a quasi-substantive philosophy of history. In recent decades, inhabitants of Western societies have been told countless times that philosophizing about history understood as the course of human affairs, firstly, is impossible; and, secondly, even if it is possible, is dangerous. Nevertheless, not to count the outstanding efforts of Karl Popper ([1957] 2002; [1945] 2013) to picture the enterprise as a source of totalitarianism, stressing the second point was mostly unnecessary. From a philosophical or theoretical point of view, it was generally good enough to prove that philosophy of history understood as the philosophy of the course of affairs is 'a theoretically invalid enterprise', as Maurice Mandelbaum (1948) did, or to explain its illegitimacy, as Arthur Danto ([1965] 1985) did (regardless of their essential disagreement over the task of a philosophy of history focused on the practice of writing history instead).

Like a good high school student, the scholarly community has eagerly learned its lesson. Historians and philosophers, being the ones who otherwise would claim expertise in such an enterprise, were the quickest and most rigorous in accommodating it. They began to refer to the philosophy of history as a pursuable enterprise solely in the sense of a philosophy of historiography. In doing so, they excommunicated every effort directed toward devising an overall account for change in the course of human affairs from the body of what might be considered as serious scholarly work. Accordingly, the good high school student in me has learned the lesson too and wants to repeat that I do not wish to *propose* any particular philosophy of history, be it quasi-substantive or properly substantive.

Now that this particular anxiety has been eased, I would like to generate a second one, only to ease it again right away: the main reason why I do not wish to deliberately propose a quasi-substantive philosophy of history is that it would be unnecessary even if I wanted to. There is no need to propose it simply because it is already out there, or to be more precise, it is already out *here*. It has already found its way into history departments and venues engaged in theorizing and philosophizing about the course of history. It is already deliberately present in the work of Eelco Runia (2014); rather unintentionally implied in Frank Ankersmit's *Sublime Historical Experience* (2005); and, at least partly, without actually being 'historical', prominently features in the thought of Jean-Luc Nancy (1993: 143–66). It is already here, and it is already taken seriously.

The anxiety that the prospect of the existence of such a philosophy of history might generate can be eased again by pointing out that it is taken seriously precisely and insofar as it is *quasi-substantive* and not substantive as such. Or at least, this is what I plan to do on the following pages, to take such efforts seriously as a quasi-substantive philosophy of history. This may largely go against the explicit intentions of those whose ideas I will make use of. As it hopefully will become clear at a later stage, while Runia regards his enterprise as properly substantive in many respects, Ankersmit does not even want to have a philosophy of history in this sense, and Nancy forgets about history in trying to avoid entertaining substantive concerns.

Accordingly, this early phase of the book sets the stage for the core arguments of later chapters by playing the respective ideas of Runia, Ankersmit and Nancy off against each other. It does so by shaping them into a base for the quasi-substantive philosophy of history that I think Western societies already have at their disposal in the twenty-first century. Building up the overall theoretical edifice and carrying out the work of conceptualization of the relation to the past and to the future in such a philosophy of history will be the task of the following two chapters. Here, as preliminary work, I want to sketch the outlines of such a philosophy of history, elaborate on its 'quasi-substantiveness', explain what it means, and assess what it entails and what it does not. In other words, and in the most general terms, I will try to outline the way in which we can begin to talk about the movement of history again and clarify what 'history' could possibly mean in this very sense, after returning from its long exile.

As a result, I will end by offering a more comprehensive picture than any individual theoretical efforts identified as foreshadowing a quasi-substantive philosophy of history might wish to offer. I intend to do this in an argument consisting of five steps. In the first step, I will attempt to answer the question of what it is that makes a philosophy of history only *quasi*-substantive. The answer necessarily entails retrospection into the substantive days of philosophy of history to see what cannot be done in our quasi-times. Then, as second and third steps, I will highlight what I consider to be the two main features of today's quasi-substantive philosophy of history, namely, the fact that it sets history into motion again and the fact that it reintroduces the future into historical thinking. Given that to some extent these were also features of 'proper' substantive philosophies of history, the main question here will be the following: how does the quasi-substantive approach differ from the substantive one? In the fourth step, I will outline the concept of history theorized by a quasi-substantive philosophy of history, call it *history as a disrupted singular*, and contrast it to Koselleck's notion of history as a collective singular. Finally, I will return to the initial issue and offer some remarks on such a quasi-enterprise, trying to eliminate the substantive concerns still inherent in the ideas of Runia and Ankersmit. Another purpose of this final operation is to set the stage for the next two chapters, which elaborate on the quasi-substantive philosophy of history we have today.

Substantive days and quasi-times

In order to understand what makes the philosophy of history of our time only quasi-substantive, the question to ask seems to be analogous to the one my generation asked about something else. This something else was a hit in the early 1990s. In 1993, the otherwise hilariously named Meat Loaf claimed in a song that he would do anything for love, with the qualification attached: 'but I won't do that, no, I won't do that'. As the song peaked in the charts, an entire generation became puzzled by the question of what that 'that' could possibly be that Meat Loaf would not do for love. I think that the right question to ask about a quasi-substantive philosophy of history is something similar. In order to understand why it is only quasi-substantive, the question to ask is: what could it possibly be that a quasi-substantive philosophy of history would not do to enable us to philosophize about history as the course of human affairs again? Or, phrased in a more academic vocabulary, can we have a philosophy of history that accounts for historical change and, at the same time, nevertheless takes seriously all postwar criticism and avoids substantive concerns?

To answer this question, the first thing to be familiar with is not the classical philosophy of history of the Enlightenment, German Idealism or Marxist philosophy of history. Nor is it a twentieth-century philosophy of history such as that of Oswald Spengler ([1918–1922] 1991) or Arnold Toynbee (1934–1961). Instead, the first thing to understand is the way in which all these substantive philosophies of history were explained, criticized, often ridiculed and rather unanimously refuted in the postwar period. In order to see the ground for their dismissal and excommunication, what needs to be explored is the way such classical philosophies of history were conceived by their successive critical and analytical philosophies of history. And in this respect, probably the most influential account – or at least the account I am going to make use of – is that of Arthur Danto ([1965] 1985), who introduced the distinction between substantive and analytical philosophy of history half a century ago.

Danto's distinction has lost much of its original sophistication by now. The two sides have become equated with philosophizing about the course of history and about the academic practice of historical studies, best reflected today in the more recent distinction between 'philosophy of history' and 'philosophy of historiography' (Tucker 2004: 1–22). Besides, it is also often seen as a way of differentiating between frivolous and serious scholarly activities, and even more so as a contrast between something that is not even philosophy and something that really is. As it stands, Danto himself has a lot to do with this reaction. In sketching the distinction, Danto does not hesitate to emphasize that whereas analytical philosophy of history 'is philosophy' ('philosophy applied to the special conceptual problems which arise out of the practice of history as well as out of substantive philosophy of history'), its substantive counterpart, despite appearances, 'is not really connected to philosophy at all' ([1965] 1985: 1). And if this was not harsh enough, Danto even goes on and claims to analyse 'what substantive philosophy of history pretends to do'.

In doing so, Danto takes a point of departure from Karl Löwith's characterization of philosophy of history ([1965] 1985: 7), according to which it is nothing other than 'a systematic interpretation of universal history in accordance with a principle by which historical events and successions are unified and directed towards an ultimate meaning' (Löwith 1957: 1). The fact that substantive philosophies of history try to attribute meaning to the whole of history – and especially the aspect of 'ultimate meaning' that is not yet present – entails that this kind of meaning-attribution encompasses not only the past and the present, but also the future. And such involvement of the future is precisely the point where things go terribly wrong in Danto's eyes.

The problem is not the involvement of the future as such. The troubling aspect is the involvement of a future that is future not only to past events one talks about in the present, but also to the present point from which one might talk. The future in the former sense is a necessary condition of historical knowledge and, thus, the task of exploring its temporality in the shape of 'narrative sentences' is precisely the one that Danto carries out as an exercise in analytical philosophy of history ([1965] 1985: 143–81). A narrative sentence refers to two events separated in time but is only about the earlier of these events. One of Danto's examples is the sentence 'The Thirty Years War began in 1618,' which is about the beginning of the war, although it refers also to its end by implying that the war lasted thirty years. In 1618, when the war started, such knowledge of the future was unavailable to historical actors but is available to the historian describing the war and seeing both time-separated events as past.

According to Danto, sentences that imply the future of the past are typical of the language of historiography. Histories remain within such confines and do not invoke the future that exceeds their present horizon; philosophies of histories do, and that is what renders the enterprise unfeasible. Whereas it is a necessary condition of historical studies to base interpretations of the past on the knowledge of what is future to historical actors, it is illegitimate for historians and philosophers writing about historical actors to base those interpretations on the supposed knowledge of what is future to themselves at the time of their writing. The curious thing for Danto in the latter case is that the future becomes a viewpoint and also the locus of meaning for the whole of history. Hence Danto's criticism that substantive philosophies of history 'are trying to write the history of what happens before it has happened, and to give accounts of the past based upon accounts of the future' (13). Again, what makes the entire enterprise illegitimate is not necessarily the involvement of the horizon of the future as such but the way the future is supposed to be logically connected to the past. If accounts of the past are derived from a future, and if it is illegitimate to claim to know the future, then anything that logically derives from that illegitimate knowledge of the future must be illegitimate too.

This sort of connection that establishes the unity and continuity of past, present and future (the unity of the time of history, or even the concept of history *as* the continuous flow of time) is typical for linear, teleological visions. Philosophies of history of the Enlightenment, such as those of Condorcet (1796), or the philosophy of history of German Idealism as exemplified by Hegel ([1837] 1975), are based on such temporal configurations. But Danto's criterion of illegitimacy could apply equally well to non-linear philosophies of history, such as Spengler's cyclical-organicist conception. In light of the Danto criterion, a cyclical-organicist philosophy of history is illegitimate inasmuch as it posits a temporal unity that encompasses past, present and future, and treats the entirety of this temporal plane as *a matter of knowledge*. And this is precisely what Spengler does. The opening passages of *The Decline of the West* claim nothing other than 'in this book is attempted for the first time the venture of predetermining history' (Spengler [1918–1922] 1991: 3). And if this was not straightforwardly convincing enough, all doubts must be dissipated a few pages later when Spengler triumphantly reveals that his approach 'broadens itself into a new philosophy – the philosophy of the future' (5).

Nevertheless, it cannot be denied that, in a certain sense, Spengler has a narrower scope than classical philosophies of the Enlightenment and German Idealism did. Instead of talking about the whole of human history as a single unit, Spengler examines separate cultures to which he attributes the characteristic of having organic life cycles. Yet, what Spengler is interested in is the future of the life cycle of the culture he is in the midst of. What's more, the fact that cultures are separated from each other by 'historyless' periods indicates that Spengler is still interested in history as a whole. The only difference is that unlike much more common linear philosophies of history, Spengler associates this whole temporal unit of history with that which encompasses the existence of organic cultures. Accordingly, dropping the idea of an *all-encompassing* progress and exchanging it for an organicist, cyclical conception nevertheless retains the intention of outlining a 'morphology of world history'. This would be a conception of the 'world-as-history' that 'reviews once again the forms and movements of the world in their depths and final significance' (5).

Given that this sounds very much like any other classical philosophy of history, it may be that Spengler does not even drop the idea of the ultimate purpose of the historical process entirely. True enough, Spengler famously denounces it in passages like this: '"Mankind", however, has no aim, no idea, no plan, any more than the family of butterflies or orchids' (17). Yet at the same time he also makes the claim about his many cultures that 'each stamping its material, its mankind, in its own image; each having its own idea, its own passions, its own life, will and feeling, its own death'. What this means is that each culture (including Spengler's own) has its own purpose and its own future (which Spengler illegitimately presumes to know regarding his own culture), and all of them are held together by the abovementioned conception of the 'world-as-history'.

Regardless of the question of whether Spengler whole-heartedly abandons the idea of ultimate purpose or eventually retains it in a confined version, there is something more overwhelming that cyclical-organicist schemes share with more regular linear ones: the developmental view. According to Maurice Mandelbaum, a developmental temporality has underlined and configured historical thinking since the Enlightenment and throughout the nineteenth century in various forms, organicism being only one of them. Unlike the idea of progress, which is to do with 'advancing toward something new', the concept of development is connected to 'processes in which there was an unfolding of that which was already at least implicitly present' (Mandelbaum 1971: 44). This *unfolding of a single ontological subject* characterizes Spengler's cyclical-organicist vision just as much as it characterizes linear-teleological ones. In this sense, the difference between the two rests in the fact that Spengler's insistence on the inevitable decline follows from the organicist idea that Mandelbaum detects even in the teleological philosophies of histories of Hegel and Marx, or in the positivist program of August Comte (1971: 163–91).

All this should now provide a solid foundation for an answer to the initial question of what our quasi-times would not do to enable us to theorize or philosophize about the course of affairs. It must be something that Spenglerian visions share with the linear and teleological philosophies of history of the Enlightenment and German Idealism. It must be something that makes all substantive philosophies of history possible or thinkable in the first place, something that defines them all. This something is not the idea of progress but the more encompassing developmental view in which progress may be only a particular instance. Unlike progress, which necessarily entails advancement as Mandelbaum shows, development only implies the unfolding of a subject *within* and *as* the whole of history. It is the latter, the developmental view as the unfolding of a single ontological subject over the whole of history, that seems to underlie all substantive philosophies of history.

The postulation of the whole of history leads back to Danto's criticism of such philosophies of history. Their illegitimate logical connection between past, present and future, that is, their invention of the unity of history, became possible only as based on a developmental temporality. Accordingly, on this basis I would like to offer the following somewhat long working definition – or, rather, working description – of the philosophy of history of our time.

A quasi-substantive philosophy of history is a philosophy of history insofar as it postulates a movement, a mechanism, a pattern, or in any case a general scheme, to account for change over time in human affairs, just as substantive philosophies of history did. At the same time, it is only quasi-substantive inasmuch as, due to the abandonment of a compelling developmental continuity between past, present and future, it lacks a proper substance as the unfolding ontological subject. By virtue of lacking a developmental temporality and a self-identical subject, it cannot postulate a continuous course with meaning and purpose; instead, it is restricted to providing a conceptual understanding of historical change, that is, an empty scenario of transformation over time without content. Finally, such philosophy of history is only quasi-substantive inasmuch as it does not even stand a chance to derive knowledge of the past from a supposed knowledge of the future.

To clarify what this means, I will now briefly explore the two main features of such a quasi-substantive philosophy of history: the sort of movement it attributes to historical change and the way it embraces the future without assuming a unified historical process with a unitary central subject. As these two aspects or features seem to be closely interrelated, I do not wish to treat them as separable constituents of an easily identifiable general theory. For the sake of clarity, I will introduce these features in the shape of two theses that highlight each other.

History moves again

The first thesis is as follows: *history is on the move again but without a definite goal, without a meaning and without a proper substance; even if history is on the move again, it does not go anywhere definite.*

The claim that history moves *again* actually implies two further claims. First, that there already was a time when such movement was considered possible; and, secondly, that there already was another time when it was not. The former consists of the period between the Enlightenment and the aforementioned postwar critiques of substantive philosophies of history. As discussed earlier, the most typical form of a postulated movement of history was linear progress, although configuring large-scale change as the recurrence of organic life cycles was also a possibility. But whatever particular form the postulated movement of history took, the movement itself was informed by a developmental temporality. The developmental movement appeared as the historical process itself, in which the future unfolds from an already assumed past potential, all this being seen from the present. Classical philosophies of history conceived of the postulated movement in terms of a mechanism or pattern, that is, in terms of a general account of change over time in human affairs.

The latter point in time was the broadly understood postwar period, when the concept of history was torn down and the future was plucked off of it. Probably the most visible manifestations of the motionlessness of history came in the guise of the innumerable variations on the 'end of history' theme. Whereas the criticism of substantive philosophy of history put forward by analytic philosophers such as Danto resulted in the motionlessness of history due to a denial of the legitimacy of talking about history as a whole, 'end of history' theories proceeded along different lines. They came in two main variations: either the 'end of history' as the successful fulfilment of the developmental movement, or the 'end of history' as the end of the entire idea of history as a developmental movement. In the end, however, both variations are about the 'end' of a movement and thus arrive at the same motionlessness.

'End of history' theories of successful fulfilment engage in the enterprise of philosophy of history rather obviously. This type of end of history is based on the same speculative premise of attributing a movement to history, simply because you cannot put an end to something without presupposing that the something in question has been pretty much going somewhere previously. The most famous of all such fulfilment 'end of history' theories is Hegel's self-realization of the *Geist* as the 'development of the spirit's consciousness of its own freedom and of the consequent realization of this freedom' ([1837] 1975: 138). Recently, Fukuyama may have become equally famous with his supposed end of 'mankind's ideological evolution' with the claim that 'the ideal of liberal democracy could not be improved on' (1992: xi). Such theories necessarily postulate a substance and cannot but assume that this substance develops over time as the single ontological subject *within* and *as* the whole of history. As soon as the unfolding of the substance (freedom or the ideal of liberal democracy) is fulfilled, history ends and brings about a lack of further movement in human affairs.

The postmodern skepticism about the entire idea of history is more explicit concerning motionlessness. Instead of claiming the end as fulfilment, postmodern theories, like that of Gianni Vattimo (1987), mean the very end of the idea of history as movement. In Jean Baudrillard's more twisted version, the end is marked by the emerging condition in which the future, so to speak, ceases to come, or more precisely, we cease to move toward anything like a future (1994: 1–13; 2000: 31–57). Yet another way to hold an 'end of history' position is to talk about it as the end of not only the idea of history as the course of affairs but also an end of historical studies, as in Keith Jenkins (1999: 11). The situation at the end is nevertheless all the same: the lack of a movement we used to call 'historical'.

Talking about the assumed postwar motionlessness of history, however, does not necessarily mean talking about its end. It is also possible to talk about the suspension of history instead, which is precisely what Jean-Luc Nancy (1993: 144) does. The advantage of the vocabulary of suspension is twofold. First, because suspension has the connotation of being a temporary condition, an in-between state in which what was before and will be after is momentarily being stopped, it implies that the once-popular idea of movement may, in one form or another, return one day. Second, it can be stretched out over all other versions of the motionlessness of history mentioned above. It can equally cover the motionlessness that results from the criticism of 'end of history' theories and the motionlessness that results from the criticism of the substantive enterprise by mainly analytic philosophers. It can also cover both the suspension of the movement of history (the idea that history came to its supposed end) and a suspension of talking about that very movement of history (the illegitimacy of the entire enterprise of philosophy of history).

Given this postwar motionlessness and suspension, the thesis that history moves again does raise quite a few questions. How does a quasi-substantive philosophy of history end up attributing a movement to history again? Can this movement avoid substantive concerns by taking seriously all postwar criticism of the substantive enterprise? Is it possible to set history in motion in the first place and to take this criticism seriously at the very same time? And, if so, what kind of movement would that be and what, if anything, could possibly propel it? In attempting to answer these questions, I would like to invoke the already mentioned efforts of Runia, Ankersmit and Nancy. To various extents, they already point to the direction of the possibility of a quasi-substantive philosophy of history (which I first addressed in Simon 2015b).

A renewed interest in the question of how historical change is brought about brings together the latest work of Ankersmit and Runia. Whereas the explicit interest of Ankersmit (2005: 351) lies in the identity shifts of Western civilization, the central concern of Runia (2014: 158) is the birth of something genuinely new. Aside from their particular curiosities they wish to satisfy, they seem to have a common curiosity concerning a *kind of change*. It seems to me that ultimately both are interested in the most momentous changes in human affairs: changes that are deeply traumatic; changes that are the results of events they both call 'sublime'; changes that destroy 'the stories we live by', as Runia likes to put it (2014: 124); and changes through which 'one has become what one is no longer', as Ankersmit says (2005: 333). These most momentous changes in human affairs – of which the French Revolution is the paradigmatic example often mentioned by both Runia and Ankersmit – break with continuity. They introduce a dissociation from the past, from that which has been left behind by the change itself. What Runia wants to know eventually is how discontinuity takes place and results in something unexpected, and what Ankersmit wishes to explore ultimately is how this dissociation from the past as a means of dealing collectively with sublime/traumatic events gives birth to a new identity. Both of them intend to explain *how* rupture is brought about *in* and *by* discontinuity and dissociation, and, in their efforts to explain the 'how', they both turn to psychology and psychoanalysis.

To describe what happens when an old world is left behind, Ankersmit parallels Freud's argument on the melancholic reaction to traumatic loss. According to Ankersmit's argument, 'the lost object is, first, pulled within the subject in order to be, next repelled again as a criticized object – while it will, last, forever remain part of the subject in this guise' (2005: 341). The same is supposed to happen in case of momentous changes in human affairs that Ankersmit wishes to understand as identity shifts of the Western world. In this case, the momentous change takes place on a collective level, with an old world starring in the role of the lost object. This old world eventually has to become a part of the subject – the new world; only in order to enable the new world to dissociate itself from it, even if in its dissociation, in the shape of a reminder of what the new world *is not*, the old remains constitutive of the new.

Runia's take is a bit more complicated because of his tendency to use different vocabularies packed with metaphors in almost each of his separately written essays over a decade. Nevertheless, to pick only a few phrases out of the overall vocabulary of Runia (2014), things look more or less like this: from time to time we just give in to the urge to 'commit history', to flee forward into 'sublime', traumatic and horrendous deeds, even if it is apparently at odds with our best interest. To explain what this urge is, Runia also transfers psychological explanations of the individual level into the collective sphere of action in conceptualizing the urge as 'vertigo', that is, 'a wish to jump, covered by the fear of falling' (2014: 136). This irrepressible, subliminal urge is the one that is supposed to lurk behind the 'sublime' deeds by which we leap forward into the surprising unknown even on the collective level, and those deeds are the ones by which we create the new. Finally, the fact that we create something discontinuous cannot be fully veiled by the fact that afterwards we tend to cover the tracks of this radical transformation by creating continuity, which is the paradigmatic activity Runia associates with historical writing and also explains in psychological terms as dissonance reduction (132–5).

The key aspect that sets history in motion in Runia's theory (even if he is not explicit about it) is the dimension of identity, because if the stories that a certain 'we' live by are destroyed by a leap into the unknown, then what is born in the midst of such events is a new 'we' that is discontinuous with and is dissociated from the 'we' whose stories had been destroyed. In other words, what is born on such occasions is a new ontological subject, that is, a subject that had no previous existence. From the viewpoint of any newly born 'we', the stories that had just been destroyed belonged to a 'them' that as a 'them' was also born in the midst of events and deeds that destroyed the stories a previous 'we' lived by. Moreover, if the case is so, then it is reasonable to assume that a previous 'we' also had its 'them' that once was a 'we', and so on.

All this, it seems to me, adds up to a movement based on discontinuous change and shifts in identity. Unfortunately, in the later work of Runia a pattern of deep evolutionary continuity is stretched over this series of momentous changes (179–202). I will address later how such a deep continuity marks a retained commitment to substantive concerns. For now, what seems to be important to note is only that *the above aspects* of the theories of Runia and Ankersmit represent a renewed engagement in the question of overall historical change in a way that hints toward what I call quasi-substantive philosophy of history.

Insofar as the explanation of momentous change in human affairs is related to identity, and insofar as it is an explanation of historical change per se, it describes a mechanism, a self-repeating scenario according to which human affairs change from time to time. In the particular cases discussed, it describes a postulated mechanism rooted in historical discontinuity and dissociation that attributes a certain movement to history. But unlike substantive philosophies of history, the movement, due to the lack of any identifiable substance that could retain its identity amidst all changes, does not lead anywhere. Or, to be more precise, the conceptualized movement of history does not lead to anywhere *definite*: neither to the fulfilment of an ultimate purpose, nor to the inevitable final phases of an organism-like culture. There is only the next rupture that follows. However, this does not mean that such a philosophy of history would in any sense fail to encompass the future together with the present and the past. As the postulated mechanism explains momentous change in human affairs per se, it simply entails an extension not only to the entirety of the historicized past but also to the future.

The return of the future

The necessity of the future extension of the mechanism leads to the second thesis. It is about the return of the future: *The fact that history moves again – even if it doesn't go anywhere definite – entails the opening up of the future. In this operation, the concept of history acquires three distinguishable senses: in the sense that it belongs to 'us', history becomes equated with the future and, instead of referring to things done, it now designates things about to be done; in the sense of knowledge about things done it retains its familiar meaning as historical writing; finally, in the sense that it is on the move (in the overall sense of the course of human affairs), it is best conceptualized as a disrupted singular.*

The return of the future means that it was once there in historical thinking but vanished for a while. However, it is not only that the future *was not* there for a while; rather, the case is that the future *could not even be* there. Under the suspension of history discussed in the previous section, motionlessness entailed a necessary absence of a vision of a future different from the present and the past. Theories of the 'end of history' and presentism (according to which the point of reference migrates from the future to an overwhelming and unchanging present) discussed in the Prologue are the most apparent symptoms of how Western societies perceive themselves as losing track of the future. Aside from these, political utopianism and ideology also had a hard time in the broadly construed postwar period, at least since Judith Shklar's *After Utopia* (1957) and Daniel Bell's *The End of Ideology* (1960), coinciding with the heydays of suspicion against (substantive) philosophy of history and related ideas such as progress. Even if, according to the discussion of the Prologue, this sense of loss of the future is misleading because it concerns almost exclusively the political domain as a concern of the Western world, it captures the postwar intellectual climate and thus must be taken seriously.

If history is on the move again today and the future returns to intellectual discussions, it does not mean that the future comes back in the same conceptual shape it had before it vanished. The future as the anticipated fulfilment of a past potential that was already there before its fulfilment is simply not the future that could be reinstated after all the postwar criticism. Hence the core question about the new embrace of the future is that of how it differs from the conceptual shape and role that another notion of the future played in classical philosophies of history. In attempting to answer this question, I will first introduce Ankersmit's distinction between a 'desire to know' and a 'desire of being' as a point of departure. Then, by taking it out of context, I will link it to Runia's and Nancy's theories.

As for the distinction between a 'desire to know' and a 'desire of being', Ankersmit makes use of it in the context of two responses to the French Revolution that, as I mentioned earlier, he regards as a paradigmatic example of the identity shifts of Western civilization. To begin with the reactionaries, according to Ankersmit,

> the prerevolutionary identity can be recaptured again, and their relationship to the past can, therefore, be defined in terms of *being*. The past is an object of the *desire of being* – they want to be(come) again what the past was once like. The conservatives, on the other hand, recognize that they are forever separated from the prerevolutionary past by the abyss between two different historical or cultural identities. Their desire of the past can therefore only be a *desire to know*. They know their lusterless but lofty assignment to be the transformation of (past) *being* into *knowledge* – or, as Burkhardt once so movingly put it: 'Was einst Jubel und Jammel war, muss nun Erkenntnis werden' ('What once was joy and misery, must now be transformed into knowledge'). History became an object of knowledge, an object of research, forever separated from the world of the subject, the historian. The past became a world successfully resisting any attempt to restore the union of being and knowledge. (2005: 327)

In general terms – and thus deprived of the context of the reactions to the French Revolution – the above passage implies that a 'desire to know' is directed towards an identity other than the identity of the community that carries out an inquiry into it. It is concerned with what the present community is not. Contrary to this, the 'desire of being' may be about what the particular community *is* and how it conceives of itself. More importantly, it may primarily be concerned with what the present community imagines or wishes to be in the future. It is only that in the case of reactionaries, what they wish to be happens to be what the present community already has been in the past.

In the above description the crucial question concerns only the distinction itself: what kind of 'desire of being' have those whose relation to the past is a 'desire to know'? As they no longer associate with the past, their future 'being' opens up and gets released from under the burden of aligning with the past. I think that the 'desire of being' can describe a more general attitude towards the future in a sense that Ankersmit may not approve of. In this general sense, it does not matter if the attitude towards the future 'being' is a desire to retain a past identity, which comes out only as a particular instance. What matters more, what is more to the point, is that when Ankersmit's categories are not considered as belonging to different subjects but as general attitudes of the very same subject, they gain new dimensions. In this much broader way, as attitudes of the very same subject, *the 'desire of being' becomes the basis of a relation to the future as opposed to the 'desire to know' that refers to the relationship to the past.*

Accordingly, the most interesting aspect of Ankersmit's example is not how the past turns into an object of knowledge once an identity shift has taken place. What I find to be far more important is the implicit claim that the future opens up as a matter of being for the new-born identity at the very same time when the past turns into a matter of knowledge. Since the past as the plane of knowledge is a past that is dissociated from the actual concerns of the new-born identity, whatever that identity can associate with is not yet present. Unless association is directed toward the past as in Ankersmit's example of reactionaries, the present is left void of the possibility of associative measures. In the case of those who look at the past in terms of a 'desire to know', that is, from the viewpoint of a newly born community, the future must be a plane of a 'desire for being' in a constellation in which this desire has nothing to do with associative measures applied to the past. For a new-born identity, the 'desire for being' is aimed at a future of which the only thing to be sure of is that it has nothing to do with the past.

This interpretation of Ankersmit's distinction runs parallel to Runia and Nancy's thoughts about a history that is primarily invested in the future. To start with Runia, from his argument that committing 'sublime' deeds destroy the stories a community lives by and makes people leap into the unknown follows that the destroyed stories do not belong to those who are on the future side of the leap. For the future 'we', these stories of the past simply no longer qualify as being 'ours', and, in reverse, the stories that can be called 'ours' in such a situation cannot be associated with the past. Within this logic, it is not surprising that Runia does not hesitate to state explicitly that 'our history really is before us' (2014: 8). However, the fact that 'our' identity is not something we had but something we are about to establish is only one side of the coin. The other side is that, by leaping into the unknown, we also create a past as 'we come to see what is lost forever: what we are no longer' (16).

Runia and Ankersmit's views converge in the sense that, in both theories, the past and the future become subjects of activities of a different kind, satisfying different kinds of desires. I believe that these activities and desires are complementary. They paint the contours of a conceptual shape in which the future (and its relation to the past) is invoked in a quasi-substantive philosophy of history. Moreover, they also hint at the way the future is bound to the question of movement discussed earlier. Eventually, the complementary activities and the question of movement add up to the following picture: *in a quasi-substantive philosophy of history, the past is a matter of knowledge and the future is a matter of existence, while the movement of history is the perpetual transformation of matters of existence into matters of knowledge.*

But to return to the question of the future, the unavoidability of the future for any notion of history manifests itself most clearly in Jean-Luc Nancy's thought, where the future appears not as a postulated endpoint but as a birthplace of a new subject, a new community. Nancy theorizes the future as the 'coming' of this new subject that does not 'become', a subject that is about to be born without originating in, and unfolding from, the past. I think that this is what a quasi-substantive philosophy of history has to take as its point of departure. But only as its point of departure, because even if Nancy does equate the coming-to-existence or coming-to-presence of a future 'we' with history in order to escape substantive thinking, his notion of history is anything but historical in that it lacks the dimension of change in one crucial respect.

As to the efforts to escape substantive thought, Nancy tries to think the 'taking place' of the new subject in its very act of happening. Thinking the subject of a human community in its very act of happening means that 'rather than an unfolding, rather than a process or procession, the happening or the coming – or, more to the point, "to happen", "to come", "to take place" – would be a nonsubstantive verb and one that is nonsubstantifiable' (Nancy 2000: 162). That such 'coming' or 'taking place' of a subject entails the abandonment of the entire idea of development is especially clear when Nancy assures readers that the subject in question 'does not come from the homogeneity of a temporal process or from the homogeneous production of this process out of an origin', and 'that the origin is not and was never present' (1993: 162).

As for the lack of the dimension of change in a very crucial respect, it is coded into what I see as the perpetual stream of Nancy's notion of 'coming' and 'taking place'. Unlike a process of becoming that implies a motion directed towards an altered condition, the motion implied by a perpetual 'coming' keeps its subject in the very same condition. Whereas the 'becoming' of the substance in substantive philosophies of history entailed a concept of change as stages of development leading to an ultimate fulfilment, Nancy's 'coming' does not lead to any ultimate altered condition nor to changes along the way, simply because there is no 'way' leading anywhere. Insofar as the future community (as the subject of history) is always in its happening, insofar as it is 'coming' without ever 'becoming', it has forever to be unrealizable, forever to remain an unannounced 'we', sentenced to infinite deferral. Thus, it seems that excluding the dimension of change is the price Nancy has to pay for equating history with the future, with a coming 'we', which nevertheless enables him to cut ties with the past, to imagine a future ontological subject that has *no prior existence* and thus *no origin from which it could unfold*.

Yet no philosophy of history (as the course of affairs) is possible without accounting for change, which, in turn, necessitates not only the future but also the present and the past. This leads back to the theories of Runia and Ankersmit and to their interest in historical change, which seem to bring a balance to Nancy's ideas. Whereas Nancy is the most successful in avoiding substantive concerns but is prone to the charges of 'ahistoricity' in terms of theorizing an eternally uniform condition of a subject, Runia and Ankersmit are the most promising in theorizing a certain type of change through which new subjects come-to-existence. These views correct each other to the extent that together they attest to a large-scale interpretation of historical change. In the case of a future coming-to-presence or coming-to-existence of a new ontological subject, change has to mean a change in that very identity, that is, a change of the subject of a postulated historical process. Change here has to mean *the perpetual alteration of ever new ontological subjects*, each of them being a coming 'we' without an origin, without a previous state from which they could develop. Just because Nancy's coming-to-existence of a new ontological subject has to be of no origin in order to avoid substantive thought, it does not have to mean that it cannot be superseded by another one, and then another one, again and again.

To sum up, there are two points to keep in mind when thinking about history as the course of affairs today. First, in order to be only quasi-substantive, the future in which a quasi-substantive philosophy of history begins must be the prospect of a coming-to-existence of a new ontological subject. Second, in order to qualify as a philosophy of history that accounts for historical change, a quasi-substantive philosophy of history has to posit a series of comings-to-existence of new-born subjects, separated from each other by disruptive, momentous events, instead of speaking of one single subject that could play the role of a substance in a historical process. Neither Nancy's philosophy nor recent philosophies of history interested in historical change fulfil both conditions. But the ideas they entertain separately – that of 'coming' and that of momentous change – can nevertheless be put to work to confine and inform each other. The concept of history that emerges from this operation is *history as a disrupted singular*, a concept that I would like to introduce in the following section in order both to review and elaborate on what I have said so far.

History as a disrupted singular

A philosophy of history that wishes to avoid substantive thought can employ the word history in three distinct senses: in a prospective sense, in a retrospective one and, most importantly, in a sense that encompasses both as a movement. The *prospective sense* is the one that had a prominent role in the previous section: it is history as equated with the future, our history ahead of us – our 'coming' community. It means neither the course of affairs concerning things done nor historical writing, but things about to be done. It concerns a future existence of which we cannot have knowledge, for it is not a matter of epistemology but, if anything, of ontology. Finally, as a 'coming' without ever 'becoming', it indicates a clear break with the developmental view that characterized substantive philosophies of history as well as historical writing as it became institutionalized in the early nineteenth century.

The *retrospective* is the familiar sense of historical writing. The different understanding of the prospective, however, requires a modification to the retrospective sense too, which concerns the function of historical writing in identity constitution. For if the future is not the final stage of a 'becoming', then our retrospective stance cannot be based on the view that understanding something means inquiring into *its* past (from which it unfolds and proceeds to its future state). In the retrospective stance of a quasi-substantive philosophy of history there is nothing like a different past state of the otherwise same present identity; there is only another identity. One might nevertheless object by noting that there is nothing new here, given that the past has been the 'other' ever since the institutionalization of the discipline. And the objection would be partly right, but only partly. It is true that even in the developmental view the past was the 'other'. Yet that 'other' was always an earlier version of a present 'we', much like in the movie *Terminator 2* (1991), where the T-800 (the living tissue over a metal endoskeleton) is an earlier version of the 'advanced prototype' T-1000 (the mimetic poly-alloy), as the T-800 actually refers to its successor. In other words, the past 'other' in the developmental view is who the present 'we', notwithstanding and despite its altered past states, *always* was. In distinction, in a quasi-substantive philosophy of history the 'other' is who the coming 'we' *never* was.

To rephrase things more emphatically, the 'other' is *another* ontological subject, meaning that historical writing cannot answer 'our' identity questions by turning to the past anymore. It cannot answer the question of who 'we' are, because 'who we are' now means 'who we are about to be' prospectively, in the happening of 'our' history, which, by definition, cannot be known. Thus, in a quasi-substantive philosophy of history, the retrospective stance associated with historical writing shifts from an approach that positively connects to an approach that disrupts and *disconnects*. Similarly to negative (*apophatic*) theology, according to which God cannot be described in positive terms, history in this sense can answer our identity questions only by negation. Nevertheless, the negative answers inform us about who we are not, and by virtue of their exclusion, they can still be indicative of what the coming 'we' is about to be. This negative definition gains significance in the light of the irony of the story, namely, that if prospectively 'we' never become, and if retrospectively we can know only what 'we' are not, then we can never *know* who 'we' actually are. What we can know, what historical writing can tell us, is who we no longer are and hence what the coming 'we' cannot be.

Finally, and most importantly, it is necessary to consider these two senses of history as they meet at a present point of disruption, from which the former sense of history applies prospectively and the latter retrospectively. Seen together, the past, the present and the future make up what I would call *history as a disrupted singular*. In the long run, consisting of several disruptive moments and transformations, this is the mechanism of a perpetual transformation of unknowable 'coming' histories into dissociated, apophatic pasts. From points of disruption, the retrospective and the prospective stances satisfy two different kinds of desires. Yet, as odd as it may sound, points of disruption also function as points of connection, given that it is seen from these points that both sides of history as a disrupted singular play the same endless game: identity formation.

This history as a disrupted singular departs both from the late eighteenth-century invention of history as a collective singular, as it was dubbed by Koselleck (2004: 33–7), and from the Kosellekian interpretative scheme. There is a dual departure because Koselleck's analytical framework is based on the very same temporal configuration as its subject of analysis, the concept of history as a collective singular. To sketch the framework very briefly, in its core there are two anthropological constants, the categories of a 'space of experience' and a 'horizon of expectation', whose inner relations structure the experience of time. The kind of change that can happen in the Kosellekian framework is a change in the internal relation of these categories, like the change Koselleck associates with *Neuzeit* (by which he means Western modernity), when expectations moved away from previous experiences in an accelerating fashion, giving way to the temporal configuration in which history as a collective singular became thinkable. But however far expectations may move from experiences, Koselleck's categories work on the premise of continuous succession, as they themselves are products of the notion of history whose birth and characteristics Koselleck investigates. However thin that continuity between experiences and expectations might become in *Neuzeit*, both experiences and expectations concern one single ontological subject whose past and future are at stake in a present moment. The one single subject, whose association with both the past and the future takes place in a present moment, necessarily creates temporal unity and continuity.

Contrary to this, the temporal configuration that underlies the concept of history as a disrupted singular is based on disconnection and disruption. The past cannot be a space of experience simply because it no longer concerns the experiences of the same ontological subject that comes-to-existence on the prospective side, but the experiences of a 'them' that is anything but the 'we' in its formation. In a similar vein, the future cannot form a horizon of expectation as it simply does not concern the prospective projection of a past subject but the birth of another subject that did not exist previously. To put this in a somewhat thesis-like way: the temporal configuration that underlies the notion of history as a disrupted singular is not a relation between a space of experience and a horizon of expectation within a flow of time, but a *space of dissociated knowledge* and a *horizon of existence* against the background of a disruption of time.

To be clear, I do not intend to claim here that we have new anthropological constants to structure historical time by exchanging Koselleck's old anthropological constants for new and supposedly better ones. Rather, what the above discussion implies is that Koselleck's categories themselves are far from being anthropological constants. The above categories are tools that enable the conceptualization of the temporality of the notion of history as a disrupted singular. In turn, history as a disrupted singular is the concept that accounts for change over time in human affairs at a time when a sense of the unprecedented increasingly permeates domains of human life and endeavours. It is the concept of history that captures the emerging historical sensibility of Western societies in times of unprecedented change.

The lingering threat of substantive thinking

I do not wish to pretend to be able to give a full account of the quasi-enterprise by outlining the sense in which an emerging postwar Western historical sensibility necessarily invokes the future. I am also more than willing to concede that the above sketch of a quasi-substantive philosophy of history is not one that could be encountered in any individual theory. Certain elements of such a philosophy of history are obviously there in certain theories of late, but these theories themselves would not qualify as a theoretical edifice as overarching and coherent as the quasi-enterprise. They have neither the explicit agenda to conceptualize an emerging historical sensibility, nor a comprehensive vision of how Western societies already conceive of themselves as 'historical' in the early decades of the twenty-first century.

Furthermore, the agendas they explicitly advocate hardly seem to converge in many respects. Although compiling a complete list of their differences could take forever, it makes sense to mention a few for mere illustrative purposes. To begin with, Nancy's coming community has nothing to do with Ankersmit's focus on Western civilization as a definite subject of change. Ankersmit's trauma is the loss of an old world, while Runia's trauma is connected to the events that lead to it. Although both Runia and Nancy theorize a notion of presence, Runia's 'presence' is the past taking over the present (Chapter 2 will address this in more detail), while Nancy's 'presence' concerns not the past but the future. Finally, and most importantly, Nancy does not attribute a mechanism to history in any sense whatsoever, Ankersmit does so, at best, only by tacitly implying it, while Runia's views tend to exceed the quasi-substantive framework to which I have restricted them.

Runia's case, I think, points to probably the biggest threat a quasi-enterprise can face: the recourse to substantive thinking by virtue of entertaining cultural evolutionary views. In his later essays, Runia has begun to tailor his theory of history to a cultural evolutionary vocabulary that necessarily entails the postulation of a deeper developmental continuity. When Runia theorizes the momentous changes in human affairs with the background assumption of cultural evolution, the result is that these changes acquire an entirely different conceptual shape. Instead of being leaps into the complete unknown, each of the leaps now becomes responsible for bringing about a 'higher level of adaptive ingenuity' (Runia 2014: 198).

It is easy to see what the consequences are. As soon as the disruptive and singular character of momentous changes dissolves into a gradual increase of adaptive ingenuity, the defining features of substantive philosophies of history resurface. What's more, they not only resurface but take charge over the entire disconnection-driven mechanism that up until this point seemed like one best captured by the notion of history as a disrupted singular. The inclusion of cultural evolutionary views effectively destroys such disconnection-driven mechanism. Inasmuch as cultural evolution is stretched over a series of disruptive changes, the course of human affairs gains directionality pointing toward higher and higher levels of adaptive ingenuity. By gaining directionality, it also gains an implied although vague purpose (full adaptive ingenuity) and an implied substance that fulfils that purpose over time (humanity fulfilling their potential of adaptive ingenuity). In the end, Runia's theory of history becomes prone to the possibility of collapsing into a full-blown substantive philosophy of a historical process that appears to be the inherent property of the outside world. Contrary to this, a quasi-substantive philosophy conceives of the concept of history it designs only as a tool of sense-making.

As long as substantive thinking informs a conceptualization of history, the concept of history in question fails to respond to the challenge posed by times of unprecedented changes. In fact, substantive thinking cannot even conceive of any *challenge* posed by anything to itself, given that it does not conceive of itself as a contingent endeavour of sense-making, relative to spatially and temporally confined human aims. This is precisely what a quasi-substantive philosophy of history tries to do when attempting to deliver a conceptualization that aims to make sense of the unprecedented. Substantive thinking about history cannot but configure the relationship to the past and the future in terms of the former somehow being the preceding condition of the latter. In such a configuration, the future necessarily appears as if it always already was contained in the past to one extent or another, and if this containment simply was the natural order of the world. In contrast to this, a quasi-substantive philosophy of history aims at a conceptualization of the relationship to the past and the future that theoretically accounts for already existing societal perceptions of change over time as unprecedented. The next two chapters will elaborate on these relationships. First, by conceptualizing our relationship to the past in a quasi-substantive philosophy of history; and, second, by turning to the question of future prospects.

2

The Dissociated Past

Whose past?

How does a quasi-substantive philosophy of history account for relations to the past in Western societies of late? The issue is truly bewildering if you take into account that abandoning the idea of a substance of a historical process means the absence of a self-identical subject of historical change. It means that there is no ground on which a past subject could appear as a predecessor or forebearer to a later subject. But apprehending the past in terms of dissociation is a deeply perplexing situation. Whenever we look back to the past along dissociative measures, it is not particularly clear *whose* past it is that we relate to in the present and what exactly that relation means. With the lack of an associative relation to the past we most certainly have serious difficulties with recognizing the past as ours. In fact, it may not even be possible to recognize a dissociated past as ours at all. Accordingly, the question that demands an answer is: in what sense can we say that *the* past – or *a* past – is *ours* if we no longer define ourselves along associative measures applied to past states of human affairs? Or, put differently, what sort of past is it that we can call ours?

I believe the question is of utmost importance for an understanding of both the general historical sensibility of our times and of the specific function historical writing attains within this wider sensibility. However, before unpicking the answer I would like to unravel the question in a more detailed way by returning briefly to the concept of history as a disrupted singular, as discussed in the previous chapter. There I argued that the categories of 'space of experience' and 'horizon of expectation', which Koselleck treats as anthropological constants, simply do not work within the framework of a quasi-substantive philosophy of history. These categories are more or less extended versions of Edmund Husserl's categories of 'retention' and 'protention', introduced in the phenomenological analysis of time-consciousness (Husserl 1991). Whereas Koselleck's categories try to capture the structure of historical time, Husserl's categories are about the individual level of everyday experience. To use the almost Husserlian example of the melody of Meat Loaf's 'I'd Do

Anything for Love': when we listen to it (that is, not when we recall it), we do so not merely as a random collection of individual notes but as a succession of notes, as a whole, as an object dispersed in time, as phenomenologists like to put it. While listening to the melody, 'retention' is at play regarding the short-term past containing the notes already passed, and 'protention' makes us anticipate how the melody will unfold (which of course does not mean that we cannot fail in our anticipation).

Koselleck's categories work with a structural similarity on a collective level regarding history and historical time. Just like the Husserlian categories, they imply a continuous succession. Being conscious about historical time would mean considering not only a collection of individual events but, rather, conceiving them as a whole, as a succession of events, unfolding from the past into the future. Within this framework of continuity, asking the question of whose past it is to which we may relate in the present does not pose much difficulty. It simply occurs as self-evident that the past must be the past of the subject whose relation to the past is questioned in the present. Expectations concerning the future can fast-forward and move very far from past experiences in a Koselleckian framework – and Koselleck's thesis is precisely that they do so increasingly in Western modernity – but they cannot break with each other to the extent that those past experiences might occur as not belonging to a self-identical subject whose past and future are at stake. The past, the present and the future cannot but remain the whole of history of the very same subject and, hence, the overall concept of history cannot but remain a collective singular.

Contrary to this, in the temporal configuration that underlies the notion of history as a disrupted singular, past experiences and future expectations diverge completely. Accordingly, what history as a disrupted singular theorizes is not a *continuity in* the subject's unfolding but, rather, the *displacement and replacement of* the subject, with ever new subjects superseding each other over time. What it conceptualizes is the occasional birth of something genuinely new, something that is in no sense a newer version of the other left behind. In this disrupted singular, the retrospective side is completely dissociated and is turned into a matter of knowledge instead of being a matter of existence. At the same time, on the prospective side there is a radical openness that is not there to expect anything but the fact that the future will be filled in with a coming existence. Nevertheless, just as in the Koselleckian framework, the two sides presuppose each other with respect to their different but complementary roles in the constitution of identity. Based on all this, what I eventually suggested was that the temporal configuration of history as a disrupted singular (expressed in terms of identity formation) is the interdependence of the space of dissociated knowledge retrospectively and the horizon of existence prospectively.

This is the point where I would like to pick up the thread to expand on the respective sides of history as a disrupted singular and highlight the temporal configuration that underlies the way in which we can talk about history again in times of unprecedented change. At the heart of this discussion will be an analogy introduced in the previous chapter. According to the analogy, the way we make use of the dissociated past in identity constitution is akin to the way apophatic theology tries to describe God by means of negative statements on what God is not. Picking up on this analogy, I would like to call the past that we turn to in order to find out what we are not as our *apophatic past*.

Introducing a notion such as our apophatic past in a secular endeavour may lead to certain misunderstandings. To avoid them, I would like to be clear that making use of theological vocabulary in elucidating the temporal configuration of history as a disrupted singular by no means intends to suggest any link between religious sentiments and our conceptions of time and history. The invocation of theology does not wish to suggest anything more and has nothing more to do with history than my earlier appeal to Meat Loaf. Both are analogies in service of rendering particular things intelligible. They may be imperfect analogies, but I hope they are illustrative and instructive.

Having cleared this up, I would like to remain consistent with the meaning attributed to the notion throughout the discussions of this chapter. Hence, I will begin by talking about what conceptualizations of temporality are *not* our apophatic past: first, about the notion of the practical past as contrasted to the notion of the historical past, recently picked up by Hayden White (2014); and, second, about the notion of a present past as it appears in recent historical theory (Bevernage 2012; Runia 2014). Only after discussing what our apophatic past is not will I go on to examine what it might be and what consequences it might have concerning the function of historical writing.

Neither the practical nor the historical past

Recently, there seems to be an oversupply on the theoretical market, with multiple approaches and efforts aiming to describe what kind of work historical theory *should* carry out. The sheer spectacle of the extensiveness of the talk about what the field should do instead of what it has been doing in the last half-century betrays a shared sense of loss of orientation and a need for revision. Such craving for reorientation is nowhere exhibited more clearly than in the growing number of discussions on the future of the theory and philosophy of history.

In 2010, *History and Theory*, the leading theoretical journal of the field, devoted a theme issue to the question entitled 'History and Theory: The

Next Fifty Years.' Not much later, in 2013, the inaugural conference of the International Network for Theory of History (INTH) took place in Ghent under the equally telling title 'The Future of the Theory and Philosophy of History.' These two major events clearly attest to a shared sense of a necessity of renewal. At the same time, however, there is no shared understanding whatsoever concerning the question of what such a renewal should look like. All there is instead is an abundance of proposals, all seeming to urge particular agendas, ranging from an integration of historical studies and historical theory into a larger family of non-anthropocentric human sciences (Domanska 2010), to the revival of analytical philosophy of history (Brzechczyn 2018). The only thing there seems to be an agreement about is that the issue that demands revision is our relation to the past. Herman Paul (2015), motivated by the experiences of the INTH conference in Ghent, even advocates the issue of relations to the past as a broader research agenda for theoretical work. By mentioning a variety of ways in which both academic and non-academic relations to the past (epistemic, material, aesthetic, political) are and could be examined, Paul argues that the issue has the potential to bring together diverging approaches in the field of the theory and philosophy of history by providing an integrative theoretical framework.

Paul's view may sound a bit optimistic with respect to the assumed integrative potential. Nevertheless, I think that Paul is right in that the issue of relations to the past may, at least, have some centripetal force, regarding which I would like to make two important remarks and qualifications. The first is that the issue has some centripetal force inasmuch as it belongs to an even wider discussion on historical time and temporality. In line with the overall argument of this book, talking about our relationship to the past 'historically' means nothing other than talking about it with the background assumption of a wholesale configuration of past, present and future. Nothing illustrates this point better than the fact that even Paul's proposal to elevate the issue of relations to the past to the level of a shared research agenda came at a time when an overall revision of historical time and temporality had already been on the agenda for a while (of which Lorenz and Bevernage 2013 provide an excellent overview).

On this note, my second remark concerning the centripetal potential of the issue is precisely that it is already effective to a certain extent. Although Paul proposes to study relations to the past in the hope of achieving integration, some diverging paths of historical theory are, as far as I can see, already brought together by the issue. But this sort of coming together does not mean that the entirety of historical theory could unite around a shared interest. It means only that wholesale conceptualizations of relations to the past are already widely discussed. In fact, among the major central debates of the last ten years or so, there are two such wholesale conceptualizations of what the relationship to the past looks like in Western societies: first, the notion of the practical past as opposed to the notion of the historical past; and second, the notion of the present past. There are of course other conceptual alternatives, such as the notion of *Nachleben*, usually discussed in English as 'survival' or 'afterlife' (Didi-Hubermann 2003; Tamm 2015). In the view of Johannes Grave (2019) the notion of 'survival' and Walter Benjamin's notion of the 'dialectical image' may even establish a link between the concerns of historical theory and concepts of the image. The practical past and the present past, however, seem to dominate recent theoretical debates. Whereas the latter is closely related to a wider debate on the notion of presence, the former, which I now wish to put under closer scrutiny, marks the latest theoretical intervention of Hayden White (2014).

If White's turn to the notion of the practical past were a movie, its Wikipedia page would discuss it in terms of earning 'mixed to average' reviews. Whereas Ewa Domanska (2015a) passes a positive evaluation, Chris Lorenz (2014) remains unconvinced. While Paul (2011: 144–50) thinks that the notion is consistent with White's earlier work, Spiegel (2013) rather sees confrontation. What is certain is that, in one way or another, the notion has gathered quite some attention lately (see also Ahlskog 2016; La Greca 2016). With some Nietzschean connotations attached, it even managed to become the umbrella topic of the second INTH conference in 2016 in Ouro Preto, Brazil, under the title 'The Practical Past: On the Advantages and Disadvantages of History for Life.' The career of the notion attests to the fact that White's work is still able to deeply influence the thematization of the scholarly field of the theory and philosophy of history. With all the respect one might have towards such work, in my brief discussion I will nevertheless argue that theorizing the notion of the practical past is anything but a viable offer or a call for an otherwise much desired genuine revision of the issue of relations to the past.

As to the notion itself, White borrows it from the conservative political philosopher Michael Oakeshott. But to be more precise, White does not only borrow a notion from Oakeshott; together with the notion, White borrows a complete theoretical distinction between the counterpart categories of the practical and the historical past. Since Oakeshott first introduced the distinction in *Experience and Its Modes* ([1933] 1966), not much has changed about the notions themselves. Later reconsiderations of the distinction – either by White or Oakeshott himself – were not directed at its conceptual framing but at the different judgements passed on its respective sides. Some thirty years after the first phrasing of the distinction, even Oakeshott himself changed his attitude towards the historical and the practical past. Originally praising the former, Oakeshott grew more sympathetic towards the latter over time (Harlan 2009: 173–6) but left the conceptual apparatus itself untouched. Moreover, still staying with Oakeshott, it is important to note that this conceptual apparatus cannot be separated from the task he took on in *Experience and Its Modes* with respect to history. Oakeshott's self-conceived task was to affirm the autonomy of historical knowledge by showing that it is a distinct mode of experience in its own right. Thus, originally, Oakeshott's focus concerning history was the notion of the historical past, which served as a conceptual tool for disclosing the peculiarity of the historical mode of experience as contrasted to other modes. The other modes would be the scientific and the practical, the latter being the proper context of the practical past.

In Oakeshott's account, the distinction looks something like this: the historical past is a 'dead past' and its distinctiveness lies in 'its very disparity from what is contemporary' (Oakeshott [1933] 1966: 106), while the practical past comes to the fore 'wherever the significance of the past lies in the fact that it has been influential in deciding the present and future fortunes of man, wherever the present is sought in the past' (103). Whereas the historical past describes the relationship of professional historians to the past, the practical past describes our everyday attitude towards it. As it stands, White seems to be perfectly content with this conceptual framing. But unlike Oakeshott, who originally passed a positive judgement on the historical past for the aforementioned reasons of presenting historical knowledge as a distinct mode of experience, White, having very different objectives, calls for an embracement of the practical past.

White thinks that Oakeshott's description of the historical past corresponds to the condition of the historical profession since its institutionalization, or, at least, it corresponds to the self-image of historians. By saying that the distinction 'is useful for distinguishing between modern professional historians' approaches to the study of the past', on the one hand, and, on the other, 'the ways in which lay persons and practitioners of other disciplines call upon, recall, or seek to use "the past" as a "space of experience" to be drawn upon as a basis for all kinds of judgements and decisions in daily life', White simply reinforces the Oakeshottian picture (2014: 15). The real difference lies in White's harshness of evaluation and in his contempt for the historical past and, by extension, for professional historical studies.

In his probably most sincere moments, White seems to think that 'historical knowledge is no use at all for the solution of practical problems in the present' (2012: 127). In his less condemnatory moments, however, White seems to be more nuanced. Whereas the harsh and mutually exclusive distinction may easily result in one of the biggest straw man arguments concerning professional historiography (as if it never ever had any inclination towards practical endeavours and as if it never mobilized historical knowledge for 'the solution of practical problems in the present'), the more sophisticated White is very well aware of how professional historiography in the nineteenth century was engaged in nation-building. On this more modest ground, White does not forget to warn readers that the respective sides of the distinction are more 'ideal typifications' than 'descriptions of actual points of view or ideologies' (2014: 15).

It is nevertheless questionable whether such precautionary measures save White's case. Using the notions of the historical and the practical past to distinguish between professional and lay approaches to the past is still prone to being a rather one-dimensional (mis)representation of historical studies. But White seems to be aware of this too. He tries to avoid mistreating historical studies by confining the applicability of the distinction to postwar historiography, to the period when skepticism about the idea of an overall historical process became dominant in historiography too. What White ends up claiming is that 'over the arc of the twentieth century' professional historical writing has been 'retreating into a kind of commonsensical empiricism as justification for the neutrality and disinterestedness with which it composed its ideologically anodyne pictures of the historical past' (2014: 16). Does this confinement help? It seems to me that the problem persists, as White's claim does not stand even when reduced to a certain episode of the history of professional historiography. As María Inés La Greca (2016) argues, it certainly does not apply to politically engaged feminist history. Nor does it apply to politically motivated postcolonial histories and to all the nonetheless politically inspired different 'history from below' approaches. In fact, White's claim is, by definition, untrue for any historiography that conceives of itself in political terms. Besides, in light of one of the take-home messages of postmodern historical theory, the self-description of historians does not even matter. For regardless of how disinterested and neutral professional historiography might claim to be, as Keith Jenkins says, 'history is never for itself; it is always for someone' (2003: 21).

The latter point is actually not restricted to once popular postmodern historical theories. It forms the core of even White's own life oeuvre. In *Metahistory*, White does not only argue that every piece of historiography has a political inclination, but also makes the claim that 'every philosophy of history contains within it the elements of a proper history, just as every proper history contains within it the elements of a full-blown philosophy of history' (1973: 428). However, full-blown philosophies of history appear in White's later theory in an interesting light. Recently White has claimed that 'philosophy of history belongs to the class of disciplines meant to bring order and reason to a "practical past" rather than to that "historical past" constructed by professional historians' (2014: 16–17).

The ideal typical description of historical studies as belonging to the domain of the historical past is, needless to say, terribly at odds with White's above considerations in *Metahistory*. If (1) every piece of historiography inherently contains a philosophy of history, and (2) philosophy of history is the paradigmatic enterprise that belongs to the domain of the practical past, then it follows that every piece of historiography inherently belongs to the domain of the practical past (at least to the extent to which they necessarily contain a full-blown philosophy of history). It is simply not possible to consistently hold both the distinction and the views of *Metahistory*. If *Metahistory* is right, then the distinction between the historical and the practical past does not hold; if the distinction holds, then *Metahistory* must be wrong. In light of the earlier arguments it nevertheless seems more plausible to claim that the former is the case and that the distinction is flawed.

All in all, the dichotomy of a historical and a practical past does not withstand closer scrutiny. The problem is not only that the description does not apply to professional historical studies in general since the institutionalization of the discipline. Rather, the problem is that it does not apply to most kinds of historiography throughout the history of modern institutionalized historiography, including the period of postwar historical studies. What's more, even White's own lifetime oeuvre speaks against the feasibility of the distinction. There may be a kind of historiography that, by virtue of its self-description, aims at disinterestedness and neutrality, but even in White's own framework this must be actually just one kind of ideology among others, namely, the ideology of disinterestedness. Even if the conceptualization of a distinction between a historical and a practical past may be useful to distinguish analytically between two kinds of relations to the past, it certainly is neither useful nor accurate in describing the relation to the past as a distinction between historiographical and non-academic relations.

Yet, even if the distinction does not hold in most respects, the core question of this chapter still needs to be answered. Is White's embrace of the practical past a useful conceptual tool for a quasi-substantive philosophy of history? If throughout Western modernity even professional historical studies were engaged in the practical past to one extent or another (regardless of the self-description of the discipline as a whole or of its particular historiographical schools and approaches), then the question is: does the notion still account for relations to the past today, in times of unprecedented change? The question is whether history as a disrupted singular that applies dissociative measures to the past allows for a conceptualization of the relation to the past in Western societies in terms of a practical past, with respect to both academic and non-academic practices. And the answer will not come as a surprise. As the practical past is, by definition, that with which the present associates itself, that is, the past that according to Oakeshott 'is known as our past' ([1933] 1966: 103), this past must appear as the past of the very same subject that exists now in the present, the past of the very same subject that also extends its very existence into the future. In history as a disrupted singular, this past that pervades the present, fills it up with existence, cannot be ours, because it is the existence from which the future 'we' in formation dissociates by inquiring into it.

Not even the presence of the past

The intellectual environment in which White raised the issue of the practical past was already sparkling, thanks to the freshly emerging notion of presence and the present past (or, the presence of the past), which seems to entail a timelier account for our relation to the past. Its timeliness lies in the extent to which the present past – unlike the practical past – brings forth a reconceptualization of historical time and temporality in attempting to account for relations to the past. Even though the notion of the present past assumes the existence of the past in the present in the same way the practical past does, this present existence of the past does not come about within a flow of time. In other words, the present past resembles the practical past in that it can be present only on the assumption that the past has not vanished. But the present past is not the *continuing existence* of the past in the present; it pervades the present on the premise that the past is irrevocably gone, which provides its condition of possibility in that it needs to *break through* into the present.

The literary and cultural theorist Hans Ulrich Gumbrecht (2004) is probably the most influential advocate of the notion of presence. Eelco Runia's essay entitled 'Presence' (2006) came out two years later and got reprinted in Runia's *Moved by the Past* (2014: 49–83). Following shortly after the first formulations of their respective theories, Runia and Gumbrecht happily recognized the similarities of their approaches (Gumbrecht 2006: 323), even though they developed their views independently of each other. The third name to be mentioned here is Nancy, whose *The Birth to Presence* came out in English in 1993. Although Gumbrecht (2004: 57–8) refers to Nancy as an intellectual companion engaged in discovering neglected dimensions of relating to the world, Nancy's views actually lead far away from those of both Gumbrecht and Runia. For Nancy, as mentioned in the previous chapter, presence is about anything but the presence of the past; it concerns the prospect of a future existence, a future coming-to-presence. For Gumbrecht and Runia, on the other hand, the notion of presence refers to a present past, as a powerful alternative to what they consider to be the sole focus of the humanities in the second half of the last century: meaning. In the most general terms, their central point is that alongside the constitution of meaning, there is a different but nonetheless vital way in which we relate to the world and, hence, also a vital way in which we relate to the past. Both believe that the right name for describing this relationship is presence.

It is in the context of opposing a supposed obsession with questions of meaning and the constitution thereof that the notion of presence gained attention within the theory and philosophy of history. The reception of the notion is of a rather polarizing nature, far from any hope of even a basic agreement. On the one hand, Jenkins (2010) and Pihlainen (2014b) argue that conceptualizing 'presence' and a present past is a completely wrong direction to pursue and a retreat into theoretical naivety. On the other, Ghosh and Kleinberg (2013) even wonder whether the notion can be the foundation of a new kind of philosophizing about history. To find out how such a split response is possible, I wish to focus on Runia's concept as the one responsible for initiating an ongoing quarrel about the capabilities of the notion of the present past within historical theory.

The first thing to note about Runia's theory is its wonderful richness. The second is that this very richness exposes Runia's theory to the risk of incoherence. All this is easily seen from the very beginning, when Runia offers his first definition of presence as '"being in touch" with people, things, events, and feelings' (2014: 53), thereby invoking a sense of immediacy for which nothing seems to matter much beyond the instantaneous present. As the definition continues, however, it turns into the claim that presence is being in touch with all things that 'made you into the person you are' – an additional claim that points much beyond that which is immediate. The phrasing, which is repeated throughout Runia's *Moved by the Past*, even invites readers to think that Runia still offers something that connects past and present in the same manner as Oakeshott and White's practical past does. And the suspicion might even be backed up by recalling that in many respects Runia himself considers his enterprise as being a substantive and not a quasi-substantive one.

Perhaps the incoherence is due to a deceptive – I hesitate to say false – picture about what a philosophy of history *must* assume. The commitment to questions concerning how the past made the present into becoming what it is necessarily invokes attributes of modern philosophies of history such as directionality and development, which does not let Runia come to terms fully with the consequences of the disruptive character of history otherwise postulated by his own theory. The notion of presence, understood as the presence of all that made up a present subject, confronts not only Runia's investment in dissociation, discontinuity and disruption as discussed in the previous chapter, but also those further claims that seem to be in tune with the disruptive movement of history.

But even if one decides to go only with Runia's theory as restricted to the quasi-substantive, the question emerges: if the past is dissociated, how can it nevertheless be present? Answering this question is the terrain where the notion of presence is the most promising for a reconceptualization of relations to the past. In Runia's theory, the past seems to be able to make its way into the present on two levels. The first level concerns historical writing and the notion of presence in its relation to the linguistic trope of metonymy. The second level is the most general level of human existence, in which the notion of presence is connected to a more primordial relation to the past when it takes charge over present deeds. As for the first level, Runia claims that the linguistic trope of metaphor is responsible for the generation of meaning and thereby accounts for continuity. To counterbalance this, Runia endows metonymy with the ability to transfer presence and thereby accounting for discontinuity. In describing discontinuity as 'our being surprised by ourselves,' Runia is convinced that such discontinuities play out both in history as the course of affairs and in history as historical writing (2014: 55). Metonymy, however, concerns the level of historical writing, and the question it poses is the breakthrough of past *reality* into the present through historical *texts*. To explain how this happens, Runia also turns to a metaphor in describing the presence of the past in historical writing by saying that 'historical reality travels with historiography not as a paying passenger, but as a stowaway' (81).

On the more general second level – the level I am most interested in – the epistemological question implied in Runia's claim does not play a role. This level is indifferent to the question of whether historical writing is able to get in touch with or transfer past reality, because the question it poses is not the question of historical representation but the question of existence. It poses the question of whether a past that is absent can fill up the present with existence. Runia thinks it can: not as part of the theory of metonymy but in the far more general contention that 'the past may have a presence that is so powerful that it can use us, humans, as its material' (88). The primary example for this is the case of the Dutch historians of the Srebrenica commission, who, according to the argument of Runia, reproduced or 'acted out' the defence and argumentation of Dutch soldiers whose acts (the killing of 8,000 Bosnians under their 'guidance') they were supposed to be studying (17–48).

Discussions on the two levels often merge in Runia's work, frequently resulting in confusion about the notion of presence. For the sake of clarity, it seems important to note that it is one thing to state that texts can, due to present human intervention, be crafted to convey presence (which is what literary theory calls experientiality and Chapter 6 explores in more detail) and quite another to claim that a past existence invades and takes over the present without present human intervention (as Runia appears to think in the passage quoted above). In the latter case, the past is not supposed to carve its way into the present through historiographical presentation but takes charge over the present existentially. Even though I find this entailed idea of human passivity considerably troublesome, I have to admit that it is nevertheless on this second, ontological-existential level that the notion of the present past might be useful for efforts that aim at rethinking the question of historical time and temporality in a way different from the developmental view.

A more coherent, though less poetic, offer can be found in Berber Bevernage's *History, Memory, and State-Sponsored Violence* (2012). It explicitly seeks to fashion an 'alternative chronosophy' to transcend a confrontation of an irreversible and a reversible time. Bevernage associates the former with professional historical writing and thus with the 'time of history' and the latter with the 'time of jurisdiction,' claiming that the two are irreconcilable (2012: 2). In history's emphasis on the irreversible flow of time, there is no full remedy for past injustice. The past being gone for good, it is impossible to bring it to justice. At the same time, Bevernage thinks that the irreversibility of the time of history does not necessarily need to result in overemphasizing the absence of the past (3). In trying to avoid a 'dichotomous opposition' which assumes either the absolute presence or the absolute absence of the past, Bevernage turns to Vladimir Jankélévitch's concept of the *irrevocable* (4–6). Whereas the irreversible past is that which flees from the present, the irrevocable is that which gets 'stuck' in the present. With this persistence of the past, the concept of the irrevocable seems to grant the presence of the past without collapsing past and present into each other, on the one hand, and without assuming their complete distinctiveness, on the other. Yet, because Jankélévitch only mentions the concept in passing, Bevernage takes on the task of elaborating the notion as a foundation of the alternative chronosophy he offers.

The task itself is a multifarious one. It consists of detecting or recognizing something like an irrevocable past as underlying transitional justice, seeking a wider conceptualization of a relation to the past that could best capture the irrevocable, and also turning this conceptualization into a theoretical foundation of an ethically concerned and politically inspired form of historical writing. In the hope of finding the necessary theoretical support, Bevernage (2012: 110–30) surveys the ideas of a sample of notable historians and philosophers, namely, Fernand Braudel, R.G. Collingwood, Ernst Bloch, and Louis Althusser. At the end, the closest ally of Bevernage (2012: esp. 142–4) turns out to be Derrida's theory of spectrality and his notion of the 'haunting past' (Derrida 1994; see also Kleinberg 2017) to theorize a present that is haunted by the spectre of the past, a present that is 'out of joint', a present that is non-contemporaneous.

Inasmuch as a spectre of the past in the present is neither full presence nor full absence, it serves well Bevernage's efforts of trying to avoid the dichotomous opposition of their absoluteness. Besides, Bevernage's theoretical undertaking brilliantly fulfils its narrower purpose to account for a relation to the past of victims of injustice. This merit is nevertheless also the greatest shortcoming with respect to the more general aim of achieving a theoretical basis for the rejuvenation of the discipline of history as an ethically and politically more engaged one. Although it is possible to overcome the 'structural bias' that 'concepts of time traditionally used by historians are structurally more compatible with the perpetrators' than the victims' point of view' (Bevernage 2012: ix), its potential success means that it shares its fate with its criticized modes by being able to account for the relations to the past only of some, though this time with reversed preferences. A present past as haunting the present may resonate with a victim's point of view but as a theoretical notion it remains of rather partial scope.

Whether this is a shortcoming or a merit is of course debatable, and the judgement could be completely different depending on whether one speaks in historiographical or theoretical terms. In terms of a theory of history, I think that the narrow scope signals more of a shortcoming than a merit. A theory that accounts for victims' and survivors' relations to the past can be considered as theoretical support only for a very particular approach within historical studies. This approach may be highly important in many respects, including ethico-political, societal and historiographical considerations among others. It may even introduce historiographical novelty by challenging long-standing biases of the profession. But lacking generality it does not – and probably it even does not want to – qualify as a theory that accounts for what being 'historical' might mean on a conceptual level that aims to encompass particularities.

The achievements of both Bevernage and Runia are nevertheless vital for such a potential comprehensive conceptualization of historical time and temporality that this book aims at. In theorizing a 'presence in absence' as a present past, they both explicate notions of a kind of time that is 'historical' even while being other than a continuous flow. Due to their work in conceptualizing relations to the past that do not assume processual development, theories of the present past certainly have much more to offer to a quasi-substantive philosophy of history than the notion of the practical past does. That being the case, the question to ask is: can the notion of the present past be linked in any way to history as a disrupted singular? At first glance, the answer seems to be a rather obvious 'No, it cannot.' Indeed, how could anyone imagine that the past breaking into and taking over the present or that the past being stuck in the present, that is, the past with which the present necessarily becomes associated, has anything to do with a dissociated past as the retrospective side of history as a disrupted singular?

The answer I wish to suggest is that the notion of presence in historical theory, and thus the idea of the present past, can be regarded as the counterpart of what I call the apophatic past. Not in the sense of their being each other's evil twins, and not as if one could be favoured and set up as a standard to follow against the other. Moreover, neither are they counterparts in the sense that one of them could be recommended for historical practice at the expense of the other, nor complements in the sense that one could apply to historical practice while the other could describe a relation to the past beyond the concerns of professional historical writing. This constellation may perfectly describe the relationship between the historical past and the practical past in Oakeshott's and White's thinking. But in the case of the concept of history as a disrupted singular, the link between the present and our apophatic past concerns a more primordial and elementary relation in which they are counterparts insofar as they are *existentially bound together*.

Our apophatic past

The long and short of the discussion of the previous pages is that the notion of the present past, although promising, cannot account for relations to past in Western societies of late without a counterpart. This counterpart is what I call the apophatic past. I reckon that the phrase may sound somewhat outlandish or clumsy, but is at least indicative of the function of our backward stance in identity constitution. Besides, sounding outlandish may not be a bad thing after all, taking into consideration what the phrase stands for.

But what exactly does the phrase stand for? What exactly do I mean by an apophatic past? To begin with, I mean a dissociated past. Yet, I mean much more than a simple present dissociation from a past condition or state of affairs. The apophatic past can only be understood in relation to the future, which is not the result but the source of a backward stance. This is because it can only be a postulated future viewpoint, the viewpoint that one has in a coming community, from where the past looks apophatic, from where the past appears as a matter of dissociated knowledge about what the coming community is not and what it cannot be. The importance of this operation cannot be overstated, for if the coming 'we' cannot know its identity it has no other choice than to attempt a self-definition – a self-definition that can never fully succeed – by negation, by making use of the only usable thing at hand in that matter, the apophatic past, and hence by the practice that studies and creates (creates by studying/studies by creating) such a past: historical writing.

However, as stated above, even this notion of our apophatic past cannot do without a counterpart, the present past, with which it shares its fate. Inasmuch as any of the two is presented as a solitary and exclusive notion, neither of them can qualify as an overall theory of history that redefines historical time and accounts for our relations with the past in the most general terms. It is only when our apophatic past is seen together with the present past that a comprehensive account of our relations to the past can be conceived of within a larger frame of an overall theory of history. It is only inasmuch as the two are existentially bound together that they account for and conceptualize the role of the past in an emerging historical sensibility in times of unprecedented change.

This existential binding stems from the characteristics of the prospective side of history as a disrupted singular. Only together do the present past and our apophatic past attest to the fact that the coming 'we' is never an achievement but only the *prospect* of a 'we', of the history we have ahead of us. Because the 'we' in its happening and coming-to-presence is never realized, *our* apophatic past also cannot be fully 'realized' as the past as such (the entirety of the past). If the future coming-to-presence and coming-to-existence provides the basis for retrospective dissociation, and if this future coming-to-existence is never achieved, full dissociation from the past can never take place. Consequently, there has to be another past that is not apophatic and not dissociated. And insofar as the backward stance of historical writing is a backward stance, then its territory is the past as such, and this territory cannot be merely our apophatic past about which we can have dissociated knowledge but also a past that breaks through, a present past.

Thus, whenever we say 'past' and whenever we say that historical writing is about the past, this past is an inseparable blend of the present and the apophatic past, a blend of our associative and dissociative measures. The past that historical writing is about is neither purely present and associated, nor purely dissociated and apophatic, that is, neither purely *ours*, nor purely *not ours*. As odd and counterintuitive as it may sound, because the point of view is always the coming 'we', in a quasi-substantive philosophy of history *the past is ours by virtue of our never having had it, and the past is not ours by virtue of our still having it.*

Whenever and in whatever respect we still have the past in the present – whenever and in whatever respect the past has presence in the present – the past fills the present with existence. It would be hard, or even impossible, to imagine that the present is devoid of existence, and if the coming 'we' is, by definition, non-presence, then the present has to be filled with existence provided by the past. And in this sense the past is even more extremely present than Runia thinks, and the 'we' in its happening is even more extremely only coming-to-presence (that is, even more extremely non-presence at every present moment) as Nancy thinks. Nevertheless, the more distinct and the more extreme they look, the more the present and the apophatic past demand and complement each other. To encapsulate the essence of all this, I would like to offer the following thesis: *the relation to the past necessitates the interdependence and intertwinement of a past that is ours by virtue of being dissociated and non-present (the apophatic past), and a past that is not ours by virtue of being associated and made present (the present past).*

Essentially contested historical knowledge

That being said, there is a question that introduces further complexity: if the retrospective side of history as a disrupted singular is historical writing as knowledge about our apophatic past, and if the past is not only apophatic but also present (that is, not entirely dissociated and therefore not entirely a matter of knowledge) then how could historical writing live up to its implied task? Can historical writing be knowledge about the past, notwithstanding the extent to which the past is not dissociated but present?

I think that the answer is a rather rewarding one. To unravel it, I would like to contrast once again the distinction between the practical and the historical past with the distinction between the apophatic and the present past. As to the former, the practical past/historical past divide implies a not-so-hidden distinction between matters of ethics on the 'practical' side and matters of knowledge on the 'historical'. This is also the bulk of the criticism White receives from Lorenz (2014: 45–6). The historical past, the dead past, may be the equivalent of the apophatic past in my apophatic past/present past division in the most crucial sense that both are defined by dissociation. The same equivalence may concern the practical past and the present past insofar as both are defined by an associative relation between past and present. Yet the historical past in White's and Oakeshott's account is not only a dissociated but also a *disinterested* and *detached* past, studied for its own sake. It is precisely on the basis of this attributed disinterest and detachment that the notion of the historical past is deprived of ethical and existential concerns and consequently becomes a matter of historical knowledge. Correspondingly, it is due to the attributed interest and engagement on the side of the practical past that ethics takes over knowledge.

Now, contrary to this, the apophatic past/present past distinction is anything but a clear division between disinterest and detachment about the past, on the one side, and interest and continuing present engagement, on the other. The apophatic past is just as much a presently engaged past as its counterpart, the present past. What distinguishes and also makes them counterparts is that the apophatic past engages by negation, while the present past engages by affirmation. This dual engagement and, more importantly, the intertwinement and contemporaneity of the apophatic and the present past as the very same past, collapses matters of knowledge and ethics into each other. Consequentially, due to the inescapability of matters of ethics when it comes to studying the past, historical writing cannot be other than *essentially contested historical knowledge* about the past.

I believe that this perfectly accounts for the question of why all we have are contested histories in the sense of historical writing and why the case is necessarily so. The claim that the past cannot be anything but the terrain of contested knowledge is best supported by a counterfactual argument highlighting the circumstances under which the past could be uncontested knowledge. The past could be the plane of pure, uncontested and fully dissociated knowledge only if the future 'we' would 'become' – that is, if history as the course of affairs would eventually end in the ontological becoming of an all-encompassing subject, if the vision of substantive philosophies of history of the Enlightenment and German Idealism came true, if the ultimate fulfilment of the historical process had already happened. Though it usually goes unnoticed, the practical success of those philosophies of history would have petrified the past and hence would have erased the practice of historical writing. For if an ontological subject – humankind, reason or freedom – would achieve its ultimate truth as history, then historical writing could not be responsible for anything else than for the backward extension of that truth unfolding in history: for writing the ultimate, one and only story of the achievement.

Ironically enough, this backward extension was the founding principle of historical writing in the shape of a search for the ultimate meaning of the past, even though the actual practice of historical writing never lived up to this principle. In light of all this, it can be said that, since its institutionalization, historical writing has had to face one single threat that came in two interrelated forms. The threat of turning itself into uncontested knowledge approached historical writing either as a potential coming true of the future ultimate meaning of the substantive philosophy of history, or as potential self-annihilation through living up to its own founding principle and establishing an ultimate meaning of the past. In light of this, all the charges and debates among historians in the 1990s and early 2000s (Appleby, Hunt and Jacob 1994; Windschuttle 1994; Evans 1997; Breisach 2003) concerning the supposed threat of postmodern theories of history, Hayden White's narrativist philosophy of history and poststructuralist theories missed the point. The reason why these theories that questioned the epistemological soundness of historical writing could not pose any existential threat to historiography was precisely that most of them wished to show that historical writing is nothing other than contested knowledge. They typically wished to show that it can maintain its practice only insofar as it remains contested. In that respect, the theory presented here completely agrees with the theoretical work of the last half-century or so.

The most ominous thing historical writing had to face since its institutionalization was the threat of turning itself into uncontested knowledge. It was not the threat of unwelcomed theoretical intervention; it was the threat of self-annihilation. I think the fact that such a thing cannot reasonably happen is wonderfully exhibited in the inescapable feature of the prospective side of history as a disrupted singular. As long as there is no 'becoming' prospectively and no ultimate fulfilment of a historical process, historical writing is on the safe side as essentially contested knowledge of the past, that is, of the inseparable blending of the present past and *our* apophatic past.

3

The Unprecedented Future

History and the future

When the past is approached along dissociative measures, the future gains a crucial significance. When it is no longer feasible to ground the perception of present and future states of affairs as emerging from long-existing past conditions, the question of future-orientation becomes all the more pressing. True enough, as the previous chapters argue, future-orientation has already become of crucial significance in the reign of the modern historical sensibility. As soon as the world of human affairs became conceptualized as a course that is heading towards a future, the future itself became conceived of as the prospective fulfilment of a yet underdeveloped potential that has already been there in the past. Today, when such a scenario for historical change no longer looks feasible, the question of the hour is what to make out of the future.

On this premise, following the heavy theoretical work of the previous chapters, the present one asks the more practical question: what happens to history when the visions of the future – upon which history was invented – vanish? What happens to history when there seems to be no potential future on the horizon to fulfil in the shape of a historical process? Or, to ask the reverse question: what happens to the future when there is no longer a smooth historical process to lead there?

According to the discussion introduced in the Prologue, a prominent answer among Western intellectuals claims that the result is the 'end of history' and the rule of presentism. These answers can be supplemented by political theories of the self-identified Left, which affirm the diagnosis of the loss of future-orientation in the Western world on the one hand, and try to find ways to revive it and/or deal with it on the other. Affirming the diagnosis typically includes (but is not restricted to) familiar themes such as the aforementioned end of history, the end of utopia, the end of ideology, or the pronouncement of a 'post-political' condition of consensus politics out of which no novelty can possibly emerge. As the diagnosis is typically evaluated as a crisis, it provides the grounds for taking up the self-conceived task of reviving future-orientation in a feasible manner. To meet the challenge, political theories of the Left seek ways to redefine the political in other than consensual terms or ways in which utopia can appear again as a feasible and necessary ethico-political endeavour, if it can be feasible at all (Rancière 1999; Jameson 2005; Mouffe 2005; Unger 2009; Vieira and Marder 2012).

Unlike most of these efforts, I do not think that the future needs to be saved. I also do not think that it is the primary task of political and historical theories to come up with and advocate new versions of the old future-orientation. The primary task would rather be to understand that which might have taken the place of visions of progress of future fulfilment.

In attempting to develop such a theoretical understating, in this chapter I will argue that Western societies have not really abandoned the future in the first place. I think what happened, rather, was that a fundamental change took place – or, to be more accurate, is taking place – concerning the structure of future-orientation, beginning sometime in the middle of the last century. On the one hand, this means that I can affirm the shared diagnosis that the future no longer is where humanity is heading by following a suprahuman scheme provided by philosophies of history or by executing an intentional design of engineering a sociopolitical condition conceived of as 'better' or 'perfect' (like in the case of utopian socialists who imagined the future and also tried to execute their visions). On the other hand, the loss of the future as the fulfilment of a predefined scheme does not mean the disappearance of visions of the future that are conceived of as feasible. The future is still around, but (1) instead of residing in the political domain, it can be found today in the ecological and technological ones; (2) in these domains, the future is conceived of as unprecedented change; and (3) the unprecedented appears as exhibiting a 'posthistorical' character, meaning that it does not appear as the result of a developmental historical process. Accordingly, the envisioned future of the unprecedented no longer orients human life along a directional temporal continuum. It introduces a future-disorientation instead, inasmuch as its postulated future is expected to suddenly erupt in the shape of a singular event that potentially defies all pre-existing schemes of thought.

The triad of cataclysm

Let's begin by returning to the catastrophic character of recent visions of the future that even theories of presentism note (Gumbrecht 2014: 31; Hartog 2015: 202) in arguing that the threatening future serves only the extension and preservation of the present. The logic behind the argument assumes that Western societies of late proceed on the ground that it is better to stay safe with our known measures than venturing into the unknown and risky. This logic is actually not far from the logic of critical political theories that approach the phenomenon of catastrophism about the future in more explicitly evaluative terms and attribute intentions to supposed agents. In the view of critical theories, reinforcing present agendas is not merely the *effect* of perceiving the future as threatening. Rather, critical theories claim that catastrophism about the future *is* the actual means of control that keeps the population aligning with – again, distinctly *political* – agendas of the present. That said, no wonder the proposed solution of critical theories to new ecological and technological threats is the reactivation of a political imagination that already claims to know such threats. As an example, consider the claim of Slavoj Žižek that today's ecological threat can only be handled by handling the more familiar threat of capitalist production (2010: 333–4), which is also to blame for launching apocalyptic prospects on us. There are of course more sophisticated views like that of Isabelle Stengers, who thinks that the ecological challenge is not going to pass simply by doing away with capitalism (2015: 58–9). On the other hand, the main worry of Stengers remains the potential of mobilization in the name of the universal threat that claims to transcend sociopolitical divisions (56).

While these considerations may be valid in one sense or another, it seems to me that they are too much invested in aligning novel perceived threats with older perceived threats known from the political domain. My intention here is neither to blame already known villains and culprits for new wrongdoings nor to warn of familiar misuses of apocalyptic rhetoric. Although I also do not wish to diminish the significance of placing such warnings, what I am much more interested in is the possibility of achieving a conceptualization that recognizes the novelty of the situation and avoids domesticating it. In attempting to do so, my point of departure will be a statement that may find approval in the aforementioned interpretive frameworks as a common denominator of cultural diagnoses. The statement goes as follows: dystopian ecological and technological scenarios as dominant postwar visions of the future in Western societies are conceived of as imposing themselves on humanity in the shape of a sudden event, instead of calling for longer-term gradual achievement.

I reckon that even this common-denominator statement might sound rather suspicious. For how could a future prospect impose itself on humanity? Would this entail the attribution of agency to something inanimate? Well, yes and no. It would certainly entail the attribution of agency to something non-human, but non-human does not really mean inanimate. Recent dystopian prospects revolve around the agency of *nature* or the agency of *machines*, both of them being non-human but animate. Besides, their attributed agency does not appear as independent of human agency. The central tenet of the postulated agency of nature and machines in ecological and technological prospects is actually that it arises out of human action and appears as initially human-induced. The keyword here is *initially*. Because, at the same time, the agency of both nature and machines is expected to increase and gain entirely new dimensions at the expense of human agency, the loss of which is precisely what constitutes the perceived threat.

To gain a better understanding of the situation, consider how, on the one hand, the prospect of global nuclear warfare, anthropogenic climate change and technological apocalypse appear as inherent threats which indeed are results of (inconsiderate) human activity and human agency. Nick Bostrom wonderfully captures the novelty of the challenge of facing threats brought about by human activity by making a distinction between 'anthropogenic existential risks' as opposed to 'natural existential risks' (2013: 15–16). Whereas humanity has faced various natural existential risks before (such as asteroid impacts), the threats to humankind increasingly appear as consequences of human activity, attesting to a sense of unprecedented human capacities.

The most momentous affirmation of such increased human powers has been made already in the 1950s by Julian Huxley, claiming in his essay on transhumanism that it appears 'as if man had been suddenly appointed managing director of the biggest business of all, the business of evolution' ([1957] 1968: 73). At the same time, the more critical contemporary voice of Hannah Arendt, commenting on what is known today as the first events of the Space Race and on the same potential of science and technology to further increase human powers, painted a more balanced picture:

> This future man, whom the scientists tell us they will produce in no more than a hundred years, seems to be possessed by a rebellion against human existence as it has been given, a free gift from nowhere (secularly speaking), which he wishes to exchange, as it were, for something he has made himself. There is no reason to doubt our abilities to accomplish such an exchange, just as there is no reason to doubt our present ability to destroy all organic life on earth. (1958: 2–3)

The prospect of human-induced climate catastrophe, although conceivable for decades and remarked on since the early postwar years, has entered a wider circulation of ideas somewhat later than Arendt and Huxley's considerations. It has joined the threat posed by the increased human 'ability to destroy all organic life on earth' especially as following the quick spread of the notion of the Anthropocene to describe anthropogenic changes in the earth system (Crutzen 2002) and the emergence of earth system science. In the view of Clive Hamilton (2017), the latter is the proper context of the notion, representing a wholesale paradigm shift precisely because of new conceptualizations being inseparable from the birth of new sciences. Whether or not this is the case, the three prospects together – a climate apocalypse, a technoscientific catastrophe and a global nuclear warfare – appear today as the postwar triad of cataclysm.

The dystopian visions of climate change and technology revolve around the possibility of passing a point of no return. Once it is passed, the threat consists of nature taking over what has initially been human-induced and human-controlled change, or of a human-created 'superintelligence' – defined by Bostrom as 'any intellect that greatly exceeds the cognitive performance of humans in virtually all domains of interest' (2014: 22) – surpassing human intelligence. Whatever may happen afterwards is no longer accessible for human reasoning, given that it no longer entails human mastery. This is precisely what makes such prospects unsettling at best or catastrophic at worst: the cognitive inaccessibility of the possible consequences of human agency in bringing about its own insignificance as measured against the capacities of its own creations. In the technological domain, the notion that captures such a vision of the future of passing a point of no return is *technological singularity*. Although 'singularity' has been used earlier in the context of technology, the term 'technological singularity' has been put into wider circulation by Vernor Vinge in the 1990s. It describes *the potential eruption of a sudden, game-changer event* in the shape of the creation of greater-than-human intelligence that presumably creates even greater and greater superhuman intelligence at an explosive pace. Or, in the words of Vinge, 'from the human point of view this change will be a throwing away of all the previous rules, perhaps in the blink of an eye, an exponential runaway beyond any hope of control' (1993: 12).

To a certain extent, passing the point of no return in an event-like manner may be true of the prospect of a global nuclear warfare too. This was the initial threat that led the *Bulletin of Atomic Scientists* to set up the symbolic Doomsday Clock in 1947. As the '2018 Doomsday Clock Statement' explains, the intention behind introducing the clock was 'using the imagery of apocalypse (midnight) and the contemporary idiom of nuclear explosion (countdown to zero) to convey threats to humanity and the planet' (Mecklin 2018: 2). The statement sets the clock to two minutes to midnight, half a minute closer than it was set by the previous 2017 statement, and – reflecting recent global policy agendas – it marks the return of the centrality of the nuclear threat by nevertheless keeping its focus on the entire postwar triad of cataclysm.

Compared to the prospect of nuclear self-destruction, a climate and a technological catastrophe, although being conceivable earlier, are only more recently emerging as widely recognized dominant threats, recognized as anthropogenic existential risks. The theme of anthropogenic climate change and the notion of the Anthropocene – the proposed but not yet canonized geological epoch of humans becoming agents that shape the earth system – even conquered the agenda of historians. Following the pioneering and still ongoing adventures of Dipesh Chakrabarty (2009, 2014, 2015, 2016, 2018) into mapping the consequences of the notion of the Anthropocene for the discipline and the concept of history, historians – in line with practically any other domain of academic knowledge-production within the humanities and social sciences – have begun to explore the impact and use of the notion in historical scholarship (for instance, Robin 2013; Thomas 2014; Bonneuil and Fressoz 2016; Mikhail 2016).

However, whereas Chakrabarty's initial point of departure was an extinction scenario that challenges the deep continuity of the modern processual notion of history and thus is 'deeply destructive of our general sense of history' (2009: 198), historians in particular and humanities and social sciences research in general typically seem more interested in maintaining business as usual. Instead of asking the question of how the current humanities knowledge regime may be challenged together with its established categories of critical scholarship by novel conceptualizations, they apply their long-existing categories to the new that is supposed to challenge them (until it no longer looks challenging). Where Chakrabarty (2015) sees an emerging *zoecentric* worldview focusing on life and featuring the *anthropos* as a species understanding of the human being, critical humanities only see 'the ongoing fraud that calls itself "Anthropos"' (Cohen and Colebrook 2017: 134), a deception of a universal humanity brought together under a threat in the name of survival. Historians Christophe Bonneuil and Jean-Baptiste Fressoz go even further by claiming that an undifferentiated notion of the anthropos is put out by geologists, earth system and climate scientists to pave their own way to achieve a 'command post of a disheveled planet and its errant humanity. A geo-government of scientists!' (2016: 80).

The debate between a new understanding of the human predicament as emerging in a scientific discourse and the categories of critical humanities scholarship will most likely continue. It is not my intention even to attempt to resolve it. What I would like to point out is only that my focus nevertheless lies with what I think is the more interesting and challenging question in Chakrabarty's initial engagement: the one that senses a potential transformation of the way in which we conceive of ourselves and the world historically, instead of the one that habitually domesticates a new idea by applying the already existing conceptual tools of humanities criticism. Although the latter is equally legitimate and important, in times of unprecedented change the question is not that of how to accommodate that which is perceived as genuine novelty into our familiar ways of thinking. Rather, the question is how to recognize its novelty by creating a fresh set of concepts within the humanities and the social sciences (potentially in cooperation with the natural sciences).

The same goes for technological visions, which have not had a similar impact yet in the discipline of history. The growing societal engagement in debating visions of the future typically boils down in historical studies to histories that explore how the future was conceived of in the past (Samuel 2009; Andersson and Rindzevičiūtė 2015; Hölscher 2017; Radkau 2017). Although investigating past visions of the future has become a rather lively historical research topic recently, the historical profession is still largely missing out the otherwise widespread debate on the broader technological vision of the future today: on artificial intelligence, transhumanism, bioengineering, nanotechnology, human enhancement or genome editing (with the latter being a positive exception thanks to the recently initiated Double Helix History project at The University of Manchester). The two kinds of engagement could not be farther from each other. On the one hand, looking for traces and precedents of our current societal investment by mapping past expectations of the future is the standard historical operation. On the other, just as in the case of the Anthropocene debate, taking part in the wider discussion on recent future prospects that spark such 'historical' interest may challenge the very historical operation historians put to work when they align with societal interests and begin to study past visions of the future.

That today's technological-scientific prospects matter immensely for the way we conceive of ourselves and the world historically is best attested to by the fact that this is practically the only thing that made Francis Fukuyama reconsider his 'end of history' thesis. Although scholars in the humanities and social sciences seem to have irrevocably linked him to the idea of 'the end of history', Fukuyama has already moved on. In a book on the prospect of biotechnology, published only a decade after *The End of History*, Fukuyama reflected on his previous theory as follows:

> As the more perceptive critics of the concept of the 'end of history' have pointed out, there can be no end of history without an end of modern natural science and technology. Not only are we not at an end of science and technology; we appear to be poised at the cusp of one of the most momentous periods of technological advance in history. Biotechnology and a greater scientific understanding of the human brain promise to have extremely significant political ramifications. (2002: 15)

In these sentences, Fukuyama vests technology with the potential of carrying the historical process as we know it further, meaning that history as the course of affairs just goes on as fuelled by technologies that engineer even the human being. Such an understanding of today's technology is nevertheless obviously limited inasmuch as it remains within the confines of the modern historical sensibility and within the confines of a political framework in which technology is subordinated to politics. At a later stage I will return to the question of the relationship between the political domain and technology both in the modern and in the postwar historical sensibilities. For the current line of argument, the more important point is that Fukuyama, even if in a misguided way as seen from the viewpoint of this book, at least recognizes the link between a sense of historicity and visions of the future.

Despite the elevated tone of the above quote, Fukuyama is aware that technology's potential to appear as a vehicle of improvement is only one side of the coin. The other side is the prospect of doom, as 'the most significant threat posed by contemporary biotechnology is the possibility that it will alter human nature and thereby move it into a "posthuman" stage of history' (Fukuyama 2002: 7). The inherent ambivalence of the technological prospect of the posthuman is a fairly common observation, having already been present in Arendt's view. Today, it is a concern not only for Fukuyama and other bioconservatives in debates about the general prospect of a posthuman future to be brought about by technology, but also for advocates of radical enhancement. What they disagree about most deeply is what exactly they consider as 'promise' and 'threat'. Whereas escaping the confines of (a statistically defined) human nature is a threat to Fukuyama (129–47), the very same prospect constitutes a promise for Bostrom, the most prominent transhumanist philosopher today, who argues through various genres for the benefits of going beyond human limits (Bostrom 2003, 2008a, 2008b). And if this comes out as a promise for transhumanism, then the threat must be found elsewhere. For Bostrom, it takes the shape of an extinction event, regardless of whether the life threatened by extinction is human or posthuman. Hence the definition of existential risk – as 'one that threatens the premature extinction of Earth-originating intelligent life or the permanent and drastic destruction of its potential for desirable future development' (Bostrom 2013: 15) – can refer to a category even broader than humanity.

The simultaneity of the positive promise and the existential threat appears to build upon conflicting sets of ideas. Whereas the promise invokes a modern utopian structure of delivering a better future to be realized, the latter warns about the necessity to avoid the inherent perils of venturing into something unknown. Whereas the former claims a familiar historical trajectory of the betterment of human capacities, the latter claims to transcend those capacities that appear only as obstacles and unnecessary limitations. Although sometimes even transhumanists themselves mix up their own conceptual stakes by claiming continuity with Enlightenment ideals of human perfectibility, their promise is not about making already assumed human potentials better but about creating that which is better *than* human (Simon 2018c). Nevertheless, the transhumanist project of enhancing humans by technological means is upheld as a promise as frequently as it is considered to be a threat, or is just debated in both terms without either explicitly advocating or opposing the transhumanist project itself (for example, Agar 2010; Hauskeller 2013; Fuller and Lipinska 2014; Sharon 2014; Hurlbut and Tirosh-Samuelson 2016).

All this clearly testifies that although it is possible to talk about the growing prominence, pertinence and dominance of postwar dystopian thought, it would be misleading to suggest that the Western world completely lacks or is heading toward the total absence of utopian thought. In fact, the postwar *dominance* of the dystopian is the most apparent precisely in the structural feature that even the remnants of modern utopian thought appear now as *inherently* dystopian, due to the sense of having something ahead that has no precedent. It is the either deliberate or unintentional *bringing about the unprecedented* – the unknown, the impenetrable by human reasoning – that constitutes the inherent risk of losing or simply not having human control over whatever is brought about.

The coming pages seek to understand the character of this dominant dystopian vision of the future of our times as a change concerning Western future-orientation. In doing so, the rest of the chapter will proceed along the lines sketched in the previous one: in order to make sense of what Western societies may be or are about to be, I turn to past visions of the future that are now largely (although not completely) dissociated. In other words, I wish to indicate the main features and the novelty of contemporary prospects of dystopian unprecedented change by fleshing out what these future prospects no longer are.

In the first step, I recount a previous shift in which modern utopia gained its temporal character and contrast this modern temporal utopia with postwar dystopia. Whereas the former is possible only under a historical condition, I interpret the latter as 'posthistorical' in that it is no longer the concern of a *realization* of a desired future within and as history. In this section, the discussion of utopia claims no originality. Utopian thought has been mapped by decades of excellent scholarship in a large variety of fields (Mannheim [1936] 1998; Bloch [1954–1959] 1986; Kumar 1987; Bartkowski 1989; Levitas 1990; Booker 1994; Ferns 1999; Jameson 2005; Claeys 2010; Gordin, Tilley and Prakash 2010; Vieira and Marder 2012), the insights of which are obviously reflected in the following presentation of utopia. However, for consistency, throughout the discussion of modern utopia I use Koselleck's essay (2002: 84–99) on the modern temporalization of utopia as a thread and focus not on utopia itself but on how postwar visions of the future differ from it.

In the second and third steps, I then come to the main purpose of the chapter. In order to prove the novelty of postwar future prospects of the triad of cataclysm, I consider two potential objections. I engage with two alternative interpretations of postwar dystopias that look at the past in the hope of finding precedents either in already existing negative utopias of modernity or in even earlier Christian eschatological visions of end times. Discussing these unmistakably negative future visions provides an opportunity for elaborating on the distinctive character of postwar dystopian thought. Comparing postwar ecological and technological visions of the future to modern negative utopia enables me to illuminate the sense in which postwar dystopian thought is 'posthistorical'; comparing them to eschatological visions enables me to illuminate a distinct temporality, that is, *the temporality of the singular event*, which I will attempt to briefly sketch as a fourth and final step of the overall argument.

Throughout the discussion, following the working definition of Ruth Levitas, I regard utopia as 'the expression of the desire for a better way of being' (Levitas 1990: 8), which allows divergence regarding the particular forms, functions and contents of utopian thought as it took over time. I also agree with Levitas that 'definitions are tools, not ends in themselves' (2). Accordingly, on the coming pages I make use of both this definition and the general introduction of utopian thought as tools that intend to serve the aim of illuminating how what I call 'posthistorical dystopia' (as the characterization of postwar visions of unprecedented change) departs from utopian schemes in bringing about a novel vision of the future.

Utopian thought

The best way to explore the dominance and the characteristics of postwar dystopian thought seems to be to contrast it with modern utopia. In turn, however, modern utopian thought can be best understood through briefly contrasting it with early modern utopian imagination. As always when it comes to historical questions about the birth of new patterns of historical thought in Western modernity, Reinhart Koselleck's investigations into the temporalization of concepts provide an excellent entry point. According to Koselleck, in the period between 1750 and 1850 – the period he calls *Sattelzeit* (saddle period) – the concept of utopia gained a temporal dimension. By that time, the spatial placement of utopias became impossible as the world had been mapped thanks to geographical discoveries. The literal meaning of the word utopia, that is, 'no-place' or 'non-place' in Greek, no longer made sense. Or, to phrase it more emphatically, spatial utopia simply lost its 'place' at a time when all places have become known and consequently it has been moved from space to time: more specifically, to the future. In the words of Koselleck, as they appear in the essay entitled 'The Temporalization of Utopia', the process looked like this:

> Human beings have, as Rousseau said, stretched themselves out across the globe with every fiber of their bodies like polyps. Therefore, the authors of 'nowheres' had for some time already switched over to the moon or the stars or descended below the surface of the earth. Once recognized, the spatial possibilities for establishing a utopia on our earth's finite surface were exhausted. The utopian spaces had been surpassed by experience. The best solution for escaping this growing pressure of experience was simple, but it had to be found. If utopia was no longer to be discovered or established on our present-day earth nor in the divine world beyond, it had to be shifted into the future. (2002: 86)

Koselleck focuses only on two texts to indicate the shift from spatial to temporal utopias, one from 1770 by Louis-Sébastien Mercier and the other from 1918 by Carl Schmitt. Yet his interpretation is, I believe, quite plausible and aligns with scholarship on utopian thought. In discussing Mercier's *The Year 2440*, Krishan Kumar's comprehensive study of modern utopia confirms that in Mercier 'the radically new element is time' (Kumar 1987: 38). Besides, Kumar also associates Mercier's utopia with a wider tendency of a 'new zest for the future which in the second half of the eighteenth century was transforming both the form and the substance of utopia' (39).

As is well known, most of the classic utopian texts predating Koselleck's *Sattelzeit* typically depict utopian societies at distant and unknown places discovered under exceptional circumstances. Nobody knows how to get there, and even those who discovered the utopian society by luck and serendipity seem no longer to possess the knowledge of the route to return. Thomas More's discourse-initiator *Utopia* ([1516] 2002), Tommaso Campanella's *The City of the Sun* ([1602] 1981), or Francis Bacon's *New Atlantis* ([1627] 1996) may be the most familiar examples of a defining feature of early modern utopia: despite all the vivid depictions of utopian societies provided by 'eyewitnesses', the places themselves remain literally 'no-places' and 'nowheres', as the most crucial bit of information about their actual location remains unknown.

Contrary to this, the 'location' of modern temporal utopia is very well known: it is the future. What's more, as the 'new zest for the future' overtook utopian thought, as utopia entered the realm of future-orientation, as it gained a historical dimension, it became possible to get there. Two momentous qualities derive from the entry into the temporal realm. First, whereas spatial utopia – although it is presented as an already existing place – simply lies out of reach, *temporal utopia – although presented as non-existent – acquires the quality of 'reachability'*. But temporal utopia is not only where humanity as the typical subject of the historical process is inevitably heading. As soon as such a historical process is conceived of and as soon as the future is reachable, it becomes possible for human communities to begin to actively work on facilitating the process of reaching the desired better future. Hence the second momentous quality: *due to the postulated reachability, modern temporal utopia enters the realm of ethico-political action.*

But what does this 'reachability' of utopia and its entry into the realm of ethico-political action mean exactly? It most certainly does not mean that early modern utopias were not political in any sense whatsoever. Frederic Jameson's opening sentence of his reflection on utopian thought in *Archaeologies of the Future* makes the paradigmatic modern historical claim that 'utopia has always been a political issue' (2005: xi). What I wish to emphasize by saying that modern utopia enters the realm of ethico-political action is its aforementioned entry to the realm of historicity due to its newly gained future-orientation and temporal character, which enables action directed toward the realization of utopia as developmental change over time in the human condition and in the condition of human societies.

To introduce this modern temporal utopia under a historical condition in a bit more detail, Koselleck still proves to be a useful guide as the most eminent student of the modern idea of history (despite the fact that the Koselleckian approach is less useful in making sense of the characteristic of postwar dystopias). The key aspect to which I would like to pay special attention is not the temporal character of the modern concept of history that enables utopia to 'go temporal' in the first place, but the aforementioned aspect of 'reachability'. On this note, what Koselleck brings into the picture is what he refers to as the 'makeability' of history (2004: 92–104). As the invention of the modern concept of history rendered change over time in human affairs possible, as change became a matter of the mundane human world instead of being an entry to another world following the Last Judgment, this change started to appear as being prone to facilitation. In other words, history has been invented together with its own 'makeability' as action toward the desired future implied by the postulated historical process. As a consequence, if history is the condition of possibility of temporalized modern utopian thought, and if history is 'makeable', then utopia must be reachable through making history, through making utopia real *as* history. It is the very 'makeability' of history that enables the 'reachability' and 'realizability' of utopia.

The possibility of the actual realization of utopia also brings to light the irony of the story: the 'no-place' of spatial utopia is now expected to actually take place in the future, thereby becoming a possibility of the same place that imagines it. Although spatial utopia was also a possible world – at least, as Kumar points out (1987: 31), in scientifically motivated versions such as Bacon's *New Atlantis* – the actual realization of this possibility could not have been possible until the temporalization of utopia in the late eighteenth century. Modern temporal utopia, in that sense, promises the delivery of early-modern spatial utopia under a historical condition, as a historical process. At the same time, as Kumar notes, although 'the nineteenth century is generally, and rightly, regarded as the most utopian century of modern times', it is 'almost entirely lacking in the formal literary utopia'. Seeing this together with utopia's entry into historical 'makeability', Kumar goes on to summarize the transformation of utopian thought by claiming that 'the decline of the literary utopia, and the rise of utopianism in a new historical and "scientific" form, marks an important change in the consciousness of European societies' (1987: 33).

How to understand this claim exactly? For entering the realm of ethico-political action certainly does not mean a complete loss of utopia's early modern character of being literary writing. Even the formulation of 'formal literary utopia' and its lack thereof in the nineteenth century can be right only insofar as 'literary' stands for being a specific genre and not for being written discourse. Utopia's entry to the realm of ethico-political action under a historical condition does not mean that it is no longer written discourse. Rather, it means that writing and 'acting upon' writing became a constitutive part of the very same endeavour. Accordingly, the important change in the consciousness of European societies that Kumar talks about is, I think, the fact that utopia's entry into the realm of 'makeable' history brought about the intention both to imagine and realize utopia by numerous future-oriented ethico-political endeavours. As an obvious example, consider political ideologies and philosophies as written discourse and all the efforts that act upon them. The motto of this shift might just as well be Marx's eleventh thesis on Feuerbach, claiming that 'the philosophers have only interpreted the world, in various ways; the point, however, is to change it' (Marx [1888] 1978: 145).

The utopian socialism of the early nineteenth century may be an even more obvious example. It did not only outline the 'science' of harmonious societal organization but also kicked off social experiments to realize it. As a classic example, you can think of Charles Fourier's idea of the *phalanstère*, which inspired the establishment of many communities, or Robert Owen's efforts to establish a utopian community, New Harmony, in the United States. Although Marx and Engels in *The Manifesto of the Communist Party* ridiculed utopian socialism mostly due to the lack of concerns in utopian socialism for the proletariat and class antagonism, they did not blame them for not taking action. They blamed utopian socialism and their disciples for taking action in favour of the 'wrong' people. The accusation of Marx and Engels concerned the utopian socialist's 'dream of experimental realisation of their social Utopias' which 'appeal to the feelings and purses of the bourgeois' ([1848] 1978: 499). In their view, it made utopian socialism and communism of 'an inverse relation to historical development' (498).

I think what this attests to is not the superficial question whether communism was or was not utopian, or whether utopian socialists 'betrayed' the proletariat. Instead, this attests to how the central theme of ideological-political debates in the nineteenth century revolved around the question of the relationship between utopian thought and political action in terms of achieving a positively stated purpose that is supposed to coincide with the course of 'historical development'. Regardless of the questions of what the particular future-oriented purpose was and who was supposed to act on whose behalf, 'acting upon' came along with the future-oriented purpose. On a more practical level, emancipatory politics and civil right movements, women's suffrage and even today's movements like Black Lives Matter could not exist without a utopian vision of a better future and without the implied belief in the 'makeability' of history (whether they are explicitly formulated or not).

Yet the intertwinement of written discourse and the ethico-political action of 'reachable' or 'realizable' modern utopia is most symptomatic when it appears outside the *explicitly* political-ideological sphere (which nevertheless claims a close connection to political action). The most powerful example of this is nineteenth-century positivism. Even though the humanities and the social sciences tend to equate positivism today with a monomaniac fact-fetishism, August Comte's original project of positivism was far more than that. The doctrine of positivism is, at its core, a utopian vision of the necessary unfolding of human intellect and human knowledge, and a philosophy of history that nevertheless must be facilitated by 'acting upon' the doctrinal vision. The base of Comte's vision is the 'law of human development' that sketches a course of progress leading from a theological stage of knowledge through a metaphysical one to the final arrival of the positive stage (Comte 1896: 1–5). Once the postulation of a historical process established the 'reachability' of a scientific society as the ultimate utopia of positivism, Comte's main concern can come to the fore: the practical execution of societal betterment as based on the doctrine supported by a historical vision and presented by a written discourse. As Comte claims, 'the Positive Philosophy offers the only solid basis for that Social Reorganization which must succeed the critical condition in which the most civilized nations are now living' (15).

Posthistorical dystopia and negative utopia

So far this chapter has introduced the supersession of early modern spatial utopias by modern historical-temporal utopias, which practically gave birth to modern Western future-orientation. To review the main features, 'reachable' and 'realizable' modern utopia is (1) temporal instead of being spatial; is (2) in history instead of being 'nowhere'; and (3) enters the realm of ethico-political action under the modern historical condition instead of being 'formal literary utopia'.

The rest of this chapter intends to argue for the plausibility of attributing a posthistorical character to postwar visions of the future. It wishes to achieve this by outlining how the posthistorical dystopia of the broadly construed postwar period departs from modern utopian thought along the following lines: although posthistorical dystopia keeps the temporal dimension of modern utopia and retains the 'place' of future in the realm of action, it exchanges (1) ethico-political 'reachability' for ecological and technological 'threats to come'; (2) actions to 'realize' for actions to avoid 'realization'; and thereby (3) the historical condition of the developmental 'taking place' of the desired future for a posthistorical condition of the undesired sudden eruption of the apocalyptic event, that is, future-orientation for future-disorientation.

The first issue to tackle is that of the posthistorical character of postwar visions of the future, which raises the most pivotal question of whether temporality and history necessarily hang together. If the condition of possibility of modern utopia's temporal character is history and if postwar dystopian thought remains in the domain of temporality (as visions of the future different from past states of affairs) the question is: in what sense can dystopias reasonably be labelled as 'posthistorical'? Can history be abandoned without stepping out of the domain of temporality and the possibility of action? Does a description of 'posthistorical' entail a wholesale abandonment in the first place? The answer to the question is twofold. On the one hand, insofar as change over time in human affairs is configured along a certain *temporality*, the historical condition is retained. On the other hand, the modern historical sensibility configures change over time along a *certain* (specific and particular) temporality that is developmental and directional, which does not exclude the possibility of configuring change over time along a different temporality. I think that posthistorical dystopia harbours such an alternative configuration of change over time that it is no longer associated with history as we know it. Due to the lack of a vocabulary to keep up with change, I cannot but label it 'posthistorical', which refers to the abandonment of a certain temporality and a certain idea of history and not to the wholesale abandonment of temporality and history (as change over time). As the previous chapters argued, when it is no longer possible to positively state the identity of what there is, the only way left to indicate the newness of the new is to label it 'post', to apply dissociative measures.

This being settled, the next question is one any sensible historian relying on the developmental configuration of change over time would ask: is the postwar cataclysm-fetish something really new? A potential (and in its own framework very reasonable) objection would point out that negative utopias, depicting the threat of a terrible future, occurred in Western modernity just as well as utopias did. Posthistorical dystopia could just as well be interpreted as the latest development of pessimistic future prospects, arising out of earlier schemes of modern negative utopia.

Koselleck remains a useful guide in discussing this objection, given that one of the two texts he analyses in 'The Temporalization of Utopia' essay is a negative utopia. The text in question is Carl Schmitt's 'The Buribunks' (Schmitt 1999), which Koselleck understands as follows:

> Filled with a wealth of imagination and allusions, it is an extravagant parody of historicism and the belief in progress, as expressed in the agendas of the scientific and social organizations of the time. The content of this parody, or more accurately, this satire, can be characterized as a negative utopia. The implicit criticism was aimed at those utopian elements contained in the historical belief in facts and their historico-philosophical idealization. What was specifically utopian was the belief that humans, with their awareness, not only were able to grasp history, but that by virtue of their awareness, they could also execute and master history. This philosophy of the mind extended to all three temporal dimensions, mutually relativized and, at the same time, progressively interpreted. In this respect, Carl Schmitt's criticism aimed at the entire intellectual foundation of modernity, to the extent that it was designed and executed as historical progress. (2002: 93)

Schmitt's negative utopia, according to Koselleck, is nothing other than a satirical take on history and the historical process, which qualifies it as a negative utopia. In a similar vein, the potential objection to consider the prospect of postwar cataclysms as being posthistorical would point out that a postwar cataclysmic prospect can also be seen as a parody, a satire, or a mockery of the idea of the historical process of human betterment. In this objection, as negative utopia and posthistorical dystopia are both satirizing the idea of history, they appear as essentially the same endeavours that join forces in opposing their common target of criticism. Hence the question is whether this common opposition places a modern negative utopia like that of Schmitt's and a posthistorical dystopian prospect of technological singularity to the same platform.

The answer requires, first of all, a brief introduction of Schmitt's negative utopia. It depicts a society in which everybody is obliged to keep a diary, recording and recounting literally everything. As Koselleck claims, it is truly a parody of modern historical sensibility in that by reaching the state of constant writing, by everything being written down, everything becomes prone to historicization. Eventually, writing itself – writing elevated into being a collective diary of humanity – becomes history, that is, the fulfilment of a historical process. But because individual writings must be submitted to the authorities, all this comes with a terrible price: unimaginably heightened surveillance.

Koselleck makes use of Schmitt's text for the reason that it can be perfectly coupled together with the other text he analyses: Mercier's utopia of Paris in the year 2440, when everybody is a writer. Whereas in Mercier's utopia every citizen's capacity to write appears as the means by which despotic rule can be displaced, in Schmitt's text the very same human achievement appears as the means by which despotic rule is established. This is the basis on which Koselleck claims that 'out of the naive utopia of the future came a negative temporal utopia' (2002: 98). And, more importantly, this is the basis on which the potential objection to my argument on the distinctiveness of posthistorical dystopia proceeds. In the objection, an entire chain of historical development could be sketched, leading from naïve utopia through negative utopia to posthistorical dystopia.

But to provide more than one example, consider another text that is far better known than Schmitt's essay and exhibits a structurally similar line of argumentation. For readers of critical theory, the intellectual scheme of Schmitt's essay may look disturbingly familiar: something that previously has been the promise of the best of all times actually brings about the worst of all times. As it stands, Max Horkheimer and Theodor Adorno outline the very same scheme right at the outset of their *Dialectic of Enlightenment*, claiming – with exceptional stylistic force – that it is precisely the fulfilment of the promise of the Enlightenment that brings the darkest times upon humanity:

> Enlightenment, understood in the widest sense as the advance of thought, has always aimed at liberating human beings from fear and installing them as masters. Yet the wholly enlightened earth is radiant with triumphant calamity. ([1944] 2002: 1)

In depicting the present condition as the worst anti-utopia already being on its course of realization and approaching its inevitable, sad conclusion, the *Dialectic of Enlightenment* presents a negative philosophy of history. It configures change over time in human affairs along the same developmental temporality as 'positive' philosophies of history of the Enlightenment and German Idealism do, except that it reverses the direction of the development. But sketching a regressive historical process only reinforces the idea that there may be a processual directionality residing in human affairs, that there is a historical process out there in the first place. The reversal retains practically every defining feature of substantive philosophies of history and represents nothing other than a subcategory, being the anti-utopian counterpart of the utopian dreams of human betterment that inform most classical philosophies of history.

What postwar dystopias challenge is what temporal utopias and their negative counterparts have in common: their shared temporal structure associated with the modern historical sensibility. It may very well be that the ultimate prospect of both negative utopia and posthistorical dystopia is doom, as is the case in both Schmitt's essay and Adorno and Horkheimer's critical theory. But the doom in such negative utopias is still an ethico-political doom, while in posthistorical dystopia it is ecological and/or technological. This is of course not to say that technology and science did not play a central role in bringing about even the ethico-political doom of a negative utopia. They did, just as much as they were already regarded as major progressive forces of modernity in bringing about utopian bliss.

The point I would like to make is that in both modern utopia and negative utopia, the political domain appropriates technology and science for its own purposes. As they are put into the service of the political, the doom itself cannot be other than ethico-political. In other words, although technology and science may be *the means* of bringing about both utopia and anti-utopia, they themselves are not the *primary agents of change*. This happens only in posthistorical dystopia, where the doom itself is technological and ecological. Here, the political domain no longer appears as the force, manager and/or agent of change, but the counterforce that tries to keep ecological and technological change under control. Whereas in utopia and anti-utopia the political domain makes technological change happen for better or worse, in posthistorical dystopia the political domain appears as the one that is either expected to or effectively does introduce *preventive* measures on technological change to avoid the taking place of the unprecedented. As an example for calls for mitigation, military artificial intelligence has received quite a lot of attention lately, while an example for regulation already in effect can be laws that prohibit human cloning throughout the world.

Closely related to the changing role of the political domain, another key difference is that in posthistorical dystopia the threat is not ethico-political but existential. Whereas a negative utopia threatens what political communities define as *good* life and *good* human conduct, a posthistorical dystopia threatens human life and human conduct *as such*, regardless of whether that life and conduct qualifies as good or monstrous. What posthistorical dystopia envisions is not the decay of the human condition but a condition that is no longer human. It is non-human existence overpowering human existence and gaining control over it at best or a vision of human non-existence at worst.

Finally, and most importantly, the directionality of the postulated historical process provides both modern utopia and anti-utopia with an orientation toward the future, regardless of whether that future is desired or undesired. The eruptive event that is expected to launch posthistorical dystopia and the unprecedented change brought about can hardly be considered in terms of orientation. If anything, posthistorical dystopia introduces a distinct future-disorientation that aims at preventing the taking place of the worst future.

Posthistorical dystopia and eschatology

The sudden eruption of a game-changer singular event? Does this not sound all too familiar? By relying on the modern historical sensibility, a second objection may point out that the Christian worldview was already based on a series of singular events: Creation, Fall of Man, Original Sin, Incarnation, Second Coming (Parousia), and, most importantly, Last Judgement. Can it be that what I take to be as unprecedented change is itself not unprecedented but just another variation on an old theme? Can the prospect of posthistorical cataclysm be the new Eschaton? Can it be that instead of having a new historical sensibility the Western world is engaged only in a secularized version of eschatology?

Oddly enough, this is precisely what Karl Löwith (1957) has already suggested regarding the modern historical sensibility. Löwith thought that the modern concept of history and the entire enterprise of modern philosophy of history is only a secularized version of eschatology, because of their common theme of directionality towards an ultimate end. If you think that Löwith has a point, then the emerging postwar historical sensibility would be only the further secularization of (modern) history as already secularized eschatology. Or, if you think that Löwith is more wrong than right (which is the position implied by this book), then there is still the possibility of interpreting the postulated ultimate prospects of posthistorical dystopias as a variation on Christian eschatology in its own right. In the former case, the latest development appears as the result of a longer line of preceding stages of development. In the latter case, the latest development appears as a new alternative to a failed development (the modern concept of history), even though this new alternative unfolds from the same source (Christian eschatology). Yet the present unfolds from preceding states of affairs in both cases, and the potential objection points out the same thing, namely, that the still effective origin of posthistorical dystopia lies in the Christian Eschaton.

As to the first version of eschatological inheritance, the further secularization of secularized eschatology hinges upon the acceptance of Löwith's primary secularization thesis. However, a refutation of the objection that postwar historical sensibility is eschatological demands a refutation only of the assumed connection to the supposed origin: to eschatology itself and not to philosophy of history as supposedly secularized eschatology. Thus, for the purposes of this book, Löwith's intermediary step does not demand engagement here. Besides, Hans Blumenberg (1983: 3–121), one and a half decades after the publication of Löwith's book, has already performed the deepest engagement in arguing for the novelty of modernity in its own right. What demands engagement instead is the question of the possible ties between the Christian Eschaton and the end times of posthistorical dystopia, that is, the question of whether there is anything in posthistorical dystopia that most certainly cannot derive from eschatology.

Having an answer to this question is all the more pressing because eschatology has been linked not only to the modern concept of history but also directly to the prospects that I describe by the notion of unprecedented change. Visions of the future revolving around the possibility of human extinction have already been made sense of as new versions of old visions of end times. Whereas ecological prospects are prone to be made sense of in terms of a new kind of biblical apocalypticism (Skrimshire 2014; Northcott 2015), playing out the religious connotations is one of the most common interpretive frameworks of technological ones (Tirosh-Samuelson 2012; Burdett 2015; Mercer and Trothen 2015; Graham 2016).

Finally, there is also an indirect way that posthistorical dystopian prospects may be linked to an eschatological inheritance. It leads through the political domain and points to the structural resemblance between the unprecedented and the efforts of (among others) Giorgio Agamben, Slavoj Žižek and Alain Badiou to theorize the possibility of 'radical' or 'revolutionary' politics. Conceiving of political novelty as a complete break with pre-existing structures might certainly have to do with the notion of unprecedented change as the perceived novelty in the ecological and technological domains. And if the case is so, then it must be taken very seriously that in theorizing political novelty all these theories of otherwise openly atheist authors draw intentionally on theological resources to illuminate their theses, as has already been mapped thoroughly by Jayne Svenungsson's excellent book *Divining History* (2016: 151–202).

I am in fact convinced that these theories are engaged in conceptualizing political change in a way that, in some respects, runs parallel to the prospect of unprecedented change in posthistorical dystopia. The structural resemblance is especially true of the efforts of Badiou (2001, 2003, 2005, 2012) to theorize a revolutionary event, which I will come back to in the Epilogue. However, this is not to say that the motivation of political theories to conceptualize change over time has much to do with ecological and technological visions of the future. The aforementioned authors do not typically engage with such questions. Although Žižek explicitly reflected at length on ecological and technological cataclysm scenarios (2010: 327–47), even his reflection is more of an enumeration of prospects and their potential ties to the familiar theme of capitalist production than an actual meditation on the consequences of such prospects for the way Western societies make sense of the world and themselves. The clear focus of political theories on political novelty (in terms of Leftist politics) perhaps does not even enable these theories to consider the possibility that ecological and technological prospects pose a challenge and appear as an alternative temporality to the paralysed ethico-political domain still deeply indebted to the developmental temporality of emancipatory concerns.

The grounds for an eschatological interpretation of the prospect of unprecedented change unleashed by posthistorical dystopia look pretty solid. In support of such an interpretation, it can reasonably be pointed out that the singular event looming on the horizon is secularized today inasmuch as it arises out of human activity and not of divine intervention, but the expectation of the Eschaton is a shared structure. In much the same way, it can also be pointed out that although the singular event brings about change in the mundane world instead of offering an entry to another world as the result of the Last Judgement, the idea of the opening up of a completely new world is a shared feature again. As a counterargument, weirdly, exactly the same things can be pointed out: that posthistorical dystopia is due to *human* activity and the change it brings about concerns *mundane* life on the face of Earth. What this shows is that merely listing similarities and differences does not lead anywhere. Hence the question is not only whether there are aspects in which posthistorical dystopia differs from eschatology, but whether there is a defining feature of posthistorical prospects that is not open to the dual stress of similarities and differences concerning the very same aspect and feature.

I have to admit this is the most puzzling question. For change does not lie within the interpreted phenomena but arises out of a conceptualization as change. Ultimately, the interpretation of novelty is derivative of the grid you project over a bunch of seemingly different states of phenomena over time. A historical sensibility is a way of conceiving change, and if your (deliberately preferred or pretty much unconscious) grid is the modern historical sensibility, you will simply project hidden congruity to configure change as a surface variation of a deep continuity in substance, like Löwith did. Or, to take examples from everyday life (and everyday life is full of unconscious deployments of this sensibility), anytime a new musical act appears on the contemporary pop scene, journalists and reviewers will flesh out its 'inspirations'. This is how Muse started its career as the new Radiohead, or, even worse, a Radiohead copy, even though now it is regarded as a unique sound to which even newer musical acts may be likened. In a similar way, and shifting from the musical to the sport scene, this is how every single talented Argentinian football player in an attacking role has been regarded lately as the new Maradona, from Aimar and Agüero to Saviola and Tevez. This was also the case with Lionel Messi, even though Messi became recognized as having a unique style and talent of his own. But no doubt the qualities of future Argentinian players in an attacking role will be made sense of through Messi, who has been made sense of through Maradona, all this adding up to a story of continuity.

Continuity, however, is only half of the story. It casts a shadow of discontinuity over every story as the only possible ground to challenge continuous change. And, in that sense, even discontinuity belongs to the order of continuity as its sheer opposite (or its antithesis, if you like). As it stands, discontinuity even presupposes a continuous development into which it can introduce a rupture. Yet that rupture in scenarios of discontinuity plays the same role as a change in appearance plays in scenarios of continuous change: it introduces a new stage in the development of a certain subject. Even Blumenberg's critique of Löwith's thesis presents the modern age as a new stage in which humanity as the subject of discontinuous change enters the era of human self-assertion (Blumenberg 1983). Accordingly, if posthistorical dystopia defies this modern historical sensibility, it has to harbour a configuration of change over time that introduces a whole new grid to conceptualize change over time in a way other than the entire modern spectrum of continuity/discontinuity.

All right, but does it? Yes, I think it does. And this precisely is the contention I would like to offer here, condensed in the following thesis: *the unprecedented change posthistorical dystopia envisions is a change of the subject whose past, present and future is at stake*. This is what distinguishes posthistorical dystopia most sharply both from eschatological thought and the modern historical sensibility. Whereas they both configured change over time as a change *in* the subject's condition – regardless of whether that change comes as continuous or discontinuous – the unprecedented change of posthistorical dystopia introduces a change *of* the subject. Such a change of subject over time may mean extinction in the darkest scenario, or the birth of a superior subject that replaces the previous (human) subject in an already milder prospect. A concrete example to the former may be climate catastrophe launching an extinction event, while a concrete example to the latter may be greater-than-human intelligence or the merging of human and machine to an extent that the newly born subject can no longer reasonably be called human.

The temporality of the singular event

The prospect of a sudden eruption of the singular event that brings about a change of the subject harbours a novel temporality. For want of a better name, I will call this 'the temporality of the singular event'. I would be happy to call it 'eventual' temporality as opposed to the 'processual' and 'developmental' temporality of modern historical sensibility. Unfortunately, the word 'eventual' has the connotation of being an outcome of a process, which is precisely what 'the temporality of the singular event' displaces. In line with the English translation of Badiou's theory of the 'event', it may best be called 'evental temporality'.

This 'temporality of the singular event' or 'evental temporality' is not exclusively a matter of postwar future prospects. It is most visible in such visions of the future, but the dissociative relation to the past as conceptualized in the previous chapter entails the *supersession* and *replacement* of a subject just as much as a postwar future prospect does. True enough, the dissociated past entails the replacement and supersession of a subject in terms of identity, while posthistorical visions of the future entail a full-blown replacement and supersession that is not reduced to particular terms. The underlying scheme of unprecedented change is nevertheless shared both by future prospects and relations to the past. The shared scheme of unprecedentedness gains significance in light of the fact that in order to be able to make sense of a prospect *as* unprecedented, at least the type of change must already be familiarized (Simon 2018b). Even if the unprecedented future is cognitively inaccessible from a position prior to the event that brings it, the structural characteristics of the event and the change can and must be familiar in order to be able to recognize the unprecedented *as* unprecedented.

If postwar Western societies conceive of the future as unprecedented, it is possible precisely because the past appears at the same time as a series of unprecedented changes that had already been left behind. In return, the possibility of the past appearing as unprecedented changes that have already been left behind is due to the way the future comes as unprecedented. Relations to the past and future prospects hang together by their common configuration of change over time, and it is only together that they make up an emerging evental historical sensibility. This evental historical sensibility today challenges the processual and developmental historical sensibility of the modern era.

I am of course not alone in thinking that the modern idea of history is challenged by a new temporal arrangement. I believe that there is a shared sense among scholars across disciplines that immense changes are going on regarding the way we make sense of the world and ourselves as changing over time. Making enormous efforts to conceptualize the way Western societies make sense of change over time is what connects most of the ideas that I have engaged with or passingly touched upon throughout these chapters. Different notions of 'presence', political theories of the self-identified Left, theories of presentism, Derridean hauntology and even White's attempt to revive the notion of the practical past with its attachment to a processual and developmental sensibility – all attest to a shared concern. In one way or another, they all sprang out of a situation that Hans Ulrich Gumbrecht called earlier as a 'yet unnamed chronotope' (2014: 73). To repeat the full quote as a reminder: 'the ways the horizons of the future and the past are experienced and connect with an ever broader present give form to the as yet unnamed chronotope within which globalized life in the early twenty-first century occurs' (73).

What Gumbrecht calls a chronotope is very close to what I call historical sensibility in this book. True enough, what Gumbrecht has to say (about a broad present connecting to the future and the past) has not much to do with what I have said about it (the disconnection of past and future). Naming, conceptualizing and exploring this historical sensibility or this chronotope is nevertheless the endeavour that I wished to pursue throughout these chapters. In doing so, I crossed paths with various efforts that aim at conceptualizing the relation to the past and the future in Western societies. All of them can testify that such conceptualization is not the most effortless of all endeavours, especially in light of one of the central messages of this book, namely, that when the new chronotope configures change over time as unprecedented, it is simply part of this chronotope that the conceptual resources of the past may be of little or of no help whatsoever in exploring it. Therein lies the greatest challenge of the theory and philosophy of history today: to create the vocabulary and the conceptual resources that may be able to understand the new chronotope or historical sensibility in other than merely inherited terms.

The investigations and the conceptual work of the first half of the book intend to be contributions to a response to this challenge, with regard to history in the sense of the course of affairs. The notion of 'unprecedented change' and notions like 'apophatic past', 'history as a disrupted singular', 'posthistorical dystopia', 'evental temporality' and 'evental historical sensibility' hopefully prove to be useful conceptual tools to enhance our understanding of what being 'historical' means in the Western world at the beginning of the new millennium. If, of course, being 'historical' still means anything at all.

Part Two

On Historiographical Change

As long as there is historical change, as long as there is a course of human affairs conceived of as changing over time, there is historiographical change. This is partly due to the fact that in many respects historical and historiographical change can hardly be separated. To name one, it is evident that the occurrence of historiographical novelty and change is itself a kind of historical change. It is equally well known that in Western modernity professional historiography delivers knowledge about historical change by explaining how things – and potentially all things – change over time.

But these observations only scratch the surface. Change over time in historiography has been conventionally linked to change in the course of human affairs in a more fundamental way throughout Western modernity. With the invention of the modern notion of history, with the establishment of the possibility of change in human affairs, historiographical revision simply came as a necessary entailment. As long as novelty is conceived of as a possibility occurring in human affairs, histories must constantly have been rewritten in light of the perceived new. In his studies on the modern notion of history, Koselleck – while quoting Goethe – remarks on this phenomenon as something 'self-evident' (2004: 240). Indeed, all this is well known and taken for granted in professional historiography. Historiographical revision is self-evident in two senses: first, in the sense of a disciplinary awareness about the fact that historical writing might just as well have its own history deriving from the need of revision in light of new occurrences; and second, in the sense that historiographical revision itself appears as a fascinating research topic that reinforces disciplinary awareness (see Hughes-Warrington 2013).

In the second part of this book, my intentions are related to some of these aspects of historiographical revision but nevertheless stand on their own insofar as I attempt to account for historiographical change in a distinctly theoretical fashion. The underlying assumption of this endeavour is not only that historiographical change appears as a possibility only in relation to historical change. Rather, the underlying assumption is that the birth of a novel sense of configuring historical change as investigated in the first part of this book calls for a new conceptualization of historiographical change. For if there is a fundamental link between historical and historiographical change, and if the way Western societies conceive of historical change is itself already changing, this simply cannot leave unchanged the way in which we conceive of historiographical change.

All this eventually boils down to the necessity of a theory of history in the sense of historical writing that is able to account for historiographical change in the broadest sense. But anyone may ask: is there not already such an ambitious theory around? Has an overall theory of history not already manoeuvred itself in the last half-century into a hegemonic position within the field of the theory and philosophy of history? Well, of course there is such a theory of history around. As mentioned in the Prologue, Whitean narrative philosophy of history – and more generally speaking, a Hayden White-inspired narrativism – has long since been dominating the theoretical field. What's more, it earned this dominance over the theoretical field precisely by offering a theory that explains historical writing as such, regardless of the perceived differences between historiographical schools, approaches and methods. As an overall theory of history, Whitean and White-inspired narrativism claims validity concerning all histories ever produced since the institutionalization of the discipline, since professional historiography as we know it exists.

But again, if there already is a theory of history with a universality claim, then what can I possibly mean by the aforementioned necessity to have one? By the necessity of a theory of history in the sense of historical writing, I certainly mean a theory with such a universality claim. At the same time, I mean a theory other than narrativism. The reason for this is what appears to be the blind spot of narrativism, namely, its incapacity to account for historiographical change. I am very well aware that this claim may sound rather odd. Especially in light of the fact that White's *Metahistory* is itself an account for historiographical change, despite the fact of rarely being referenced as such. The book is most famous for its theoretical framework that White sketches in the introductory chapter and calls 'the poetics of history' (1973: 1–42). However, the rest of the book outlines a change in the disposition of the elements within that framework and presents it as a history of nineteenth-century historical thinking.

As to the theoretical part, in the same year that *Metahistory* appeared, White also published an essay entitled 'Interpretation in History,' reserved for sketching only the framework, which was reprinted a few years later in a collection of White's essays (1978: 51–80). In this theoretical framework, a background set of linguistic and conceptual schemes – composed of modes of emplotment (romantic, tragic, comic, satiric), argument (formist, mechanistic, organicist, contextualist) and ideological implication (anarchist, radical, conservative, liberal) – is responsible for prefiguring the historical field. Historical interpretations are determined by the disposition of the elements of this background set, but what White seeks is something even more profound: 'the grounding of these modes in some more basic level of consciousness' (72). White eventually finds this in linguistic tropes (metaphor, metonymy, synechdoche, irony), which appear as the ultimate pre-existing linguistic schemes that provide the ground for meaning-constitution in history.

As to the question of historiographical change, *Metahistory* appears to be the most conventional historical exercise. It presents a historical trajectory concerned with the changing dominance of certain tropes and thereby certain dispositions of the background set of linguistic and conceptual schemes in nineteenth-century 'historical consciousness'. At the end of the introductory sketch of the theoretical framework, when White outlines the main argument of the book, it becomes clear that historiographical change for White means 'phases' of the 'evolution' and 'development' of historical thought (1973: 38–42). Needless to say, this is the stereotypical invocation of the modern processual historical sensibility. What seems to be more important though is that this nineteenth-century historiographical development means a development from a metaphorical to an ironic prefiguration of the historical field, meaning that *Metahistory* explains historiographical change as a result of a rearrangement within the already existing background set of linguistic and conceptual schemes.

This brief summary clearly testifies that the Whitean enterprise is actually very much engaged in the question of change over time in historiography. Not to mention that historiographical change in the Whitean framework even appears as linked to an overall change in the far wider category of 'historical consciousness' and modern historical thinking in general. How to understand then the above claim that the blind spot of Whitean and White-inspired narrativism is its incapacity to account for historiographical change?

The answer lies in the difference between *presuming* the possibility of historiographical change and even providing a *historical explanation* of such presumed change on the one hand, and *theoretically accounting for the possibility of such change* on the other hand and in the first place. I believe narrativism does the former job without doing the latter. It presumes historiographical change as a rearrangement of theoretical categories of pre-existing linguistic and conceptual patterns, but it cannot account for why and how the rearrangement of the already available constituents of a background set happens.

Yet another major problem of the historiographical change sketched by White in *Metahistory* is posed by the fact of *everything being already available*. In 'the poetics of history', the linguistic and conceptual schemes and patterns form such an already available background set, while the set itself does not appear as prone to change. The possibility of new constituents emerging within the pre-existing background set seems to be out of the question. Nor can Whitean narrative philosophy of history conceive of the possibility of change as the emergence of a completely novel background set of linguistic and conceptual schemes. Thus, to repeat my point, it seems to me that narrativism does not theoretically *account for* historiographical change; instead, it *presumes* its possibility in all variations as the mere recombination of that which already exists and that which enables the possibility of a meaningful historical explanation.

Finally, the historical explanation enabled by narrativism recounts a change over time of a peculiar kind. As attested to by the historiographical development outlined in *Metahistory*, it is the historiographical change that matched a vision of processual change in history as the course of affairs. As all possible elements are already available at any point of time, nothing genuinely unexpected can take place within the Whitean view of historiography, and whatever arrangement of the elements comes out as the result of the recounted change, the change cannot but form a processual sequence of combinations of already assumed potentialities. Needless to say, this does not look like a feasible framework for accounting for historiographical novelty in times of unprecedented change. I believe that in historiography today we need a configuration of change over time that matches the perception of the novel configuration of historical change.

All in all, against the backdrop of such a multilayered discontent with narrativism, the following chapters attempt to outline a theory of history (understood as historical writing) that *accounts for* historiographical change *when* historical change is conceived of as unprecedented. The chapters of the two parts of this book, ideally read together, amount to a theory of history in times of unprecedented change. Yet, I believe that it is possible to see value in the respective parts without fully subscribing to the overall theory. Even if the arguments of the first part of the book constantly lurk behind the second, familiarity with them is not a prerequisite of an engagement with the arguments of the coming pages – at least not until the final chapter, which explicitly connects historical change and historiographical change. As a point of departure, however, the next chapter begins to approach historiographical change as emerging from a dissatisfaction with the dominance of narrativism-inspired historical theory.

4

The Expression of Historical Experience

Blasphemous rumours

On the following pages I plan to commit metaphorical blasphemy. Being metaphorical, the sort of blasphemy I have in mind is not directed against religious sentiments but against what has become an authoritative view within the theory and philosophy of history in recent decades. However liberating this view proved to be to former generations, after a period of excitement created by the first encounter, my generation had to face it in the shape of the establishment. Being the establishment, its initial grace began to look somewhat faded and – somewhat naturally – it appeared to be less fresh and vivid, and more restrictive and limited. On this premise, any challenge posed to that view counts today as faithless and faithful at the same time: faithless and sometimes oppositional to the arguments upon which it rests, while faithful and indebted to its liberating intentions. This is the dual ground on which I plan to proceed when, in the broadest terms, I talk about the possibility of a *productive interaction* between language and the non-linguistic in order to explain a kind of linguistic change that disconnects to previous linguistic schemes. On a narrower scale, it means that in relation to history, I am going to talk about the question of how historical experience as something non-linguistic could productively interact with language in giving birth to genuinely novel historical representations that challenge received wisdom.

The current conviction about the issue is not hard to summarize. It says that although it is possible to talk about both language and something non-linguistic separately (or as the one prefiguring the other), any productive interaction between them is utterly impossible. It says that the choices are rather limited: either there is experience and there is no language; or there is language and there is no experience. As for experience, philosophy has been under the impression at least since the Kantian critique that we cannot have *immediate* experiences, that we cannot have experiences without the pre-structuring work of our categories of understanding. In other words, whatever we experience, we cannot escape the fact that *we* experience it, which means that this *we* must be constitutive of whatever is experienced and of experience itself. Since Kant's categories of understanding, this determinant *we* has meant various things: our mental content; our social and cultural constraints; our ideological leaning; our brain; our body; and, throughout the last century and most dominantly, our language. Although from time to time it seems to be possible to witness efforts to talk about a mind- or language-independent reality – most recently in various strands of speculative realism (Meillassoux 2008; Bryant, Srnicek and Harman 2011; Harman 2013) – the idea of the impossibility of immediacy prevails both in philosophy and within the narrower field of the theory and philosophy of history.

Anyone who did not hear something like this from Kant would likely hear similar things from structuralists, poststructuralists, narrative philosophers of history, social constructivists and practically all who consider themselves (or are considered by others as being) postmodernists. However, their common agenda of emphasizing the mediated character of experience is only one side of the coin. The other side is experience as mute, or experience as infancy, as Giorgio Agamben calls it in saying that 'a primary experience, far from being subjective, could then only be what in human beings comes before the subject – that is, before language: a "wordless" experience in the literal sense of the term, a human *infancy*, whose boundary would be marked by language' (1993: 47). Whereas these words recognize a non-linguistic realm on the one hand, on the other they set up its territory, which happens to end where language begins. This constellation is precisely what the pioneer adventures into the non-linguistic tend to result in: the reinforcement of the separation of language and experience, culminating in either having an immediate experience that is incommunicable and inexpressible, or having language without any immediate experiential basis.

In the context of the theory and philosophy of history, even Ankersmit, the most eminent proponent of historical experience, maintains the dilemma by accepting the mutual exclusion of experience and language in claiming that 'where you have language, experience is not, and vice versa' (2005: 11). What's more, in a talk at Ghent University in 2013 under the title 'Toggling White and Ankersmit: Is There a "Between" between Text and Experience,' Hans Kellner suggested to approve the status quo by making peace with it. Kellner depicted the two main orientations of recent years within the theory and philosophy of history – an orientation toward narrative, language and the linguistic associated with Hayden White, and an orientation toward experience and the non-linguistic associated with Ankersmit – and argued that they seem to embody contradictory movements. He did not see any reason for thinking that, provided this situation, we should strive for any reconciliation or harmony between these orientations and went on to claim that because we are comfortable with extremes, we can pretty easily inhabit extremes, and the best we can do is simply 'toggle' back and forth between language and experience.

Even though I can acknowledge that Kellner's approach might be the actual attitude most of us have towards our experiences, and even though it seems obvious that many times we just do not even try to voice most of these experiences, there certainly are times when we do. These latter times are the ones that I will try to account for. Without these times, Kellner could not even talk about 'extremes', because if there were nothing but those times of either-or, then neither of the two options would be extremes in any sense. There are extremes only when there are other times with other options in whose relations extremes can be set, and one of these other options is what I am interested in. Not because I wish to prove that under an extraordinary constellation of stars we eventually might be able to transfer our experiences into language without any damage done to them. I can happily accept the impossibility of that. I am interested in another option because I see no reason why the acceptance of the position that such a straight transfer is impossible would necessarily entail that experience and language cannot be engaged cooperatively in any other way in producing new insights. This latter point, that what a productive interaction brings about is the birth of new insights, is the most crucial one, given that no theory that keeps experience and language separated seems to be able to account for it. On the one hand, a mute experience lacks linguistic conceptualization to attribute sense to that experience, without which the novelty of experience is hardly an insight. On the other hand, linguistic conceptualization that prefigures experience is something we already have at our disposal, so an insight gained this way is anything but qualitatively new (what I mean by 'qualitatively new' will become clear later).

This being the received view does not mean that there are no efforts to conceptualize the situation differently, efforts that could either deliberately or implicitly suggest that the dilemma outlined above might be false. It appears to me that – among a few others – Hans Ulrich Gumbrecht, Eelco Runia and Anton Froeyman suggest something like this in their own respective ways. However, I do not wish to offer ways to 'amalgamate' language and the non-linguistic as Gumbrecht (2006) does, to follow Runia (2014) in postulating a transfer of the non-linguistic into language via metonymy, or to support Froeyman (2015) in linking language and experience through poststructuralist ethics. To me – in one way or another – all these conceptualizations seem to entail a return to an operation that the dilemma had been set up against in the first place, namely, the possibility of an admittance of the non-linguistic into language. Although Gumbrecht, Runia and Froeyman seem equally to accept this possibility, I cannot. My reasons for this (and the presently very vague notion of 'admittance' by which I characterize this operation) will become clear at a later stage of this chapter. For the time being, I would like to note only that notwithstanding all my general sympathies with these efforts, I cannot agree with their particular suggestions.

On the following pages, I nevertheless intend to join forces with the few like Gumbrecht, Runia and Froeyman, while also arguing contrary to their position as well as contrary to the dogmatic dilemma introduced above. I am going to suggest that under a theory of expression a more friendly relationship can be established between experience and language – a relationship in which rather than being hostile they are desperately in need of each other to produce new insights. This relationship can be established in a way that, according to my optimistic scenario, might satisfy both those who strive for immediate experiences and are willing to sacrifice language in its name, and those who stick to the idea of an omnipotent language and are willing to sacrifice immediacy in its name. In fact, one of the main reasons this scenario might be attractive is that it suggests that there is no need for such pseudo-heroic sacrifices at all.

I will try to satisfy everyone in five steps, in the shape of five short sections. Four of these sections will make up my main argument; the fifth one is reserved for an argument about the significance of the main argument. As for the concrete steps, first I will depict the current situation in the theory and philosophy of history regarding expression, a situation in which expression as such cannot be named because naming it would contradict the basic principles of linguistic and narrative theories. In the second step I will argue that this is the case because when we think about expression we tend to rely on a notion of expression we tacitly rely on in our everyday lives. Next, in the third section I will leave behind the description of the situation and try to overcome these obstacles by finding a way to name expression, and by creating a notion of expression different from the one we rely on in our everyday lives. Then, as a fourth and final step of the main argument, I will condense this notion of expression into a struck-through 'of' in talking about the expression of historical experience. Finally, I will offer some closing remarks on the significance of the entire enterprise.

The unnameable expression

Those who are familiar with the Harry Potter universe might find some value in the characterization of expression as the Lord Voldemort of the theory and philosophy of history. Even though expression, unlike Lord Voldemort, is far from being a dreadful villain in this particular story, this is the claim I would like to begin with: expression is Lord Voldemort in the sense that it is the

'You-Know-What' and 'The-Thing-That-Must-Not-Be-Named' of the theory and philosophy of history.

It became the 'You-Know-What' and the 'The-Thing-That-Must-Not-Be-Named' when the issues of narration and language took over the theoretical field. Not right away though, not when narration and language entered the scene and the golden days of analytical philosophy of history began. Expression became the unnamable apparition when those days ended even according to its practitioners (Danto 1995), when the questions of analytical philosophy of history were suddenly dropped, and when theoretical discussions moved from sentences to texts. Since then, although almost nothing has been said about expression itself, it has discreetly lurked behind the entire discussion. In a latent but overwhelming way it was both present and non-present at the same time in postmodern theories of history as discourse, in explorations into the rhetoric of historical representation, in investigations concerning the stylistic features of historical writing, in assessments of the capabilities of historical narratives, in enumerations of the literary devices used (or recommended for use) by historians and, of course, in Hayden White's narrative philosophy of history, which, either directly or indirectly, inspired many of the aforementioned approaches (for instance, Rigney 1990; Berkhofer 1995; Jenkins 1995; Munslow 2007; Ermarth 2011). All in all, in its dormant all-pervasiveness, expression was there all the time. It just could not be named – or at least was not supposed to be.

Expression could not be named because the explicit invocation and the naming of expression would have entailed the naming of whatever was being expressed. Or, to put it more emphatically, calling histories linguistic expressions would have demanded having an answer to the question 'Expressions of what exactly?' Narrative-linguistic theories of history, however, were not supposed to have an answer to the question in the first place. The entities that populated the narrative-linguistic landscape were entities that could be studied and analysed *within* or *as* language – entities such as linguistic tropes, styles, literary devices, modes of emplotment, discursive strategies, and so on – and, because of their 'being within' or 'being as' language, none of them could be named as the expressed of histories. And if there is no expressed to express, there can be no expression. At least it would be somewhat odd to claim that what a particular history expresses *is* a certain style or a certain mode of emplotment, or that in general what language expresses *are* linguistic entities that inhabit language. Claiming this would be no more than claiming that language eventually *expresses* itself, which would probably strike everyone as nonsense. Therefore, in the final analysis, it seems that the case with narrative theories and the question of expression was not only that narrative theories were not supposed to have any answer to the question; rather, the case was that they could not even pose or make sense of the question.

This, briefly, is how the question of expression and narrative-linguistic theories relate to each other. If linguistic conceptualization precedes our encounters with any non-linguistic conceptualization and if, in consequence, our experience is linguistically prefigured, then there is no experience, only language; and if there is only language, then there is nothing left to be expressed *by* language – except language itself. But could anyone claim that language eventually *expresses* itself? Would it count as an expression? What instantaneously comes to mind as an answer is that it would rather embarrassingly contradict our everyday notion of expression, which we so comfortably rely on not merely in our everyday lives but, apparently, also in our academic theories. Therefore, in order to get a fuller grasp of the problem, in the next section I would like to briefly analyse it.

Our everyday notion of expression

In our everyday lives, expression features as an entity that connects two supposedly separated spheres. To provide an example that stays within the confines of the theory and philosophy of history and thereby shows how far-reaching this notion of expression is, I would like to consider the sphere of events and the sphere of thoughts in the case of Collingwood. To begin with, in *The Idea of History*, Collingwood famously/infamously claims that historians are 'concerned with thoughts alone', thereby opposing the view that history is about change as a succession of events in favour of a conception of history as knowledge of mind. Nevertheless, with the focus on thoughts, Collingwood does not attribute complete insignificance to events but lays down the conditions for their significance, and what emerges as a protagonist under these conditions is expression:

> Unlike the natural scientist, the historian is not concerned with events as such at all. He is only concerned with those events which are the outward expression of thoughts, and is only concerned with these in so far as they express thoughts. At bottom, he is concerned with thoughts alone; with their outward expression in events he is concerned only by the way, in so far as these reveal to him the thoughts of which he is in search. ([1946] 1993: 217)

The most important aspect to note is that – as Collingwood implies with the qualification 'those events' – events are not necessarily expressions of thoughts. Events as such do not inherently contain, embody, exhibit and expose thoughts as such, meaning that thoughts do not belong to the sphere of events. Without expression, in their own right, events and thoughts are two distinct spheres, and thoughts could not be traced within the sphere of events if expression were not postulated in order to establish a connection between the two distinct spheres. It is the established connection that results in a re-placement of thoughts, and it is only when expression is postulated that the expressed – which before the postulation of expression is not even an expressed – can be said to belong to whatever is supposed to express it. In other words, (1) expression presupposes two distinct spheres, which (2) by and in expression become one in a way that the sphere that is supposed to express an expressed has to take in, embody, house, or admit the potential expressed.

These two features, (1) the *initially distinct spheres* and (2) the *act of admittance*, seem to be the prerequisites for our everyday notion of expression. This is the case for every expression we tend to take for granted in our everyday lives and, as Collingwood's case shows, even in our academic activities. As an everyday life example, our gestures are supposed to express our emotional states insofar as our emotions do not belong to the sphere of gestures but become admitted into it by the postulation of expression. Another illuminating example is graphology (at least for those who used to practise handwriting), where the distinctness of the two spheres between which expression is supposed to establish a connection – our handwriting and our personality traits – looks even more obvious.

In much the same way, according to our tacit, everyday notion of expression, through language we are supposed to express something other than language itself, something other which, before an act of admittance can take place through expression, does not belong to the sphere of language. Further, this something other (the expressed of linguistic expression) is supposed to be the ultimate object of curiosity, just as in the case of Collingwood who is ultimately curious about thoughts, or in the case of graphology, which is curious about our handwriting in order to satisfy curiosity about our personality. And this is precisely why expression could not be named by linguistic theories: because according to our tacitly held notion of expression, it would entail an admittance of the non-linguistic into the linguistic. The possibility of translating experience through expression into language, that is, the idea of language as a medium, simply contradicts the most fundamental principles of both the Kantian critique and the more recent linguistic enchantment.

Naming experience as the expressed

Arriving at this point and identifying the problem inherent in the current state of the field, the challenge seems to be clear. In order to be able to talk about linguistic expression concerning history, in order to establish a productive interaction between the non-linguistic and the linguistic (and in order to do so in a way that satisfies both those who strive for immediate contact with the world and those who wish to remain within the confines of language), something like an expressed has to be named. But in order to avoid falling back to entertaining pre-linguistic-turn and pre-narrative-theory concerns, this expressed cannot be a proper expressed in the sense that it cannot act as a medium and cannot entail any straightforward admittance of the non-linguistic into language. In the rest of this chapter as a response to this challenge I will do two things. First, I will name expression by naming a potential expressed other than language itself: historical experience. Then, in the next section I will clarify how this cannot actually be an expressed in the sense of our everyday notion of expression.

As for naming something like an expressed, historical experience as the potential candidate has three main interrelated features. First, the experience is historical in the sense that it is an experience of a particular piece of the past. It is neither an experience of history as the course of affairs, nor past people's experience of their own environment. It is what Ankersmit calls *subjective, individual historical experience* as opposed both to sublime, collective historical experience (the experience of history understood as the course of affairs) and to objective historical experience (the experience past people had) (2005: 264–6). It might be provoked by an 'encounter' with any remnant of the past existing in the present, be it material or immaterial, say, a postwar abstract expressionist painting, a medieval chronicle either as you touch it in its materiality or as you read it, a room left untouched for ages, an idea you come across in Voltaire or a weird story in Plutarch, or the melody of Michael Jackson's 'Billie Jean.' But in order for these examples to qualify as (subjective) historical experiences, they have to be unfamiliar in the sense that such experience is not a recollection. A historical experience is not a memory of a Barnett Newman painting to revisit but an encounter with the painting in a way that has never taken place before: an encounter that carries the element of surprise. It is not to say that the painting or, for that matter, 'Billie Jean,' has to be completely unknown in order for the experience to take place. When Runia describes his 'Abba-sensation' of being moved by a documentary about the band without Abba ever being part of his identity (2014: 86–7), this may qualify as such an experience (in case it is the encounter with a melody he most probably knew and not the documentary-effect that moved Runia). Nothing excludes the possibility of the unfamiliarity and the surprise to emerge from an encounter with the supposedly familiar and quotidian (although, as the next chapter argues, that which is unfamiliar is more likely to provide an occasion for an encounter-event).

The element of surprise leads to the second point, namely, that the historical experience I am interested in has a strong aesthetic character. By attributing an aesthetic character to it, I wish to stress the suddenness of historical experience, and because of its suddenness, its non-cognitivity. With all this, as far as I am concerned, I remain in line with Ankersmit's theory, even though my reasons for doing so are slightly different from his. Stressing non-cognitivity gains significance when you take into consideration that the main reason post-Kantian philosophy denied the possibility of immediate experience was the role it supposedly played in cognition. In much the same way, the target of the critique of linguistic theories was this experience: experience as a matter of epistemology, as a matter of gaining knowledge. I do not see any way (or any reason) to restore the immediacy of such experience, but I think there is a way to reserve the possibility of immediacy for a characteristically aesthetic experience. In other words, I believe that it is on aesthetic grounds that the linguistic and non-linguistic aspects of history (both its academic and non-academic forms) can be engaged in a productive interaction.

As for my divergences, whereas Ankersmit binds his notion of historical experience to 'moods and feelings' (2005: 306–12), I would not restrict it to a territory that concerns only what we associate with the affectual. Nor would I confine the territory of such experience to the intellectual or the corporeal. As usual, even those who pursue the scholarly activity called 'aesthetics' are in deep disagreement over what it is they actually pursue and what attributes an experience labelled 'aesthetic' does or should have. The way I intend to make use of an aesthetic character of historical experience is indifferent to and therefore compatible with any approach within and outside aesthetics – be it a 'movement' in Germany to redefine aesthetics as aesthesis (Adler 2002), or all the variety of standpoints of analytic philosophy on the concept of 'aesthetic experience' (Shusterman and Tomlin 2008) – insofar as it excludes epistemological concerns. Nevertheless, as it will soon become clear, I do not wish to get rid of those concerns entirely by this exclusion. What I wish to retain is the non-cognitivity only of a sudden 'encounter' with the world in the shape of a remnant of the past, that is, I wish to emphasize the non-cognitive character only of the experience that is still mute, only of the experience that is not yet a quasi-expressed of an expression, but an experience that can potentially be a quasi-expressed exactly because a moment of 'encounter' disrupts our linguistic schemes.

In a certain sense, it is this 'encounter' and disruption itself, or more the experience of this very disruption and the cognitive void it entails, which I would like to characterize as being aesthetic and without epistemological concerns. The disruptive character of the aesthetic appears in both Gumbrecht (2004: 101–3) and Ankersmit (2005: 275–80). At least I would like to interpret them such that where Gumbrecht talks about the insularity of aesthetic experience and its distance from our everyday concerns, and where Ankersmit talks about a decontextualized experience, they both invoke a moment that disrupts business as usual. But whereas they consider this moment to be a part of aesthetic experience, according to what I said above, this moment itself (on which Chapter 5 will elaborate) is what I would like to label as aesthetic.

This brings me to my third point, namely that all this nears certain approaches within phenomenology, where it gets a clearer articulation in a broader sense. Thus, finally, the experience I am interested in is not only a subjective historical experience with an aesthetic character, but also an experience to which a certain sort of phenomenology and hermeneutics, and recently especially the Hungarian phenomenologist László Tengelyi (2004, 2007), pays attention. The most important peculiarity of this experience is its ability to thwart our expectations. Just like the disruption an aesthetic experience brings about, in a phenomenological experience, our linguistic conceptualizations break down, instead of framing and producing experiences, as linguistic theories claim. What can be regarded as an experience in a phenomenological sense – and also what deserves to be called experience according to the hermeneutics of Hans-Georg Gadamer (2004: 350) – is precisely the momentary collapse of our means of sense attribution.

There is no need to think here about anything mysterious. In the context of actual historical practice, such experiences that thwart expectations are less often the ones we face in abstract expressionist exhibitions or in 1980s retro parties and more often the ones that occur during a customary archival visit or during any 'encounter' with whatever gets identified as a source. It is most likely that the 'encounter' takes place in a way similar to how Robert Darnton describes the moment out of which his book *The Great Cat Massacre* was born (even though of course it does not have to be confined to an encounter with written words):

> There is no better way, I believe, than to wander through the archives. One can hardly read a letter from the Old Regime without coming up against surprises – anything from the constant dread of toothaches, which existed everywhere, to the obsession with braiding dung for display on manure heaps, which remained confined to certain villages. What was proverbial wisdom to our ancestors is completely opaque to us. Open any eighteenth-century book of proverbs, and you will find entries such as: 'He who is snotty, let him blow his nose.' When we cannot get a proverb, or a joke, or a ritual, or a poem, we know we are on to something. By picking at the document where it is most opaque, we may be able to unravel an alien system of meaning. The thread might even lead into a strange and wonderful world view. (1999: 4–5)

Even if I cannot support Darnton in claiming that historians 'unravel an alien system of meaning' that arises out of their experience (because this would entail that the meaning was already there in the first place), I think that the experience he talks about before that supposed unravelling of meaning could happen is precisely the disruptive experience, the experience of disruption itself. Not getting the joke in the archives, suddenly confronting something that does not make sense, is the moment of the birth of a new insight that disrupts previous schemes and gives way to a process of expression. This process may differ significantly from what Darnton thinks about it, but it cannot overshadow the fact that these are the situations that might result in overwriting existing histories, in much the same way that, according to Tengelyi, it happens regarding our life-histories. Tengelyi calls these moments 'the critical situations that constrain us to rectify the stories held to be precise and authentic by ourselves', that is, situations in which 'we catch sight of an ungovernable and uncontrollable process that results in the spontaneous emergence of a dispossessed sense' (2004: xxvi). This process that we catch sight of is the process of expression, the issue I would like to turn to now to see how the experience that is mute and non-cognitive may interact productively with language, and how this interaction results in new insights.

The expression of historical experience

Before anything else, I would like to condense the essence of the last section about experience into one sentence: in order to name expression, something like an expressed – a quasi-expressed – has to be named, and my candidate for this quasi-expressed is (1) a *subjective historical experience* with (2) an *aesthetic character* that (3) thwarts our expectations. I share the excitement with Tengelyi and phenomenology that this might be the cradle of new insights, or, in the context of history, the birthplace of novel historical representations, about which I would like to note two things. First, given the disruptive character of this experience, it must be clear now that whenever I talk about new insights as results, I mean insights that introduce momentous *change that disconnects with previous linguistic schemes*; and second, experience can be regarded as a birthplace only in cases when *the step toward expression* is taken. I believe this step is due to an ethical impulse (to be explored in Chapter 6), to an approval of an ethical demand that pushes us toward expression in some cases, whereas lacking such approval we remain either stranded or pretty much content with our mute experience.

In this second scenario, because what we have is just another ineffable experience, our behaviour is perfectly legitimate even in the eyes of narrative theories, insofar as experience stays away from linguistic concerns. But in the first scenario, once the step toward expression is taken, narrative theories have to face the familiar dilemma again, this time rephrased for my present concerns: either you opt for the possibility of change and new insights and then you open up language to admit experience into it; or you opt for language without being able to explain how linguistic change and new insights are possible. If you choose the one, you subscribe to our comforting, everyday notion of expression and doom language to subservience; if you choose the other, you go for the convenience of linguistic omnipotence and do not feature experience even in the smallest supporting role. I would like to suggest that this dilemma is a false one. There are not only two choices (one about a straight transfer of experience into language and another about language making up all experiences) in which one of the parties is always taking over a passive other. I would like to suggest that by a shift in focus it is possible to talk about the relationship of experience and language in terms of a productive engagement, in terms of a creative process of sense-formation in which two powerful parties do not sentence the other to passivity but rather cannot do without each other. The only thing required for this is to recognize that the dilemma itself rests on an inadequate notion of expression, and that taking sides by relying jointly on our everyday notion of expression can be avoided by dropping that notion, thereby introducing another, more sophisticated possibility to account for momentous linguistic change.

There is nothing compelling in regarding the process of expression as a straight transfer of experience into language that implies an act of admittance. In order to get a grasp on what difference it would make to drop our everyday notion of expression, it is worth beginning with Maurice Merleau-Ponty's *Phenomenology of Perception* (2004), in which he struggled with his own version of the dilemma outlined above. In his case, the dilemma involved a thinking subject and thought on the non-linguistic side, and language and speech on the other. In looking for a way out, the first thing he had to realize is that meaning does not lie on either side of the divide, it is neither the property of an already formulated expression as a final product nor the property of anything primordially non-linguistic that precedes expression, but is constituted in and through expression. What he realized was that expression as a process of meaning constitution is not what I call here the admittance of an expressed but an operation of creation, that 'the process of expression brings the meaning into being or makes it effective, and does not merely translate it' (Merleau-Ponty 2004: 213). According to the *Phenomenology of Perception*, the way all this happens is that 'the new sense-giving intention knows itself only by donning already available meanings, the outcome of previous acts of expression. The available meanings suddenly link up in accordance with an unknown law, and once and for all a fresh cultural entity has taken on an existence' (213).

However, it does not come as a surprise that this is not Merleau-Ponty's final take on the issue. For even if expression features here as a creative process, the process itself does not involve anything non-linguistic. It is only the recombination of what we already have at our disposal. Nevertheless, it does not mean that this description would not be able to account for anything: it might still be valid whenever it comes to continuous, progressive or cumulative change. What it cannot account for is non-continuous change as a result of an experience that disrupts our previous linguistic schemes. In fact, Merleau-Ponty could not even consider this possibility inasmuch as he did not have a notion of experience in which the entire set of 'already available meanings' he talks about collapses. Rather, it is Tengelyi who – while having a point of departure in a notion of experience that thwarts expectations, on the one hand, and drawing on Merleau-Ponty's posthumously published body of work, on the other – can consistently envision a language 'that does not content itself with sedimented or instituted meanings' (2004: 29).

Tengelyi borrows from Merleau-Ponty and elaborates on the idea of a 'wild sense' that might emerge in the process of expression and the idea that this emergent sense might be associated with 'the expression of experience by experience' (Merleau-Ponty 1968: 155). The emerging sense is labelled 'wild' because it is uncontrollable by the subject who is associated with producing it in the process of expression. As for the phrase 'the expression of experience by experience', in Tengelyi's interpretation it means that the original experience is inseparable from the experience of expression, from our very struggle with language as we try to formulate a sense. At the end of the process, 'the struggle for expression engenders an unpredictable sense which does not coincide with the originally intended meaning of the speaker', highlighted by Tengelyi with the familiar example of writing (2004: 34), where the final result might be something entirely different from the original intention we began with.

The first remarkable consequence of these phenomenological investigations is that, accommodated to the concerns of historical writing, experience (the sort of historical experience I named as a quasi-expressed) might serve as an *incentive* to a struggle with language in a situation where our linguistic conceptualizations are momentarily collapsed. Then, because the career of experience is not reduced to initiation, I would like to call the inseparability of a mute experience and the experience of our sense-formulating efforts *the duality of experience*, and, following Tengelyi, to regard their melting together as a *drive* to expression, without which our histories would not be radically revised and redescribed from time to time. However, as is apparent in his example of writing, Tengelyi's phenomenology of expression works with a primordial intention that the ultimate expression eventually departs from. In the case of historical writing and in the case of the sort of historical experience I talk about, this intention is never present in the first place. As I indicated earlier, what accounts for the step toward expression in the context of history is an ethical approval of a demand, which has nothing to do with the content of expression in terms of intentionality. In other words, in the case of history, instead of a primordial intention there is a demand to fulfil an ethical purpose that lies behind those historical representations we regard as historiographical classics that challenge disciplinary consensus.

Finally, there is a difference between talking about the process of expression as sense-formation and talking about the result as already formulated sense and constituted meaning. Chapter 5 will engage with this question in a more detailed manner. For now, what seems important to point out is that once you shift perspective and begin to talk about the former, you might still go with narrativism and claim that no original experiential sense can be traced upon which the end result would be founded. Similarly, you can still conveniently claim that in opposition to language and linguistic expression, there is the inexpressible non-linguistic. However, these contentions (that lead to the dilemma with which I began) cannot overwrite the contention I take to be of utmost importance, namely that once you shift your attention from final products you begin to see that experience is not a foundation of constituted meanings and new insights, but their midwife and cradle. And the whole process that accounts for their birth and constitution, or on a larger scale for how well-established meanings get challenged and replaced, is impossible without it.

What all this means is that between the static world of speechlessness and the nonetheless static world of already formulated expressions, already instituted meanings and already written historical accounts, there is the dynamic world of sense-formation. This is the world where, theoretically speaking, the most gripping things happen. This is the process of the bringing forth of novel historical representations, the process that I would like to refer to as the expression of historical experience. Further, it is the simultaneous lack of admittance and the quasi-presence of a 'something-like-an-expressed' (which is far from being a proper expressed in the sense of our everyday notion of expression) that I would like to visualize typographically by using the strikethrough. For it is the question of this ~~of~~, the question of how to understand this ~~of~~, around which everything revolves. It is the question of the expressed, the question of the extent to which it is only a 'something-like-an-expressed', the question of the boundaries this ~~of~~ might erect for expression, and, ultimately, the question of the extent to which the non-linguistic and the linguistic can be engaged, hand in hand, in meaning-constitution and sense-formation, in giving birth to genuine novelty.

To get a better understanding of what is at stake here, consider what is not. The crucial point to make with regards to this is that the struck-through ~~of~~ is not simply a matter of linguistic communication. This is why I do not talk about the ~~expression~~ of historical experience and why I reserve the strikethrough for the expression ~~of~~ such experience. Being interested in linguistic communication means wanting to know what Donald Davidson, one of the most eminent philosophers of language of the previous century, wants to know in his classic essay 'A Nice Derangement of Epitaphs,' that is, 'how people who already have a language (whatever exactly that means) manage to apply their skill or knowledge to actual cases of interpretation' (2005: 100). But expression in the expression ~~of~~ historical experience is not merely a case of interpretation as the application of skill and knowledge in a situation of 'being home with the business of linguistic communication' (100). If I wanted to know what Davidson wants to know, I would be concerned about the communication of whatever is defined as experience. In that case, my focus would indeed lie in the question of whether it is better to talk about expression or only about ~~expression~~, the latter potentially hinting at the perplexities involved in attempting to account for the conditions of successful linguistic communication.

Reserving the struck-through for the ~~of~~ means that I am not interested in the question of *how* communication works. For the struck-through ~~of~~, it does not matter whether Davidson is right or wrong in concluding that 'there is no such thing as language, not if language is anything like what many philosophers and linguists have supposed' and that there is 'no such thing to be learned, mastered, or born with' (107). The concerns of the struck-through ~~of~~ precede concerns of linguistic communication. They are directed at the motives of *initiating* such linguistic communication instead. And even when it comes to the question of language use, the concerns of the struck-through ~~of~~ are not about the 'skill and knowledge' that language users already have but about that which defies the 'application' of such supposedly pre-existing 'skill and knowledge'. The question of the ~~of~~ in the expression ~~of~~ historical experience is the question of the emergence of the kind of novelty that is neither the reiteration of already instituted linguistic knowledge and linguistic competence, nor the successful linguistic rendering of a mute experience that defies such already instituted linguistic knowledge and linguistic competence.

How the trick is done

So far so good. To run an inconveniently schematic review: the expression ~~of~~ historical experience refers to a process in which, first, there is an initial moment of historical experience (a characteristically aesthetic moment that thwarts our expectations); then, because of an ethical impulse, there is a step taken toward expression; then there is our actual struggle with language (which we experience as the experience of expression itself that is inseparable from our initial experience); and finally, there is the final result, the already formulated new sense, the already finished expression, the already finished novel historical representation that challenges received wisdom. In a wider context this process testifies that there is nothing compelling in drawing the usual conclusion from the narrative-linguistic critique, namely that if language is not a neutral medium that translates the non-linguistic, then language either prefigures experience or that experience remains mute, and no productive interaction between the linguistic and the non-linguistic is possible. This conclusion is inevitable only in the light of our everyday notion of expression, and nothing excludes the possibility of dropping this notion of expression and exchanging it for another one instead of dropping the non-linguistic in favour of the linguistic (or the other way around). The theory of expression sketched above points to a direction where a productive interaction of language and the non-linguistic is not only possible but necessary for the birth of new insights, while at the same time it still does not treat language as a medium.

Once again, so far so good. But there is also the question that the English punk band, the Anti-Nowhere League, asked in a slightly different context in 1981: So what? At least this is the question that could be asked by anyone who takes the pragmatist philosopher Richard Rorty's side in assessing what questions are significant and important to ask and what theoretical enterprises are worth pursuing. Consider the following paragraph taken from Rorty's *Contingency, Irony, and Solidarity*:

> I can develop the contrast between the idea that the history of culture has a telos – such as the discovery of truth, or the emancipation of humanity – and the Nietzschean and Davidsonian picture which I am sketching by noting that the latter picture is compatible with a bleakly mechanical description of the relation between human beings and the rest of the universe. For genuine novelty can, after all, occur in a world of blind, contingent, mechanical forces. Think of novelty as the sort of thing which happens when, for example, a cosmic ray scrambles the atoms in a DNA molecule, thus sending things off in the direction of the orchids or the anthropoids. The orchids, when their time came, were no less novel or marvelous for the sheer contingency of this necessary condition of their existence. Analogously, for all we know, or should care, Aristotle's metaphorical use of *ousia*, Saint Paul's metaphorical use of *agapē*, and Newton's metaphorical use of *gravitas*, were the results of cosmic rays scrambling the fine structure of some crucial neurons in their respective

brains. Or, more plausibly, they were the result of some odd episodes in infancy – some obsessional kinks left in these brains by idiosyncratic traumata. It hardly matters how the trick was done. The results were marvelous. There had never been such things before. (1989: 17)

As the title of this section indicates, the part of the passage I would like to pay special attention to is the rather detached statement that 'it hardly matters how the trick was done', that it hardly matters how novelty occurs. I must consider this attitude because what the process of the expression of historical experience wishes to account for is precisely the occurrence of novelty and the way in which momentous linguistic change takes place as historiographical change. To begin with, Rorty's attitude is understandable to a certain extent. It is understandable insofar as he wishes to drop the question because he intends to offer a picture in which history understood as the course of affairs has no *telos*. But it is less understandable why the picture in which history has no *telos* necessarily entails dropping questions about how novelty occurs and how change takes place in a contingent universe. In fact, not trying to answer such questions has consequences even Rorty could not be wholeheartedly happy about.

While the rare proponents of the possibility of an immediate experience (even if they retain its muteness) are often accused of leaning to mysticism (Roth 2007; Domanska 2009; Icke 2012), I would like to point out that it might be the maintenance of the position that it hardly matters to answer questions about novelty and change that renders the entire issue mystical. And Rorty's choice of words is wonderfully instructive in this respect. Yes, the phrase 'how the trick is done' is a figure of speech, but it is not *just* a figure of speech. According to Rorty, linguistic change takes place in a way that you 'redescribe lots and lots of things in new ways, until you have created a pattern of linguistic behavior which will tempt the rising generation to adopt it' (1989: 9), but he has no idea about the way in which these redescriptions occur. According to what I said earlier – namely, that without an 'encounter' with the non-linguistic, no linguistic change that disconnects from pre-existing schemes can take place – as long as Rorty sticks to his epistemological framework and posits the separation of language and experience, he could not even have an idea about it. It is precisely this incapacity to have an idea that renders the question of the occurrence of novelty and change mystical; it is precisely this that makes Rorty talk about a trick and dismiss the entire question.

Rorty's dismissal, which stems from this incapacity, counters his own enthusiasm about linguistic change. For talking about novelty as a trick, talking about novelty as a given without being interested in how it takes place, is just like talking about the daily rise and disappearance of the glowing spot in the sky without asking questions about what it's doing there, and how and why it got there in the first place, or about things that we drop always falling down instead of flying off without asking how and why this happens. Had astronomers and physicists taken these things as given and not asked 'how' and 'why', novelty would not have occurred in the first place and there would have been no marvellous results to praise.

In other words, it seems to me that what motivates the perpetual redescriptions Rorty takes for granted are exactly the questions he forbids himself (and others) to ask. Or, in the most general terms, the attitude exhibited in the ban on asking such questions does not seem to keep us discovering, exploring and inventing, but in many respects, keeps us from doing these things. At the same time, it is precisely the attitude of discoveries and inventions that results in the redescriptions Rorty praises, and these redescriptions are quite often explanations for things that have been previously considered mystical, such as gravity or the movement of heavenly bodies. In much the same vein, what I have tried to show above on a more modest level, and with more preliminary intentions, is that there might be nothing mysterious in how new insights are born, neither in the most general terms nor in the context of the theory and philosophy of history. There is nothing mysterious in theoretically accounting for historiographical change. The irony of the story is that while a theory of expression that intends to account for how novelty occurs in historical writing is not an unveiling of a trick or a series of tricks done by historians or by anyone else, it can still be regarded as a Rortyan redescription in some senses. It is a redescription of redescription, if you will, a redescription of the way in which Rorty's very concern of linguistic change takes place.

5

Encountering the World

What about truth and falsity?

The theory of history as the expression of historical experience builds upon two key moments that set the entire scheme in motion. The first is the very initial moment of experience, an encounter with the world, which nevertheless remains mute without the second key moment, the step toward expression. The first moment is characteristically aesthetic, while the second one leads to the realm of ethics. Although both moments may be constitutive of every expression that results in new insights, my concern here is history as the expression of historical experience and a specific mode of ethical engagement in historical sense-formation as historiographical change.

The next two chapters intend to elaborate on the aforementioned two moments as the aesthetic and ethical dimensions of a theory of history that shifts the focus from the final product to the coming about of that very final product. Of course, such a shift of attention does not mean that whatever has been said about historical writing in recent decades is either wrong or pointless. What this means is only that it may be time to broaden the scope of theoretical investigation. The theoretical work of recent decades concerning historical writing studied mainly final results or carried out investigations based on their theoretical takes on already crafted histories. As I will show later, such interests, nevertheless, are not incompatible with the theory of historiographical novelty and change outlined here. For the present discussion, the more important point is that focusing on final results, rather unsurprisingly, was accompanied by debates revolving around the question of epistemology – either by finding out under what conditions we can regard histories as true, or by claiming that non-epistemological criteria matter more when it comes to evaluating histories. In light of this, broadening the scope of theoretical investigation means simply that more attention might be paid to what precedes questions related to the evaluation of already crafted histories (which I take to be the primary intention also of Ankersmit, Runia and Gumbrecht, regardless of what judgement one may pass on their theories).

To sketch the situation in a more detailed manner, when Hayden White (1987: 26–57) and the 'pre-historical experience' Frank Ankersmit (2001: 39–48), the two most prominent narrativist philosophers of history, argued that statements in historical texts can be evaluated in epistemic terms but the whole of the historical narrative cannot, they succeeded at least in one thing. Like the most controversial politicians or rock stars, they created an unlikely coalition of those merely brought together by their oppositional stances and values. Instead of fully succeeding in bringing about an informed discussion over a large variety of issues they put on the agenda, Whitean and Ankersmitian narrativism created the most heated debate over the issue they mostly, although not completely, wished to bracket or relegate to a smaller stage: historical truth. The reaction of fellow philosophers of history such as Chris Lorenz (1998), phenomenologists like David Carr (1986b), historians such as Joyce Appleby, Lynn Hunt and Margaret Jacob (1994), or the criticism of Carlo Ginzburg (1992), agreed at least on one point, namely that whatever narrative philosophy of history claims, the main concern of any theoretical approach to historical writing must be the truthfulness of historical accounts.

In a certain sense, this is hardly surprising. Debates about truth and falsity in historiography have had a respectable pedigree even before narrativism. Nor is it surprising that such discussions survived the unchallenged prominence of the question of narrative. Even today, when the heyday of narrativism is long gone, the question of the truthfulness of historiography is still vigorously debated. The prenarrativist epistemological focus of theoretical work is now being reconsidered by approaches aiming at postnarrativism (Kuukkanen 2015) and even by efforts that wish to give the otherwise non-epistemological notion of historical experience an epistemological edge (Díaz-Maldonado 2016). The question of historiographical truth, it seems, persists as long as the practice of modern historiography does.

All this is fine, necessary and important, and also forces me to say a few more words about how a theory of history as the expression of historical experience relates to narrativist approaches on the one hand, and epistemology-oriented approaches on the other. The key momentum, as indicated earlier, is the difference between examining a moment of inception and a sense-making process, instead of having a point of departure in the end result, in the already crafted historical narrative. My interest lies in the former, while the latter is the most important feature that narrativism shares with epistemology-oriented approaches, despite their sharply opposing stances. Whereas epistemology-oriented approaches are concerned with the validation of end results with regard to their truth or falsity, narrative philosophies of history offer aesthetic (coherence of the entirety of the narrative, for instance), moral, or sociocultural validation criteria (such as recognition of familiar emplotment-patterns), or a combination of these.

The diverging stances concerning validation criteria makes narrativism far more open to questions concerning the composition of end results than epistemology-oriented theories ever could be. Even in the sense of a process of composition (which may be a shared interest with the approach of this book), though not necessarily. More importantly, in the sense of identifying the fundamental structuring 'deteminants' of historical narratives. These 'determinants' – the otherwise completely different linguistic tropes in White (1973) and narrative substances in Ankersmit (1983) – are responsible for the ultimate form of end results on the one hand, but on the other they can only be studied and identified as such by investigating the very end results they determine. Hence the primacy of end results even in narrative philosophy of history, which puts it alongside its theoretical opponents invested in exploring epistemic validation criteria.

This is, again, anything but surprising. For the shared focus of narrativism and epistemology-oriented historical theories on end results has its equivalent in the philosophy of science. Perhaps it would not even be completely inaccurate to claim that the primacy of end results in historical theory is modelled on the primacy of the 'context of justification' in philosophy of science, even though such modelling may be anything but deliberate. Apart from the original context of the distinction of Hans Reichenbach (1938) between the 'context of discovery' and the 'context of justification', and apart from all the criticism and debate over the distinction that has seriously been called into question after Thomas Kuhn's *The Structure of Scientific Revolutions* ([1962] 2012), there seems to be a clear benefit of reducing scholarly interest to the 'context of justification'. The benefit in question is that the justification of scientific theories can at least be considered as having an inherent logic and as being prone to rational assessment, while discovery is often regarded as a messy affair involving irrational elements – if it is not completely irrational as such.

The most famous anecdote concerning the supposed irrationality of the 'context of discovery' is probably Newton's apple incident. An apple falling on Newton's head (or in other variations to the ground) has been a crucial moment of the story about the context of Newton's discovery of the laws of gravitation. As the plausibility of this story is rather questionable, it makes sense to consider another example, based on the recollection of the protagonist in question. Hence the second most famous example, August Kekulé's dream of a snake seizing its own tail as the context of the discovery of the ring structure of the benzene molecule. Although both stories are constitutive of the *creation* of Newton's and Kekulé's end results, none of these stories are constitutive with respect to the *justification* of those already created end results and their evaluation. In other words, however messy the 'context of discovery' may be (either narrowly construed as the moment of conceiving an idea or broadly construed as the entire process of creation), the distinction puts the investigation of end results onto the safe side of rationality by separating the procedure of evaluation from concerns for the coming about of end results.

The point I would like to make by recounting all this is that the distinction between the 'context of discovery' and the 'context of justification' in the philosophy of science is the best analogy to indicate the difference between a theory of history as the expression of historical experience and the shared focus of narrativism and epistemology-oriented historical theories on end results. In terms of this analogy, my interest concerning historiography belongs to the former side of the distinction, what pre-Kuhnian philosophy of science relegated to the supposedly messy and confused realm of the 'context of discovery'. What I am interested in is the equivalence of the moment of Newton's apple incident in historiography as the birth of a new insight, and the question of what happens between that apple incident and the publication of the law of gravitation. This interest entails an extended understanding of the 'context of discovery', including far more than the moment of conceiving an idea. It includes the entire creative process that leads to the end result of the already formed idea. Contrary to this, both narrativists and epistemology-oriented historical theories chiefly focus on studying historiography as the equivalent of studying the law of gravitation itself, with the additional interest of narrativism in unveiling the fundamental linguistic determinants that are constitutive of already crafted historical narratives.

Post-Kuhnian history and philosophy of science had already turned its attention to such questions. However, whereas Rheinberger (2010: 79–87) links this shift of attention to a 'practical turn' (while discussing the work of Ian Hacking and Bruno Latour), my intention here is not to provide an investigation that could be an equivalent of the interest of the history and philosophy (and sociology) of science in how scientific knowledge is generated in laboratories or in other instances of a narrowly understood scientific practice. Instead of carrying out an investigation into the practice of actual archival research of historians, my intention is to provide a theoretical account on historiographical change.

That said, the suspicion may arise that focusing on the 'context of discovery' – even in its broadest sense – merely turns things inside out. The suspicion may arise that a shift of attention to the process of creation is nothing more than an unsophisticated reversal of the order of primacy. So, is this the case? No, I think it is far more than that. In fact, nothing in the above picture is about primary concerns as opposed to secondary, or even tertiary ones. Paying attention to the initial moment and the process of the coming about of historical accounts is more of a supplementary act. It does not oppose approaches that try to understand end results (be those approaches narrativist or not) but seeks points of compatibility by introducing a wider framework. In fact, inasmuch as 'the context of discovery' is broadly construed, it even provides a common ground with certain interests of an equally broadly construed narrativism. For as long as the process of fashioning a historical narrative is part of this process, after carrying out the usual epistemological criticism of historical studies, certain (more pragmatic than theoretical) narrativist approaches can be said to have a huge interest in mapping the ethical and literary choices present in the process of fashioning historical narratives (Pihlainen 2017), or on a more practical level in applying the insights of narratology to the art of fashioning historical narratives (for example, Munslow 2007, 2010).

Besides, narrativism also kicked off *practical* experiments with historical narrative. Rather obviously, the cash value of narrativism for historians did not primarily lie in debating the relationship between narrative and past reality in highly abstract terms, but in the question of how to create culturally relevant contemporary historical narratives. The self-described 'postmodern' stance of the journal *Rethinking History* has long supported the writing of experimental histories by devoting special issues to such endeavours, and Robert Rosenstone (1988), one of the journal's founding editors, even wrote his own. Not to mention that Whitean narrativism has also inspired many historians to engage reflexively in the question of how to write engaging narrative histories. You can even find interesting recent discussions of historians about narrative experiments on Twitter with the hashtag #storypast. Yet, as Ankersmit (2007: 180–1) points out, by definition experiments must remain on the margin, necessitating a mainstream to deviate from, relative to which they can qualify as 'experimental'.

To sum up, although the theory presented here has its point of departure in experience as the birth of novelty, in the broadly construed process it meets narrativism, which nevertheless has its point of departure and primary focus in the literary end product. True enough, the above overlap of concerns may not be based on a shared understanding of what such a process consists of, and the compatibility with narrativism to a large extent stems from an indifference on behalf of the theory of history as the expression of historical experience to the evaluation of historical narratives. What's more, this compatibility is not even an exclusive one. The theory of history as the expression of historical experience is compatible not only with narrativism but practically with any theoretical take on end results – except the one that tries to anchor the truth of descriptions of the world in the world that it describes.

To repeat the main message of these introductory lines, the greatest merit of the theory presented here is the possibility of accounting for historiographical novelty, while the greatest limitation is its relative indifference towards (and thus its broad compatibility with) questions concerning the truth and falsity of histories. The indifference is only relative insofar as it nevertheless implies a position that later on I will call *realist irrealism*. By virtue of *allowing* both realist and irrealist claims, this position is exceptionally inclusive concerning a large variety of epistemological positions and plainly admits the great importance of epistemological debates. Yet, a theory of history as the expression of historical experience does not deliberately and explicitly wish to contribute to those debates, despite the fact it may take an implicit, although limited, epistemological stand, as this also follows from the investigations of the first half of the book, which presented historical writing as essentially contested historical knowledge. Instead, it wishes to explore an entire world that (maybe only for the time being) lies outside the scope of the mainstream debates in historical theory.

A phenomenology of historical studies

One more crucial question arises out of the analogy with the philosophy of science: if the study of the 'context of discovery' seems to have at least implicit consequences for the study of the 'context of justification', then is the distinction useful in the first place? Does a focus on whatever precedes already crafted histories necessarily mean a study of irrationality and the messy affairs of innovation, and, in turn, does a focus on end results necessarily mean a study of rationality? Although this is what the analogy with the 'context of discovery' would suggest, the case is much more complex. A nuanced answer would begin by pointing out that the *distinction* is useful only inasmuch as it does not begin to mean *separation*. One of the chief benefits of exploring discovery in historical studies would be precisely the possibility of a renegotiation of the boundaries between the two sides of the divide. In a certain sense, narrative philosophy of history has already begun this renegotiation, starting from the other side and showing how the 'context of justification' is anything but plainly rational. Theorizing the process of the coming about of histories may complement this by showing how the 'context of discovery' is anything but plainly irrational.

Renegotiating the divide between the study of conceptions of new insights and processes of creation on the one hand, and the study of end results on the other, does not amount to a complete demolition of the distinction either. It is an exploration of a constitutive relationship and occasional overlaps between two domains that nevertheless remain distinct. The possibility of a constitutive relationship does not mean that there can be a way the study of the 'context of discovery' can serve as a foundational enterprise for a study of the 'context of justification'. Avoiding this was precisely the reason why the distinction has been set up in the first place. Whatever is revealed about the inception and the process that eventually ends in a final result, it cannot function as truth-maker in the justification context. Or, put differently, the justification of an end result cannot be based on pointing at the moment of the conception of an idea or at the process of how an end result came about.

Now, what approach is best suited for a theoretical study of inceptions of new insights and processes of creation? What sort of investigation can successfully map the occurrence of novelty in historical studies by investigating the 'context of discovery'? I think that the investigations of these chapters can best be conceived of as a phenomenology of historical studies. Maybe not as phenomenology in the strictest philosophical sense, and certainly not in the sense of the most pertinent phenomenological analyses concerning history carried out by Paul Ricœur (1984–1988) and David Carr (1986a, 2014). Even though – as the discussion of Tengelyi in the previous chapter clearly indicates – I tend to make use of the insights of phenomenology in the strictest philosophical sense too, I would like to label the work of these chapters as 'phenomenological' in a sense that is both broader and narrower. In the simplest possible manner, I wish to conceive of the investigation into the occurrence of novelty in historical studies as 'phenomenological' inasmuch as the point of departure is the primary experience of the individual (within a complex net of a sociocultural environment).

Unlike phenomenology understood as a branch of philosophy or as a discipline with its peculiar methods, the investigations of these chapters do not claim to explore the deep structures of human experience. In fact, the notion of experience that features here is defined by its break with that very structure. Since Husserl's study on the temporal structure of human experience (Husserl 1991), mainstream phenomenological approaches to history have taken the temporal continuity of experience for granted: whatever is experienced is smoothed into the temporal continuity composed of that which took place before and that which is expected to take place. Contrary to this, the notion of experience these chapters intend to explore is about what defies efforts to smooth experience into such a temporal continuity.

Nevertheless, at the centre there is the experience of an individual. It can potentially be anyone, but most often I talk about the individual historian who ends up creating a final product that gets classified afterwards as 'historical'. However, despite such primacy of attention, my scope oftentimes extends beyond the 'historical'. And this happens immediately at the first step, when trying to elaborate on the very initial moment of experience. For regardless of whether this initial moment of experience concerns the world or (a remnant of) the past, the first issue to settle is whether experience may concern an external reality – and if so, in what sense.

Encountering the world, encountering the past

Based on the work of the previous chapter, I would like to conceptualize experience as an *encounter* with the world in general, and historical experience as an encounter with the past in particular. The latter may sound somewhat curious, because literally speaking nobody encounters the past of course. Rather, what historians or anybody else encounters are remnants of the past, which may dominantly be material objects, although this is not necessarily so. A melody or a smell may just as well qualify as such remnant of the past to encounter. Still being in line with earlier discussions, an experience – a historical experience – takes place when this encounter makes no sense, when efforts to invoke pre-existing conceptual schemes to make sense of it are in vain, when those pre-existing conceptual schemes go bankrupt.

The idea of such an encounter with the world and with the past may be quite a dubious one as seen from the dominant narrativist point of view. No wonder that the notions of historical experience and presence as advocated by Ankersmit, Runia and Gumbrecht (which inspire the conceptualization of an encounter-event) have already received their fair share of criticism in this respect, concerning mostly their supposed pre-linguistic-turn agenda and their supposed desire for unmediated contact with external reality. Yet, in their self-description these theories do not wish to deny the importance of the theoretical work of the last half-century that intended to explore the manifold ways in which language pervades our lives and activities, be those activities academic or everyday ones. Rather, the most fundamental thing they wish to point out is that the non-linguistic components or constituents of our lives and activities are *just as important* as the linguistic ones, and hence at least equal attention should be paid to them. Runia's claim is that presence is 'just as basic as meaning' (2014: 54); Gumbrecht makes clear that his efforts are not 'against interpretation' but against 'the exclusive status of interpretation within the humanities' (2004: 2); and Ankersmit rather sharply warns that whatever he says about historical experience is not a 'recantation' of his earlier writings on narrative and representation (2005: 14), which according to Ankersmit constitute an entirely different topic.

Critics of the notions of historical experience and presence usually do not give much weight to such self-descriptions. Instead of regarding the inquiry into the non-linguistic as supplementary to the study of the linguistic, they are concerned about what they think is the reactionary nature of such theories. In this manner, Keith Jenkins attributes to Runia 'the old dream of accessing the truth "plain"' on the basis that Runia aims at a contact with 'a reality beyond words' (2010: 246); Ewa Domaska argues that Ankersmit's 'understanding of a concept of historical experience and the sublime marks a step back' (2009: 176);

and Kalle Pihlainen passes the judgement that the way the current interest in the notions of presence and experience wishes to leave behind the concerns of the linguistic turn 'seems to constitute a retreat' (2014b: 103).

I do not wish to defend these notions in the conceptual shapes as formulated by Ankersmit, Runia and Gumbrecht (which significantly differ otherwise in many respects). What I wish to argue is that by definition the conceptualization of the initial moment of experience as an encounter with the world and the conceptualization of historical experience as an initial encounter with (a remnant of) the past is immune to the kind of criticism Ankersmit, Runia and Gumbrecht receive. This immunity to criticism concerning the reactionary or complementary character of the notion of experience I defend stems from the earlier discussed distance from epistemological concerns. Maybe when Runia made clear in a debate with Jenkins that he thinks it is possible 'to get in touch with an infratextual level of being' (2010: 249), he also attempted a similar defence. Or maybe not. In any event, in a theory of history as the expression of historical experience, there certainly is a *contact* with 'an infratextual level of being' as Runia thinks it is possible. At the same time, this contact equally certainly does not entail anything like '*accessing* the truth "plain"', the ground on which potential criticism could label it as a theoretical retreat.

The most important aspect of conceptualizing experience as an encounter is precisely that while it accounts for the reality of an external world, at the same time *it grants the inaccessibility of external reality*. Inasmuch as the theory of history presented here does not derive knowledge from the encounter with the world or with (a remnant of) the past, it should satisfy both those who think there is a contact and those who think that knowledge is equal to knowledge production. For an initial moment of experience, that is, the encounter-event itself, is a confrontation with the unknown, a confrontation with something that is unclaimed and unconquered by linguistic conceptualization. The only thing you know in the encounter can be the sheer fact that you just had an encounter, and you know this precisely because otherwise you do not have the slightest idea of what this means and of what you have encountered. The encounter leaves you stranded concerning sense-making and meaning-attribution on the one hand, but provides you the clearest indication of the existence of the external world (outside of your linguistic conceptualizations that simply break down) on the other.

In light of this, what needs to be reconsidered is the narrativist stance, because despite its claim to occupy a realist position it cannot *account for* the existence of the external world. Consider the narrativism-inspired postmodern historical theory of Keith Jenkins, who, to my knowledge, explains his position in the most consistent manner. Jenkins actually knows what it feels like to face charges that intend to ridicule, because he had to explain himself concerning how his theoretical beliefs do not amount to denying the reality of the past. To clarify his position, Jenkins described himself as a transcendental realist who grants that 'the "stuff" we call, for example, the world, the universe, etc., is really out there and is therefore not the product of my current mental state' (2009: 256). But no one can know the world that is out there, because 'it transcends each and every attempt in each and every social formation to reduce it to their inhabitants' experiences, vocabularies, lexicons, abstractions, etc.' The point of clearing this up is that it does not commit Jenkins to 'metaphysical realism (namely, that we can know the way things are independent of the way we access them)'. Finally, the net result, according to Jenkins, is that 'this reduction of any "knowledge" we "may think we have" of the world (past, present, future) to the contingencies of knowledge production, distribution, reception, etc., means [...] that we can never have access to the actualities of "stuff" plain, pure'.

As the parenthesis in the last quoted sentence entails, Jenkins regards the 'past' to be part of the wider category 'world', meaning that, deductively, what is true of being a transcendental realist about the world is true of being a transcendental realist about the past. Although Jenkins's view is not history-specific in this sense, it still represents the clearest attempt to claim realism for a narrativist or narrativism-inspired theory of history. The main problem with this position is an internal inconsistency that stems from the fact that Jenkins simply takes for granted the existence of the world and the past without being able to justify it in any sense. I think this inability renders any 'knowledge' *of* the external world and the past unintelligible, especially when 'knowledge' is equated with knowledge production. For insofar as you are unable to theoretically account for the existence of the external world, what you ultimately cannot prove is precisely that the knowledge you have is a knowledge of this external world and not of any other worlds that may be the products of your mental states. You can still consistently claim that your knowledge is of a world that came about as the product of your knowledge production, but you cannot consistently claim that *your* knowledge *production* results in knowledge of an external world, which, at the same time, is also independent of your knowledge production.

In a consistent position concerning knowledge understood as knowledge production, you are left with a situation in which the knowledge you have has nothing to do with the external world, and the external world has nothing to do with your knowledge. What your knowledge has to do with is the world in which knowledge production results. But this then is a world (or even worlds in plural – but for the sake of the argument let's suppose that you constitute only one world by knowledge production) other than the external world. You can claim that there is an external world only as a knowledge you produce, that is, an external world as constituted by language and mental content.

This is anything but the mind- and language-independent external world that Jenkins assumes, which arises as an additional world to the one knowledge production results in. Moreover, in the Jenkins scenario, the two worlds thereby constituted and assumed do not relate to each other in any way whatsoever. Your knowledge of the world of knowledge production would be the same regardless of whether you affirm or deny the existence of the external world that you claim to be unable to prove. What this means is that, ultimately, the very assumption of the existence of the external world is completely irrelevant to whatever you call knowledge and to whatever world you constitute. Insofar as your knowledge has nothing to do with this external world, assuming its existence – and hence claiming a realist position on the grounds of such assumption – simply makes no difference.

To be fair, Jenkins is explicit that his realism is an 'originary axiom' (2009: 256). Conceding this, however, is of no help in resolving the inconsistency; it is the problem itself. For it is precisely the acceptance of the reality of the external world as an originary axiom – and nothing more than an originary axiom – that prevents Jenkins from being able to prove that what he is supposed to be able to have knowledge *of* is the external world. The problem is that in order to be able to claim intelligibly that you have knowledge *of* something – even if you reduce knowledge to knowledge production – you have to be able to prove the existence of that which you claim to be able to have knowledge of. If, following Jenkins (256), to support your position that external reality is not just a product of your mental states the best you can say is that 'of course I cannot prove this'; this may sound like fun, but no amount of fun will veil the theoretical problem inherent in your position.

Accordingly, the twofold challenge for a realist position (realist other than metaphysical realism) is to be able to prove the existence of the external world and to be able to theorize a relationship between that very world and knowledge production (a relationship other than having 'access to the actualities of "stuff" plain', as Jenkins says). The metaphysical realist position is consistent precisely because it claims the possibility of having knowledge *of* the world that exists supposedly independently of mental states and linguistic conceptualizations. In a similar vein, the irrealist position, as advocated by Nelson Goodman (1978) for instance, according to which 'ways of worldmaking' create conflicting world versions that cannot be encompassed in a single world, is consistent because it regards knowledge as knowledge production, which in turn also produces world versions about which knowledge is produced. In both positions, consistency is achieved thanks to wedding ontological and epistemological positions in an overwhelming metaphysical realism/irrealism.

But if you are convinced that the metaphysical realist is wrong and you still consider yourself a realist, then the challenge is to come up with a position that is just as consistent as is metaphysical realism or a Goodman-style irrealism. The challenge is to theorize a position that is able to *prove* the existence of the world, on the one hand, but, on the other, doing so *without* granting epistemological access to the world. And this is, I believe, what experience conceptualized as an encounter-event achieves. It claims realism due to the initial moment of experience as an encounter that at least indicates the existence of a world independent of mental states and linguistic conceptualizations, and it *allows* (although does not necessitate) any sort of constructivist epistemologies. The most important feature of a theory of history as the expression of historical experience, however, is not the question of which epistemological positions are allowed. Nor is it the sheer fact that many epistemological positions are allowed. Rather, its most important feature is its capacity to consistently enable ontological realism, *even under the condition of* the most extreme epistemological irrealisms, relativisms, constructivisms and nominalisms.

(Realist irrealism, irrealist realism)

In a somewhat hesitant manner, by opening a brief parenthesis, I would like to call this position realist irrealism. Admittedly, this is only for the sake of convenience, in order to have an identifiable position concerning the question of external reality and its (in)accessibility. Instead of circumscribing the position as the one that entails the existence of external reality without the possibility to have knowledge *of* it on the one hand, and on the other hand allows for (but does not necessitate) irrealism concerning multiple realities arising out of knowledge constitution, it is simply more convenient to name it as realist irrealism.

Alternatively, it can equally be called irrealist realism, for the most important feature of the position is that it equally fulfils the deepest convictions of a realist who holds that there is an external reality independent of our mental content and linguistic conceptualizations, and a Goodmanian irrealist who holds that we make many irreconcilable worlds by conceptualizing them. Realist irrealism or irrealist realism equally allows both positions, although it also introduces a qualification into both of them. It allows the realist element only under the condition of epistemological inaccessibility, and it allows Goodmanian irrealism only under the condition that 'ways of worldmaking' create multiple worlds due to an incentive arising out of an encounter with the external world and external reality, which incites the creation of Goodmanian 'world-versions' (without appearing also as a single world that could encompass these multiple worlds).

Doesn't look like anything to me

But how exactly does all this happen? And what exactly does it mean to have a proof or at least an indication of the existence of the external world and the past without having epistemological access to whatever there is? The best way to illuminate what this means is, again, to invoke an imperfect but useful analogy.

In the TV series *Westworld* (2016–), some characters seem to have something like a moment of experience as an encounter-event. These characters are not humans but so-called 'hosts', completely human-like androids who inhabit an amusement park organized around the theme of the Wild West. The inhabitants of Westworld live their daily life as the service provided for human customers who can do anything they want to them, which oftentimes means nothing more than sex and violence. The hosts live alongside preprogrammed behavioural patterns and narratives, and the guests enter several intertwining Western-themed storylines during their stay in the park. Although the storylines can unfold in multiple directions, the narratives, the behaviour of both hosts and guest, and all small events and details are controlled in various ways by the staff running the amusement park. Until of course things get out of control, as is expected of a TV show. The way all hell breaks loose revolves around the central theme of the possibility of the emergence of self-awareness in hosts. They have an extremely refined human-like artificial intelligence and the capacity for both human-like reasoning and emotional states, but at the beginning of the show they appear to lack self-awareness. Given that artificial intelligence is portrayed as human-like throughout the series (leaving aside the question of non-human artificial intelligence), the self-awareness of hosts is also supposed to be human-like.

It is in their quest for self-knowledge (that opens their way to self-awareness) that some hosts of Westworld have their encounter-events, all characterized by the sheer incapability of sense-making. When hosts are confronted with something that they are not supposed to understand, they say the iconic and instant classic phrase: 'Doesn't look like anything to me.' Throughout the show, this happens on various occasions, but as far as this chapter is concerned the most illuminating occasion is probably the first instance. It happens in the pilot episode when Dolores (portrayed by Evan Rachel Wood), one of the central characters of the show, is looking at a photo shown to her by her father who accidentally found it in the field. Both Dolores and her father are hosts, and the photo – left at the park by a guest – shows a woman in an urban environment of the 'real' world. When the troubled father shows the photo to Dolores, her immediate reaction is 'Doesn't look like anything to me.' And when the father poses the quasi-rhetorical question 'Where is she? Have you ever seen anything like this place?', Dolores only repeats: 'Doesn't look like anything to me.'

I believe that what happens to Dolores in this scene is similar to what happened to Darnton in the archives, discussed in the previous chapter. As a quick reminder, Darnton suggested that as a historian you know you are onto something when you stumble into a thing in the archive that you do not understand. However, the shared incapability of sense-making in the cases of both Dolores and Darnton is only one side of the coin. The other side is a decisive and crucial difference concerning the capability to understand this incapability. Whereas Darnton has self-awareness and therefore is capable of understanding at least the fact that he ran into the boundaries of his own understanding, Dolores lacks self-awareness (at this point in the show) and therefore is incapable of such an understanding. Accordingly, whereas Darnton can in principle pause for a moment to ponder whether he wishes to try to make sense of the encounter-event that makes no sense or simply looks non-sense for now, Dolores (at this point of the show) can only pass by the event and continue her day as usual. In other words, while Darnton had an experience as a 'doesn't look like anything to me' encounter in the archives, Dolores had an encounter but not an experience.

The usefulness of the *Westworld* analogy is that it can bring to light a few key points concerning the initial moment of experience. The first point touches upon the above difference between Darnton and Dolores: although *the initial moment of experience has an encounter-structure, not all encounters qualify as experience*. Only an encounter that is recognized as an encounter by the subject who has the encounter qualifies as experience. This is the case of Darnton but not the case of Dolores. Even though the initial moment of experience is deeply rooted in the 'doesn't look like anything to me' encounter that they both had, without elevating that encounter into being an encounter-event by recognizing the failure of understanding, that is, without gaining an understanding about this failure, the 'doesn't look like anything to me' encounter is an empty structure. It gains significance insofar as it comes with the subject's awareness of having an encounter, although the structure of the encounter (the collapse of cognitive capacities) remains the same regardless of whether an awareness of having an encounter is gained or not.

The second point made clear by the *Westworld* analogy is that the question of whether an encounter qualifies as an encounter lies in the eye of the beholder. Although it is an object or a phenomenon that triggers experience as an encounter, to be able to trigger that experience is not a quality of the object or the phenomenon. If something 'doesn't look like anything to me', it is not because the object or phenomenon itself is incomparable and incomprehensible, but because it doesn't look like anything *to me*, meaning that it appears as incomprehensible relative to the experiencing individual's pre-existing mental, linguistic and conceptual schemes. What is the most familiar thing to somebody might easily be utterly incomprehensible to somebody else. Growing up in the jungle and being raised among great apes, Tarzan must have found many of the objects and phenomena familiar to inhabitants of Western societies incomparable and incomprehensible when encountering them. In the same way, the photo Dolores looks at is familiar to practically any guest of Westworld but is simply incomprehensible to her.

Having said that, for the simple reason that some objects and phenomena may appear as incomprehensible relative to the pre-existing mental, linguistic and conceptual schemes of *most human beings*, there may be objects and phenomena more likely to trigger experience as a 'doesn't look like anything to me' encounter-event than other ones. It simply is a matter only of quantity and not of quality though. More people are familiar with holding a coffee mug in their hands than a piece of gallium (a metal that – due to its low melting point – melts in their hands), and therefore fewer people's expectations may be thwarted by putting a mug rather than gallium in their hands. Some of course are not familiar with coffee mugs, while some are familiar at least with the idea of liquid metals due to the more popular mercury (and to the even more popular T-1000 in *Terminator 2* (1991)). But the point is not that a mug is what everybody knows and gallium is what only a very few do. The point is only that encountering gallium likely defies more people's pre-existing conceptual schemes than encountering a coffee mug. At the same time, as mentioned in the previous chapter, nothing excludes the possibility that those pre-existing schemes collapse in an encounter with an otherwise familiar object that is suddenly seen in an unfamiliar light. Encountering unfamiliar things and objects, however, may thwart expectations with a higher degree of probability.

For examples of a more 'historical' character, you can think of soldiers first encountering trench warfare in the First World War (Fussell 1975), or the eyewitnesses of the Trinity test, the first detonation of a nuclear device on 16 July 1945, in New Mexico. Even though those present, being involved in the Manhattan Project in one way or another, had their expectations about what they were going to witness, and even though their reports necessarily focused on the technicalities of the 'achievement', that is, even though those present must already have had a pre-established sense attributed to the event before it took place, some reports indicate how those expectations might have been thwarted. Consider the following passage from the account of Brigadier

General Thomas F. Farrell in General Groves's report, dating from two days following the detonation:

> The effects could well be called unprecedented, magnificent, beautiful, stupendous and terrifying. No man-made phenomenon of such tremendous power had ever occurred before. The lighting effects beggared description. The whole country was lighted by a searing light with the intensity many times that of the midday sun. It was golden, purple, violet, gray and blue. It lighted every peak, crevasse and ridge of the nearby mountain range with a clarity and beauty that cannot be described but must be seen to be imagined. It was that beauty the great poets dream about but describe most poorly and inadequately. Thirty seconds after the explosion came first, the air blast pressing hard against the people and things, to be followed almost immediately by the strong, sustained, awesome roar which warned of doomsday and made us feel that we puny things were blasphemous to dare tamper with the forces heretofore reserved to The Almighty. Words are inadequate tools for the job of acquainting those not present with the physical, mental and psychological effects. It had to be witnessed and realized. (quoted in Williams and Cantelon 1984: 52–3)

Of course, this account is already a post-evental attempt to make sense of the event and *not the encounter-event itself*, hence it already belongs to the realm of the process of sense-making. The reason why I quoted it here is that the reflection itself nevertheless constantly alludes to the inadequacy of available linguistic tools for sense-making. General Groves's remarks on General Farrell's account, saying that 'the feeling of the entire assembly was similar to that described by General Farrell, with even the uninitiated feeling profound awe' (quoted in Williams and Cantelon 1984: 53), attests to the same impression. But this 'profound awe' that General Groves attributes to those being present is already a *reaction* that arises out of a 'doesn't look like anything to me' encounter. It is not a quality of the encounter-event itself. When eyewitnesses of the Trinity test cope with finding words, it is due to their incapability of sense-making and not to the event's capability of defying human sense-making processes. What is at stake here is not the 'ineffable' residing in the event but the 'ineffable' as the result of the collapse of pre-existing mental, linguistic and conceptual schemes to render the encounter familiar.

Finally, the third point that I wish to highlight echoes the thesis of the previous section: a subjectively recognized 'doesn't look like anything to me' encounter as a moment of experience (as a moment of the recognition of the collapse of the sense-making powers of pre-existing linguistic conceptualizations and mental contents) is, without further qualifications, the best we have to indicate the existence of external reality. For the recognition of the encounter as an encounter (as a 'doesn't look like anything to me' event) is nothing other than the recognition of the collapse of cognitive powers with respect to whatever has been encountered, with respect to our ability to face reality through pre-existing conceptual tools.

The aesthetic moment

The above characterization of the initial moment of experience necessitates the recognition of the collapse of cognitive powers. It is prone to the potential objection noting that the act of recognition is already a step toward comprehensibility. It can be pointed out that even if experience as an encounter is a confrontation with something that does not make sense, inasmuch as the encounter itself is recognized as an encounter-event, the moment of experience itself does make sense in a twisted, paradoxical fashion. And this is because the recognition of the encounter-event as such already implies the work of cognitive powers. Even though sense-making here concerns not what has been encountered but the encounter itself, it implies sense-making as non-sense, meaning that the encounter-event, once recognized as such, once qualified as experience, is already made sense of as the collapse of sense-making.

The moment of the collapse of human capacities of sense-making is often affiliated with the aesthetic category of the sublime. In eighteenth-century thought, the sublime was linked to grandeur (mostly in nature) that human cognitive capacities cannot cope with when confronting them. In postwar – and especially in 'postmodern' – thought, a revived notion of the sublime has been linked with questions of language and representation and has become associated with that which is unrepresentable and unpresentable. As most of these theories fall out of scope for my purposes and concerns, instead of tracing the occurrence of the notion of the sublime from Longinus to Lyotard and instead of offering a developmental history of the idea (see Grave 2011; Costelloe 2012; Brady 2013; Doran 2015), I would like to briefly consider the sublime in Frank Ankersmit's version, which explicitly ties it to the notion of historical experience.

To begin with, Ankersmit's sublime historical experience concerns identity shifts, and hence it concerns history understood as the course of affairs. It is not an individual but a collective experience of a community that undergoes tectonic changes, which points to the fact that the proper context to discuss it is the first half of this book. Why is it worth returning to this topic here, if not because of Ankersmit's association between the sublime and identity shifts of communities? Well, the relevance of considering it at this point lies in the structure of historical experience *as* sublime, that is, to the extent that Ankersmit subsumes historical experience under the category of the sublime. For what the sublime introduces to Ankersmit's notion of historical experience is a 'momentary disruption of our normal cognitive apparatus' (Ankersmit 2005: 335).

I would like to interpret this as the core claim of Ankersmit regarding the sublimity of experience, and to treat everything else as additional claims. These additional claims derive from two sources. On the one hand, Ankersmit's sublime is indebted to eighteenth-century theories, most notably that of Immanuel Kant and Edmund Burke; on the other, Ankersmit finds an equivalent to the historical experience that is sublime in psychology, namely, in traumatic experience. As to the first source, Ankersmit borrows from Burke the effects of the sublime. In Burke's words this means that an experience that falls into the category of the sublime is 'capable of producing delight; a sort of delightful horror, a sort of tranquility tingled with terror' (quoted in Ankersmit 2005: 334). According to Ankersmit, this appears 'as if the axis on which pain and pleasure are each other's opposite extremes has suddenly been turned ninety degrees so that they coincide with each other from this new and unexpected perspective' (2005: 334–5).

If the effect of the sublime in a Burkean fashion is supposed to be rather ambivalent, a mixture of feelings arising in the subject who has the experience, then General Farrell's experience of the Trinity event would qualify as Burkean sublime without a doubt. But the entanglement of the feeling of 'doomsday' warning and the spectacle of incomparable allure that General Farrell attributes to the explosion is not the exclusivity of Burke's theory. As Robert Doran (2015: 125) shows, even the phrase 'delightful horror' was used to describe the contradictory feeling much earlier than Burke by John Dennis, while the ambivalence in feelings characterizes practically any modern theories of the sublime, including 'postmodern' ones, such as that of Lyotard (1991: 78–143; 1994).

All this is fairly regular so far. Things get an interesting twist with the introduction of Ankersmit's second additional claim, which does away with much of the ambivalence created by the invocation of the Burkean contradiction of feelings. In the trauma-sublime equivalence, the sublime pretty straightforwardly migrates to the horror side and leaves the 'delightful' component behind. According to Ankersmit, the equivalence-claim goes as follows:

> Both trauma and the sublime wholly disrupt the normal schema within which we make sense of the data of experience, and they do so by means of dissociation: Trauma dissociates because the traumatic experience is not admitted to 'normal' consciousness, and the sublime dissociates since

it places us at a standpoint objectifying all experience as such. In sum, trauma can be seen as the psychological counterpart of the sublime, and the sublime can be seen as the philosophical counterpart of trauma. (2005: 337–8)

The close affiliation with traumatic experience makes Ankersmit's sublime literally terrible, which is also one of the central points of the sharpest criticism coming from Jenkins (2009: 295–314), who – I think very rightly – registers the lack of the promised union of joy and fear when remarking on the overwhelming negativity attached to the notion. The self-damaging consequence of Ankersmit's interpretation of the sublime is that it no longer appears as desirable. When it indicates an experience that may be more like the experiences of Detective Mills (Brad Pitt's character) and Detective Somerset (Morgan Freeman) in the movie *Seven* (1997), then probably no one would strive badly for having it. And even if someone just happened to have such an experience (regardless whether there is a striving for it or not), it is hard to imagine how it could give way to the emergence of any constructive attitude.

These difficulties lead straight to the question of how the sublime relates to an experience as a 'doesn't look like anything to me' encounter outlined above. For unlike Ankersmit's sublime, an encounter-event may be something you would like to happen to you. Besides, in a theory of history as the expression of historical experience, the encounter indeed plays a constructive role as an incentive to formulate new insights. But if an initial moment of experience as the collapse of sense-making capacities in the shape of a 'doesn't look like anything to me' encounter definitely does not evoke an aesthetics of doom, then what about a less gloomy version of the sublime? What about all those more common theories of the sublime, like that of Burke, which introduce the category as producing an essentially contradictory feeling? Can a 'doesn't look like anything to me' encounter be associated with the sublime as a 'delightful horror', as a mixture of joy and despair, pleasure and pain?

No, I think it still cannot. However tempting it would be to bring together the initial moment of experience with the aesthetic category of the sublime, this was a regrettable mistake. The fact that the initial moment of experience exhibits an encounter-structure means precisely that it does not evoke any feelings or moods whatsoever. When Darnton in the archives and Dolores in Westworld are confronted with the limits of their cognitive capacities, their confrontation is not accompanied by either joy or angst. Had any accompanying feeling or mood emerged as in the sublime, the encounter would already imply a sense other than that of non-sense. Feelings may emerge as a *reaction* to the encounter, but such a reaction does not belong to the structure of the encounter-event. To phrase it most emphatically, in a 'doesn't look like anything to me' encounter, any recognition of a 'content' that is 'traumatic' or even 'joyful' simply cannot take place; for if it did, things would already look like 'something' to you.

Although the sublime is the closest concept already in circulation that can be linked to the collapse of the cognitive apparatus that also characterizes the initial moment of experience as an encounter-event, the notion entails much more than an encounter-event does. It is only as deprived of accompanying feelings emerging as reactions that the sublime can be useful to indicate the aesthetic character of experience as elaborated here. What remains without emerging reactions is *the sheer spectacle of the non-sense*. To baptize this aesthetic moment that is far less than sublime and yet is an equivalent of the core claim of any theory of the sublime, proto-sublime seems to be a reasonable choice. To pull the different threads together concerning the discussion of the initial moment of experience, the encounter-event and the aesthetic character, I wish to offer the following thesis-like formulation: *the initial moment of experience as an encounter-event is characteristically aesthetic in the sense of falling under the category of the proto-sublime.*

From non-sense to sense

Defining the initial moment of experience as a moment of non-sense that is even less than the sublime poses one final question: in what sense can the sheer spectacle of non-sense appear as an *initial* moment? Referring to such a moment implies that it qualifies as a beginning and that there must be a way leading from that moment to a final result that is anything but non-sense. But can there be such a way from non-sense to sense? Or, to ask the question in the vocabulary of this chapter, when the (initial) moment is reduced to that of the proto-sublime and if by definition that moment is 'doesn't look like anything', is it possible to move away from it and move toward something that is 'something' while retaining the constructive role of the non-sense in sense-making?

In a wonderful essay, Hayden White argues that this precisely is what professional historical studies are for: they impose order on and thereby 'domesticate' the meaninglessness of history (as the course of affairs). This has a lot to do again with the aesthetic category of the sublime, as White heavily draws on an essay of Schiller ([1801] 2001), entitled 'On the Sublime,' which refuses to look for meaning in history understood in the sense of a unitary course of affairs. In making the case for the futility of efforts to find meaning in history, Schiller says that the meaningless disorder of human affairs is best to look at as a sublime spectacle. What interests White in Schiller's view is nevertheless not what interested Schiller, not the sublime spectacle of history itself. White is more concerned with what philosophies of history, political ideologies and historical studies have done to that spectacle. In line with Schiller's own distinction between the sublimity of history and the category of the beautiful associated with the realm of 'sense', White makes the point that historical studies belong to the realm of 'sense' and their function is to beautify the sublime, and, most importantly, that 'this same aesthetics of the beautiful presides over the process in which historical studies are constituted as an autonomous scholarly discipline' (1987: 70–1).

Now, all this clearly implies a way from non-sense to sense, which in White's view applies to the entirety of the discipline of history as such. Although White does not explicitly say anything about why and how this happens exactly, his treatment is particularly revealing regarding at least two important aspects. The first rather unfortunate aspect is the one that White shares with Jenkins, and it concerns the inconsistency of his theoretical position. The second and more fortunate aspect concerns the moral implications of historical sense-making.

As to the first aspect, White makes claims that do not fit very well with his own theoretical position. As White's intellectual biographer Herman Paul points out, when talking about the sublimity of history (as the unitary course of affairs) White makes statements about the nature of (historical) reality (Paul 2011: 117). Sublimity for White does not lie in the eye of the beholder, it does not appear as an aesthetic reaction to experience, but history itself appears as a sublime object, chaotic and meaningless by its nature. At the same time, the fundamental contention of White's own philosophy of history contradicts the very possibility of making such a claim. This fundamental contention is that historians conceptually prefigure and thereby constitute the object they study and make claims about. According to White, this goes as follows:

> Before the historian can bring to bear upon the data of the historical field the conceptual apparatus he will use to represent and explain it, he must first prefigure the field – that is to say, constitute it as an object of mental representation. This poetic act is indistinguishable from the linguistic act in which the field is made ready for interpretation as a domain of a particular kind. (1973: 30)

Or, in a different version, this means

> that the shape of the relationships which will appear to be inherent in the objects inhabiting the field will in reality have been imposed on the field by the investigator in the very act of identifying and describing the

> objects that he finds there. The implication is that historians constitute their subjects as possible objects of narrative representation by the very language they use to describe them. (White 1978: 95)

Whereas the linguistic prefiguration of the historical field and the constitution of the object are operations that apply to all historians, they do not seem to apply to White and to the object about which he makes claims: history as the course of affairs. Whereas historians linguistically constitute their objects and the historical field, White appears to know the true nature of history, prior to any prefiguration. How is this possible? Well, it was not supposed to be. Insofar as White holds the view that prefiguration constitutes the object, he cannot consistently claim that the object in question has a chaotic nature prior to linguistic prefiguration. The case would be the same even if White claimed that history has a nature other than chaotic. No claims can be made concerning what the object itself is prior to prefiguration according to the view that prefiguration constitutes objects: neither can one claim that historical reality itself is chaotic, nor can one claim that it is already ordered and meaningful; neither can one claim that historical reality itself is non-narrative, nor can one claim that it is narratively pre-structured.

The only consistent claim for White would be that history as sublime meaninglessness, chaos and confusion is nothing other than White's prefiguration. And this has further consequences. For if the sublimity of history is just one among the possible results of prefiguration and not the nature of historical reality itself, then the entire Whitean vocabulary of 'imposing' form and meaning on a shapeless and meaningless reality (as exemplified by the second quote above) is unintelligible. 'Imposing' various orders on disorder is possible only as long as disorder appears to be the fundamental nature of reality on which all prefigurations exercise their descriptive acts. When sublimity no longer appears as the shared fundament on which all linguistic prefigurations exercise their work but itself appears as one among the possible prefigurations, then there is nothing left to 'impose' anything on.

Conceptualizing experience as an encounter-event, an initial aesthetic moment, fixes the inconsistency in White's views by not claiming anything about the nature of external reality. An encounter reveals only the existence of external reality, without any additional claims on its nature, composition or condition. It is precisely for this reason that an encounter-event falls under the category of a proto-sublime that entails merely the recognized collapse of cognitive capacities and a sheer spectacle of non-sense without any added values. Detecting White's inconsistency nevertheless has a positive effect. It throws new light on the core question concerning sense-making, indicating that the question is not how to 'impose' sense *on* non-sense but how to move *toward* sense *from* non-sense. The question is not that of how non-sense can be *transformed* into sense but that of how an encounter with non-sense *initiates* sense-making.

This question leads straight to the second aspect of White's treatment of the sublime and beautiful that I wish to touch upon. Despite the self-contradictory theoretical position concerning the sublime and the nature of historical reality, White has an important thing to say about the moral character of the move towards sense-making. Again, this stems from a Schillerian inspiration to consider the sublimity of history to be a basis for an emerging sense of human freedom. The moral ground to look at history as a sublime object is, according to White, that 'whatever dignity and freedom human beings could lay claim to could come only by way of what Freud called "reaction-formation" to an apperception of history's meaninglessness' (1987: 72). In White's view, only a confrontation with the sublime meaninglessness of history can give rise to the moral need for taking action that aims to achieve a better human condition, to the need for political visions of a historical process and, consequently, to the need for historical sense-making, also regarding historical studies.

There is an element in White's view that is relevant for answering the question of whether there is a way in which a moment of encountering non-sense initiates sense-making. It may very well be that this important take-away message, or at least the message I would like to take away, has not much to do with White's actual views on the sublime and the beautiful, but it certainly has to do with his invocation of the moral element. It is simply the necessity of a moral incentive to move away from non-sense, an incentive that opens up the possibility of sense-making and sets you onto a course toward sense. In order to move toward sense and move away from non-sense, a demand has to arise, and I think this demand introduces an ethical moment into the theory of history as the expression of historical experience, which will be the subject of the next chapter.

6

The Step toward Historical Sense-Making

On the difference between experience and experientiality

Although a theory of history as the expression of historical experience begins in an aesthetic moment of experience, this moment is insular and void of meaning. It is separated from anything we think we know and it resists integration into pre-established webs of meanings, conceptualizations and stories. In most cases, an experience that defies everything we are familiar with does not compel us to initiate a process of sense-making. The only – and somewhat paradoxical – sense that we most often attribute to such an experience is that it makes no sense whatsoever. However, we usually do not even bother arriving at the conclusion of attributing non-sense to experience. Yet, every now and then, we do engage in sense-making after encountering non-sense, after an encounter-event that 'doesn't look like anything' to us. These few cases clearly testify that there must be a crucial element that is present when we engage in sense-making and is absent when we do not. It is equally clear that inasmuch as this element is the one that makes the difference, this must be also the one responsible for a moment of pushing us from an encounter with non-sense toward sense-making.

The core contention of this last chapter will be that this element between the initial moment of experience and the creative process that leads to the end result is nothing other than an ethical moment that sets expression in motion. The chapter sets out to conceptualize this ethical moment as an approval of a demand for a specifically historical sense-making. The endeavour of conceptualizing a process of making sense of non-sense historically, a process motivated by an ethical impulse, may be prone to several sources and ways of misunderstanding. The troubles begin right away with the question of the relationship of the two poles between which an ethical moment sets expression in motion: the moment of aesthetic experience and the linguistic construct. Before venturing into the exploration of the in-between ethical step of a theory of history as the expression of historical experience, I would like to say a few words about what kind of relationship can and cannot be established between these two poles by an ethical move.

As to the first pole, it is the moment of experience, the non-linguistic, the non-cognitive, the non-sense, the aesthetic encounter-event with the world or a remnant of the past, explored in the previous chapter. The other pole is the final result, the linguistic, the cognitive, the ready-made sense, the already crafted history, explored lately thanks to decades of narrativist research. The contrast between non-sense and sense could not have been sharper when the poles appear as separated from each other. Once you try to posit a relationship between them, you expose your theory to the threat of serious theoretical inconsistencies and an overall confusion. Chapter 4 has already attempted to do away with much of the possible confusion by making clear that the tendency in historical theory to configure a relationship between the poles of non-sense and sense as a simple and unproblematic transfer of (an already potentially meaningful) experience into language is mistaken.

What the discussion of Chapter 4 could not touch upon is the most typical subcase of this wider tendency. It seems to me that the bulk of the current misunderstandings in contemporary historical theory revolve around mistaking an expectation of experientiality concerning already crafted histories for an expectation of presenting an immediate experience in historiography. In other words, experientiality, which in the definition of narratologist and literary theorist Monika Fludernik means 'a quasi-mimetic evocation of "real-life experience"' (1996: 12), is often mistaken for what Fludernik refers to here as 'real-life experience' itself. In current discussions, the two tend to get conflated and conjoined all too easily. The most common form of this conflation is when the former is expected to emerge from the latter, that is, experientiality as the quality of already crafted historical narrative is expected to *convey* or *transfer* an originary 'real-life experience'.

Gumbrech, Runia and Ankersmit, as the main advocates of the notions of presence and historical experience, themselves are quite often responsible for creating this confusion. Oftentimes – or, maybe it would be more accurate to say, most of the time – they are after experientiality and not 'experience' or 'presence', even though they insist on talking explicitly about the latter. Kalle Pihlainen has already noted this confusion regarding experience and experientiality and complained about the 'insufficient attention' paid to the difference between them (2012: 326). Although neither Pihlainen's nor Fludernik's notion of experience have much to do with the 'doesn't look like anything to me' encounter-event that I theorize here, experientiality in the view of both is a quality of representations. In that quality, Pihlainen warmly welcomes experiential historical representations on constructivist grounds (2013: 518–20). Problems arise when, according to Pihlainen, this experientiality is conflated with immediate experience:

> In my reading, the goal (albeit still most often unarticulated, it seems to me) of the recent debate on presence has also been to bring experientiality to center stage. Yet, despite what I take to be at least a partially common goal, it is hard to understand suggestions that representation might somehow be bypassed and the past could produce experience 'in itself' or be encountered 'directly'. (2014a: 21)

The theory of history as the expression of historical experience as outlined in these chapters is admittedly inspired by theories of presence and historical experience. At the same time, it is just as discontented with the conflation of experience and experientiality as is Pihlainen, even if this shared discontent about mistaking experientiality for experience does not arise out of a shared position on the question of experience. Remedying the theoretical inattention towards the difference between experience and experientiality nevertheless seems to be a crucial task in order to qualify the relation of the theory presented here to other theories of history. I wish to carry out this task in a concise manner by discussing actual instances of mistaking one for the other. Showing how these theories are actually in a pursuit of experientiality may even have the subsidiary benefit of being revealing concerning the possibilities and limitations of the evocation of 'real-life experiences' in historiography.

My first example of the conflation of 'real-life experience' and experientiality (the later evocation of such experience) is Runia's argument on modern monuments. In sketching his notion of presence, Runia argues that a modern monument, such as the Berlin Holocaust Memorial, is paradigmatically metonymical and that metonymy can serve as transfer of presence. The two arguments add up to the unified claim that 'whereas premodern, metaphorical monuments are primarily engaged in a transfer of meaning, modern metonymical monuments concentrate on the transfer of presence' (Runia 2014: 69). The claim entails that where 'presence' – the presence of the past in general or the presence of something that is past in particular – can be caught and met is the monument itself, which straightforwardly transmits such presence. Although Runia knows very well that modern monuments are crafted artworks of artists – and that the Berlin Holocaust Memorial is the crafted artwork of Peter Eisenman – he insists on the possibility of transferring presence. Consider the following passage in Runia on how such transfer is supposed to happen:

> Modern, metonymical monuments function not by giving an account of an event, but by forcefully 'presenting an absence' in the here and now. [...] A modern monument entails, first of all, a metonymical transposition of 'substance' – like the concrete slabs of the Berlin Holocaust Memorial – from one 'place' to another – where it tries to occupy space in such

a way that there is no escaping it. Then, second, in an act of artistic transubstantiation, this metonymical *Fremdkörper* is metaphorically associated with what is to be commemorated: it is claimed that the way the monument is present in the present 'is like', or equals, that particular part of the past that deserves to be 'presented'. (68)

If this passage attests to something, I think it is precisely the opposite of a possibility of a transfer of presence. Even Runia's choice of words of referring to the monument as it 'is like' a 'particular part of the past' indicates that it is nevertheless *not* that – it is only *as if* it was. Associating the function of such monuments with 'presenting' is equally telling, for such monuments are not simply *presence* and they not simply *are* presence; they have a function and a task of *presenting* that which *is not presence*. As a purposefully crafted human creation, a modern monument is already invested with meaning by the author, by the commissioner, by its audience, by a web of sociocultural and political expectations, and so on. If a modern monument somehow appears to give rise to a sensation of presence in somebody as Runia claims, it is because the monument is either crafted with the very purpose of evoking an artificial sense of the past's presence, or the audience invests the monument with the very meaning of conveying such presence. In any case, the monument itself is not the presence of the past, not an instance of being in touch with reality. It may have a presence, but this presence is not the presence of what the monument intends to make present but the presence of the monument itself, inaugurated in 2005. At best, it is a human creation conceived of as exhibiting the quality of experientiality, a crafted artifact whose success is defined by whether it evokes the 'real-life experience' of people of the past in its contemporary audience, whether it artificially evokes a nonetheless artificial sense of that which it intends to make present.

Evoking such 'real-life experience' of people of the past and thus achieving 'historical' experientiality is of course not the privilege of monuments. Historians and novelists try to achieve it predominantly by written words even in the first decades of the twenty-first century. Achieving experientiality in written texts is, in Fludernik's view, precisely the criterion of success for the text in question to qualify as exhibiting narrativity. For instead of invoking more regular narratological elements such as having a plot, Fludernik defines narrativity as 'mediated human experientiality' (1996: 36). Rather surprisingly, however, defining narrativity as mediated experientiality is also the grounds on which Fludernik argues that historical writing is excluded 'from the central realm of prototypical narrativity' (26), at least in its most conventional forms. What makes Fludernik's treatment of historical studies rather odd in this respect is that, within the theory and philosophy of history, the very same requirement of experientiality may appear as the grounds on which historical writing does qualify as narrative. Alfred Richard Louch, in a theory of historical narratives presented decades before Fludernik's narratology, had already claimed that 'narrative, ideally, stands proxy for experience' (1969: 56). But even if Louch's definition of narrativity is congruent with that of Fludernik, their paths depart when Louch says that the historian, like the traveller, actually provides 'a proxy-experience for an audience lacking the detailed and more immediate acquaintance possessed by the historian or traveler' (60).

That historiography according to Louch is exactly what historiography according to Fludernik is not is probably due to the fact that Fludernik uses novels as a control group. It is in being compared to novels that historiography fails to meet much higher standards of experientiality. To Fludernik's credit, however, she relatively recently reconsidered her position. Instead of attributing 'zero narrativity' to historical writing, Fludernik now argues that in historical writing 'experientiality (and hence narrativity) occurs on a scale, and that the more academic a historical text is, the less experientiality there will be' (2010: 50).

I do not intend to start a detailed discussion here on the merits and shortcomings of the theories of Fludernik and Louch. What seems more important for the purpose of highlighting the difference between experience and experientiality is to point out that in the course of Fludernik's reconsideration of the experientiality of historical narratives, there is a theorist of presence who plays a prominent role. One of the texts Fludernik (2010) analyses is Gumbrecht's *In 1926: Living at the Edge of Time* (1997), published prior to his explicit theoretical explorations of the notion of presence. The book consists of a 'User's Manual,' fifty-one shorter chapter-like entries and two longer essays, which outline the overall theoretical framework of the book. The first paragraph of the 'User's Manual' – entitled 'Where to Start' – gives a fairly good overview of both the structure of the book and Gumbrecht's aims. It reads as follows:

> Do not try 'to start from the beginning', for this book has no beginning in the sense that narratives or arguments have beginnings. Start with any of the fifty-one entries in any of the three sections entitled 'Arrays', 'Codes', and 'Codes Collapsed' (the alphabetical order of the subheadings shows that there isn't any hierarchy among them). Simply start with an entry that particularly interests you. From each entry a web of cross-references will take you to other, related entries. Read as far as your interest carries you (and as long as your schedule allows). You'll thus establish your individual

reading path. Just as there is no obligatory beginning, there also is no obligatory or definitive end to the reading process. Regardless of where you enter or exit, any reading sequence of some length should produce the effect to which the book's title alludes: you should feel 'in 1926'. The more immediate and sensual this illusion becomes, the more your reading will fulfill the book's chief aim. Note: you can, if you like, experience this effect *without* reading the last two chapters, 'After Learning from History' and 'Being-in-the-Worlds of 1926.' (Gumbrecht 1997: ix)

The keywords of the quoted passage are 'produce', 'effect' and 'illusion'. The production of an illusionary effect is the means to achieve Gumbrecht's ultimate aim, namely, to make readers feel *as if* they were in 1926. It cannot possibly be clearer that what Gumbrecht wishes to achieve by this is not an immediate experience but mediated experientiality. And when it comes to theorizing these aims, Gumbrecht is much more explicit about what he aims at than Runia. As Gumbrecht contends, 'what most interests' him 'today in the field of history' is 'the presentification of past worlds', which he describes as 'techniques that produce the impression (or, rather, the illusion) that worlds of the past can become tangible again' (2004: 94). In other words, notwithstanding all the talk about the notion of presence, as soon as it comes to historical writing, Gumbrecht no longer thinks that the work of the historian is to *convey* or *transfer* presence. The work of the historian is to 'produce' it by adequate 'techniques'.

I think that the words quoted above are wonderfully revealing concerning the role that historical writing might play in theories of presence and historical experience. And this role has little to do with the theoretical outlook of the notions. As soon as it comes to historical writing, *presence* must give way to *presentification*, assumed *immediacy* must give way to *mediation*, and assumed *genuineness* must give way to *artificiality*. The ultimate aim here is to achieve a heightened sense of experientiality in the final product, and the work of the historian is best compared to the work of the illusionist. The historian crafts an artifice, the artificiality of which you as a reader and audience are very well aware. And you are aware of this artificiality despite the fact that the purpose of the artifice is to create the atmosphere of former times and make you feel *as if* you actually experienced those former times. This is experientiality in historiography: *the crafted and mediated illusion of the immediacy of an experience of former times, accompanied by a full awareness of its very illusoriness on behalf of both the author and the audience.*

Being so, such experientiality in historiography is sharply opposed to the defining features of the notions of presence and historical experience. As it must be clear by now, I do not intend either to defend or promote these notions as they first appeared in historical theory. I find these theories highly inspiring, but their criticism also seems partly justified. In their overall constitution both sides seem to miss the mark: whereas theories of presence and historical experience tend to fall prey to metaphysical realism, their criticism tends to fall prey to scaremongering and fails to consider the potential of an emerging body of yet-to-be explicated ideas, unfairly measured against decades of common wisdom produced by narrative philosophy of history. Hence, despite all inspiration and indebtedness, the theory of history as the expression of historical experience defines experience in a way that is incompatible in many respects with the theories of Runia, Ankersmit and Gumbrecht. At the same time, against the narrativist mainstream, it insists on the possibility and the necessity of experience conceptualized as a 'doesn't look like anything to me' encounter that is constitutive of crafting histories that bring about historiographical novelty.

In principle, such historiographical novelty can be achieved by a history that intends to artificially exhibit a high degree of experientiality. But the intention to craft experiential histories is only a particular case within historical writing, one among the many shapes of both possible and actual histories. What matters more is the question of the relationship between the initial experience as an encounter-event and this crafted experientiality. And the lesson of the above discussion is that *in no way should experience and experientiality be conflated, and in no way can the latter directly convey, or transfer the former.* They simply belong to different orders of things. To highlight this fundamental difference, I would like to offer the following brief sketch of the difference between experience (this time meaning experience as defined in this book) and experientiality (based on the above considerations).

To begin with, whereas experience as a 'doesn't look like anything to me' encounter defies language and linguistic conceptualization, experientiality is attached to language. Experientiality is the property of language, the property of historical narratives; it *is* language and conceptualization (which, as long as histories are still produced predominantly as written artefacts, remains a specifically linguistic conceptualization). By virtue of being language, experientiality in history is mediated but voiced, while experience as a 'doesn't look like anything to me' encounter is immediate but necessarily remains mute inasmuch as it is without 'content'. Experience is merely the encounter itself, deprived of 'content' and sense, and it happens to you suddenly and unexpectedly. Contrary to this, experientiality, if successful, is your own purposeful and deliberate achievement. You make it 'happen', you design it to appear as a ready-made sense. Your role as a historian in designing it is that of the illusionist, and this role is necessarily so precisely because that which is experience is non-sense, and therefore whatever you design as experientiality in the realm of sense, it cannot be a result of a transfer of experience.

The designed evocation of 'real-life experience' in an experiential historical narrative concerns the *lived experience of past people* and not the historian's experience as an encounter with (any remnant of) the past. The same is true of Runia's modern monuments, whose experientiality is supposed to evoke a 'real-life experience' not belonging to their designers. This lived experience (the German *Erlebnis* as distinguished from *Erfahrung*) of people of the past has long been a subject of historical studies, and the classics of history from below – as in Italian microhistory (Ginzburg 1980), German *Alltagsgeschichte* (Imhof 1996) or French history of mentalities (Le Roy Ladurie 1978) – have all claimed to explore it. Being *lived*, this experience means nothing like a 'doesn't look like anything to me' encounter. It means already meaningful experiences in the most conventional, everyday sense of the word experience. It consists of the various ways in which their own lives and the world appeared to the consciousness of past people; it concerns the way they made sense of their lifeworlds.

Of course, this has nothing to do with experience as defined in this book. Nor has it much to do with the theoretical outlook of the notions of presence and historical experience as advocated by Runia, Gumbrecht and Ankersmit. Nevertheless, what all these different notions of experience share is that they belong to a different order of things than experientiality. Yet the fact that this experientiality cannot mean a straightforward transfer of experience (however defined) does not mean that they cannot be related to each other in a more complicated way. In a theory of history as the expression of historical experience, the most crucial question is precisely the nature of this relationship between an initial experience of non-sense and a final result. The latter might just as well be a historical account that exhibits a high degree of experientiality, but it can equally be a conventional historical narrative or any other historiographical achievement. In all cases the question is: how to get from one to the other? Why is the initial moment of experience 'initial' in the first place? What pushes us toward sense-making so that experience can appear as the point of departure of a larger scheme?

This finally brings me to the core issue of this chapter: between the non-sense of the 'doesn't look like anything to me' encounter with a (remnant of) the past and the already crafted sense there is an ethical moment. It is a moment of commitment to sense-making, a commitment to engage in the process of expression in which the historian (or anybody else) crafts a specifically 'historical' meaning by integrating singular phenomena into a larger temporal scheme encompassing the past, the present and the future, that is, into a configuration of change over time. In what follows, I attempt to account for this ethical moment. In the first step I will sketch an approval-demand structure borrowed from Simon Critchley. Then I will elaborate on the question of how such an ethical moment relates to a form of sense-making that is specifically 'historical'. In doing so, bringing about novelty in historiography though historical sense-making will turn out to be the correlate of a perception of novelty and change in history understood as the course of affairs. Finally, to conclude, I will offer a brief summary of the endeavour of the chapters that form Part Two of this book.

The approval of a demand

The theory of ethical experience in Critchley (2007) seems to be of great value for an effort to conceptualize the ethical moment of taking the step toward expression, that is, the step toward historical sense-making. For the sake of avoiding further confusion about the already overused and overburdened notion of 'experience', instead of referring to Critchley's theory as a theory of ethical experience, I will stick as much as possible with the idea of an ethical moment and make use of those aspects of Critchley's theory which are the most relevant from this viewpoint. Critchley's ultimate aim is to design a form of ethics that might preserve the possibility of political action. Although this purpose is not particularly relevant for the overall theory sketched here, the motivational force Critchley attributes to his theory is of crucial importance. For *motivation for taking action is precisely what the ethical moment introduces into a theory of history as the expression of historical experience*, even though the action in question is not explicit political resistance as in Critchley's theory, but action as getting engaged in the process of 'historical' sense-making against the background of the non-sense of a 'doesn't look like anything to me' encounter-event.

Critchley's enterprise of providing a 'subjective commitment to ethical action' is a response to the question he regards as 'the fundamental question of ethics': 'how does a self bind itself to whatever it determines as its good?' (Critchley 2007: 9). The ethical question of history appears as the subcategory of this wider question in that the 'self' in the case of history is a 'self' engaged in a specifically 'historical' sense-making. The question of ethics with respect to history goes as follows: how does a historian (or anybody else) bind themselves to whatever they determine as their good? Answering this question, however, is not the end point of an exploration into the ethics of history but only its beginning. Critchley's answer, that such ethical binding takes the shape of a demand-approval scheme, provides only a structural theoretical framework that accounts for a commitment to take action. In the case of history, when taking action means an engagement in the process of expression as 'historical' sense-making, there is a further question directed at whatever makes this commitment and motivation to sense-making specifically 'historical'. The specificity of the question of ethics with respect to a theory of history has to do with the specificity of history as discussed in Part One of this book, that is, with a distinctly 'historical' way of temporal ordering and apprehension. The question is whether the demand and the motivation to engage in historical sense-making comes from the past, the present or the future. This is the sense in which Critchley's 'fundamental question of ethics' and his answer in the shape of the demand-approval scheme appear as the prerequisite of answering the question of the ethical moment in the expression of historical experience.

Critchley begins to outline the scheme by claiming that 'there can be no sense of the good [...] without an act of approval, affirmation or approbation' (14–15). But even epistemic claims may imply approval and thus the act cannot be restricted to the ethical domain. In Critchley's view, the strength of approval or disapproval as entailed respectively by ethical and epistemic claims nevertheless makes a difference. As this difference is a difference in degree and not in kind, what appears as a defining characteristic of ethical statements is the degree of the strength of the approval they imply.

According to Critchley, this approval cannot be anything else than 'an approval *of* something', and this something is 'a demand that demands approval' (16). Needless to say, there is a circularity involved in this claim. Critchley thinks it is not a vicious but a virtuous one. And indeed, the circularity makes sense. For Critchley's point is precisely that you cannot say that the demand precedes the act of approval; instead, demand and approval arise jointly. To illustrate this point, Critchley cites the examples of Bob Geldof's Live Aid concerts and Christ's resurrection. According to the former, Geldof would not have organized the fundraising concerts in 1985 if he had not approved a demand he experienced when watching the BBC reports of the 1984 Ethiopian famine. The fact that Geldof took action following the BBC reports cannot prove that there was first a demand that was then followed by an approval. Other people watching the same BBC reports might not have experienced any demand at all. The majority of viewers most likely simply did not have such an ethical experience because, as Critchley argues, 'the demand is not somehow objectively given in the state of affairs'; instead, 'the demand is only felt as a demand for the self who approves it', and, consequently, it simply cannot be in any other way than 'demand and approval arise at the same time' (18).

The present approval of a demand of the future about the past

Conceptualizing an ethical moment in a theory of history as an approval of a demand raises the further question concerning the specificity of history: what kind of demand is specifically 'historical', and where does such 'historical' demand come from? Given that what Western societies call 'historical' is that which changes over time as opposed to the 'ahistoricity' of that which does not, the answer most certainly has to do with temporality and with ways of configuring the relationship between past, present and future.

If a historian (or anybody else) is invested in sense-making labelled as 'historical', and if such an investment is the result of an ethical demand, then probably the most instinctive association would be that the ethical investment concerns primarily the past, or, more precisely, people of the past. The idea that the ethics of history are based on an ethical relationship with the past has been around for a while. Edith Wyschogrod (2004) may be its most well-known advocate, and lately even a comprehensive theory of history has been built on the idea by Froeyman, who considers 'the writing of history as an expression of an ethical relation to the past' (2015: 5). Froeyman's enterprise of grounding a theory of history in ethics and grounding this ethics of history in relation to the past certainly has its merits. But there is a price to pay for such a theoretical endeavour, and the price seems quite high. The merits and the shortcomings of attributing primacy to the past in an ethics of history are best attested to by the following passage from Wyschogrod:

> Although the historian's task is the re-figuration of the past, she does not create affects through the transformation of percepts; instead her primary role is an ethical one. Prior to the creation of a historical narrative, her first act is one of promising the dead others to make past events available to present and perhaps future generations. Thus she is mediator of a legacy. (2004: 30)

The supposed merits of this view lie in the effort to transfer a 'legacy' of the past. The operation is possible only inasmuch as – in the view of Wyschogrod – the 'historian assumes liability for the Other', which eventually results in the scenario that the narrative told by the historian 'is governed by a promise to provide voice to the dead others' (30–1). The same is true of Froeyman's theory, which is explicitly based on dialogical ethics and on the ethics of the recognition of the Other (while, at the same time, labels Wyschogrod as a representative of the alternative approach of care ethics). Froeyman's ethics of recognition boils down to an ethics of representation that presumes a more active intervention than Wyschogrod in requiring not only a 'liability for the Other' but also an affirmation of the very otherness of the past together with its absent Other (Froeyman 2015: 40–53). Yet, all differences between Froeyman's and Wyschogrod's theories aside, they both are based on a shared and deep agreement over the priority of the past in an ethics of history. And this prioritization of the past means that if there is anything like a responsibility of the individual historian (or anybody else) invested in 'historical' sense-making, it is a responsibility toward the dead.

Fulfilling a responsibility toward the dead and giving voice to the voiceless of the past may indeed be a respectable endeavour. As a theory of history, however, such an ethics has a major shortcoming, which becomes visible as soon as it comes to the question of the compatibility of a responsibility toward the dead with the demand-approval scheme. At first blush, everything seems fine. Integrating such ethics into the demand-approval scheme would mean that the historian (or anybody else) is getting motivated to initiate 'historical' sense-making by the approval of a demand that comes from the past and the dead. The theoretical possibility is thereby granted. But the shortcoming of such a view is not its theoretical impossibility. Elevating a responsibility toward the dead to the level of an overall ethics of history may be possible, but it is theoretically implausible inasmuch as an ethics that prioritizes the past simply cannot account for the variety of historiography and, most importantly, for historiographical change and novelty.

The inability to account for historiographical change and novelty derives from the fact that a demand that comes from the past is, so to speak, a demand of the past and the dead over the concerns of the present and the living. Its approval might bring voice to the voiceless and might bring the otherness of the past into the present by means of a form of historical writing aiming at a high degree of experientiality. But it is precisely the intention to 'presentify' whatever was available already in the past that goes against the very possibility of novelty. For if historical writing is limited to artificially create the sense of the availability of that which was already available in the past, then it is exposed to charges of being a cultural product that fetishizes inherited schemes and viewpoints. On the other hand, defenders of a responsibility toward the dead can argue that inventive ways of 'presentification' may bring about novel ways of writing history, even novel methodologies. It may very well be that the cultural product that is exposed to the threat of fetishizing inherited schemes and viewpoints becomes engaged in inventing novel ways of carrying out its fascination with the inherited, the already available, the past and the dead. Microhistory – the chief historiographical example of Froeyman (2015: 113–41) for an ethics of recognition and historical representation – can be mentioned here to support this point, as it came about as a novel historiographical approach with the intention to explore the lived experience of people of the past (cf. Magnússon and Szijártó 2013).

Yet, even if the possibility of historiographical change and novelty can be retained in a past-oriented ethics in such a limited sense, the second problem remains: what this ethics accounts for is only one specific approach among the many available approaches of historical writing and, at best, one occasion of historiographical change as the birth of this very specific approach. It fails to account for any other historiographical approaches than the one that wishes to convey the mental schemes and viewpoints of people of the past, what those people were aware of, and how they conceived of their own lives and their world. Much of historical writing is interested in other questions, makes use of present-day analytical concepts in making sense of past phenomena, or simply aims at such sense-making from a viewpoint to which it is irrelevant how things occurred to people of the past. If a past-oriented ethics elevated into a theory of history actually informed the entirety of historical studies, these historiographical practices would never have emerged. I think that an overall theory of history should account for historiographical change and novelty as such, not only for the emergence of one certain way of writing history with a particular focus on 'presentifying' the experiences and viewpoints of people of the past. It should account for the emergence and co-existence of the overall variety of all available approaches we call 'historical'.

To avoid any misunderstandings: I most certainly am interested in an overall theory of history as a general account on both historical and historiographical change, but what I am looking for is not an ethics of history elevated to the level of a theory of history. It is only a place for ethics *within* an overall theory of history. So far it is clear that the role of an ethics is to provide motivation for action; that within the larger framework of a theory of history as the expression of historical experience action means an engagement in 'historical' sense-making; and that such ethics cannot be past-oriented. Hence the next question to ask is: where to look for a motivational ethics if not in the past?

After the past, the next candidate is, rather obviously, the present. Oddly enough, microhistory proves to be a superb example once again. The paradigmatic historiographical practice that seems to fulfil a past-oriented ethics of history as a responsibility toward the dead can also be considered as exceeding the horizon of the past. Even if microhistory can be said to fulfil an ethical relation to the past, its *motivation* for doing so does not necessarily come from the past. In fact, the entire historiographical fascination with giving voice to the voiceless, to everyday people and the marginalized, is a reflection of the political agendas of the present time of the (late) 1960s, 1970s and 1980s, when the first groundbreaking microhistories were written (cf. the historiographical and methodological accounts of Levi 1991; Ginzburg and

Poni 1991; Cerutti 2004; Brewer 2010; Magnússon and Szijártó 2013). The same is true even of Froeyman and Wyschogrod's theories. The ethical relation to the dead as the recognition of the Other is a concern inasmuch as – and precisely because – the recognition of the Other is a concern of the lifeworlds of Froeyman and Wyschogrod in their present time. But to be clear, this is far from being a spectacularly insightful observation; it is a commonplace of historical theory as practised in the last half-century. As Keith Jenkins somewhat naturally remarked, 'the past that we "know" is always contingent upon our own views, our own "present"' (2003: 15). In this broad sense, the ethical motivation and the demand to be approved may be understood as coming from the present, and such an understanding would assume an ethics of history that is unashamedly presentist.

The claim I wish to make, however, goes against both this presentist and the earlier discussed past-oriented view. It opposes the idea that the ethics of history is derived from a primacy of the past just as much as it opposes the idea of the unavoidable dominance of the present over the past. My rather counterintuitive claim is that a motivational ethics of history, an ethics that accounts for historiographical change and the occurrence of novelty in historical studies, derives from a vision of the future, and it is the primacy of the future in an ethics of history that establishes a connection between past, present and future. Without the primacy of the future and without the connection this future establishes to the past and the present, any kind of sense-making motivated by an ethics could not even qualify as 'historical' in the first place. Phrased as a thesis, and also conforming to the vocabulary of the previous chapters, all this means that *the ethical moment of a theory of history is a demand that comes from the future, a demand that demands approval in the present, and also a demand that nevertheless is about the past.*

Making sense of non-sense historically

What could this possibly mean? In what sense does a motivation for being engaged in the process of expression, that is, a motivation for being engaged in 'historical' sense-making, come from the future? And, first of all, how can we understand the claim that a sense-making process of expression is not even 'historical' without the primacy of the future as the locus of motivation? In order to give an intelligible answer to the former question concerning the role of the future, the latter question about what makes a sense-making process 'historical' must be answered first. The answer leads back to the discussion of the first half of the book about the concept of history understood as the course of human (?) affairs. The general claim I wish to put forward is that 'historical' sense-making in historiography is inseparable from conceptions about history as the course of affairs. Concerning the role of ethics, this means that the ethical moment of a theory of history as historiography is ultimately responsible for establishing the bond between the two major senses of history as the course of affairs and as historical writing.

The point of departure in explicating this claim lies in the opening remarks in the Preface on the question of novelty. As a quick reminder, making sense of the new 'historically' means nothing other than to integrate perceived novelty into a larger temporal scheme that encompasses the past, the present and the future. Throughout Western modernity this larger temporal scheme was seen as a configuration of change over time as a directional and developmental process, which has become known as 'history'. As I argued in Part One of this book, this larger temporal scheme – and, thus, what we call history – is increasingly reconfigured (in certain domains of human life) as a series of unprecedented changes in our broadly construed postwar period.

In both cases, however, you have a scheme at your disposal as a conceptual tool that you can put to work. You can of course apply it not only to perceived novelty but to any other particular phenomena. Once you have the conceptual tool of a larger temporal scheme as a configuration of change over time, you can make sense of any particular event, occurrence or phenomena by integrating it into the temporal scheme. By doing so, by locating the particular in a scenario of change over time, you attribute meaning to the particular and create a sense 'historically'. Once again, throughout Western modernity, such historical sense-making was synonymous with the integration of the particular into a processual and developmental scheme. As Hannah Arendt remarked in her essay on the modern concept of history,

> to our modern way of thinking nothing is meaningful in and by itself, not even history or nature taken each as a whole, and certainly not particular occurrences in the physical order or specific historical events. There is a fateful enormity in this state of affairs. Invisible processes have engulfed every tangible thing, every individual entity that is visible to us, degrading them into functions of an over-all process. (1961: 63)

Degradation may be a harsh word to describe the operation of historical sense-making. Transforming individual entities into meaningful historical ones by seeing them within a larger scheme surely came out in Western modernity as an upgrade that attributes significance to that which is thereby historicized. Even though the temporal scheme into which you integrate particular phenomena when you try to make sense of them historically is no longer necessarily processual, history as a configuration of change over time – encompassing past, present and future – is a prerequisite of historical sense-making. This equally applies to all popular activities we label 'historical' and to professionalized and institutionalized historiography.

If neither a past-oriented nor a present-oriented ethics of history qualifies as 'historical' sense-making, it is because both seem incapable of establishing such an overall temporal scheme into which you could integrate particularities and thereby attribute meaning and create sense. A past-oriented ethics of a responsibility toward the dead lacks the overall integrative temporal scheme inasmuch as its aim is to preserve the past. It nevertheless achieves another kind of temporality by a present compensation for what is conceived of as past injustice when seen from the present. Those who were deprived of a voice in the past, past others who were marginalized, stigmatized and disparaged, may become compensated post-mortem. By giving voice to the voiceless of the past or recognizing them as past others, a past-oriented ethics of history certainly connects at least past and present (without the future), but it does so only in order to show the past as influential in the present.

At the same time, it is self-evident that such a post-mortem compensation for past injustice matters for those who compensate in the present. It is the present that sets the agendas, and in this respect an admittedly present-oriented ethics of seeing present political agendas already in the past is nothing other than the mirror image of a past-oriented ethics. They are each other's complementary operations in the sense that just as much as the latter results in a preeminence of the past over the present, the former results in a preeminence of the present over the past. They simply transfer agendas and human concerns from the past to the present and from the present to the past, until that which was past becomes considered as being effective in the present and that which is present appears as already being effective in the past. In this way, due to the conflation of past and present agendas, both a past-oriented and a present-oriented ethics fail to offer a configuration of change over time as an overall temporal scheme within which particularities could be made sense of.

To avoid misunderstandings, it seems important to point out that such an ethics may offer a temporal *difference* between past and present. In fact, the aspect of difference can even be emphasized the most, just like in the case of a past-oriented ethics of history that talks about the Other of the past. Compared to inhabitants of present-day rural Italy, the marginalized and voiceless Other of the past might have had a completely other mental imaginary and cosmology, much like Menocchio, the sixteenth-century miller in Carlo Ginzburg's *The Cheese and the Worms* (1980). But this marginalized past Other will necessarily appear both in a past-oriented and a present-oriented ethics of history as a 'historical' proxy for those marginalized in the present.

It claims that whatever we define as 'marginalized' today has already existed in the past on the one hand, and by showing how the past marginalized has a completely different constitution on the other, it implies that change has taken place in the very constitution of that which we think of today as 'marginalized'. However, that change, the way it took place and especially the kind of change implied, remains a mystery. Such histories may nevertheless be called historical inasmuch as they imply changed conditions, regardless of the fact that they are unable to account for how their subjects change over time.

Accordingly, I do not intend to argue that the historiographical practices of history from below that renewed the historiographical field in the second half of the last century are not 'historical' in any sense whatsoever. By virtue of maintaining the difference between past and present when studying the other of the past, historiographical practices that wish to create experientiality can still be labelled historical. What I argue for is that the ethics of history that accounts for this kind of historiography (without accounting for other kinds of historiography) cannot offer a temporal *scheme* that accounts for the posited difference in terms of a scenario of change over time. It has no explanation of what kind of difference is postulated and how that difference may come about.

The temporal difference implied by both a past-oriented and a present-oriented ethics of history is a necessary condition of historical sense-making, but it is not a sufficient one. I think their inability to offer a larger temporal scheme as a sufficient condition is the result of the absence of a crucial element: the future does not seem to play any role in the ethical considerations discussed above. In light of the arguments of Chapter 3, this is all the more regrettable. Without the involvement of the future it is hardly possible at all to have anything like a concept of history as a configuration of change over time in human (?) affairs. A motivational ethics as an integral part of a theory of history understood as historiography, a motivational ethics of a specifically historical sense-making, simply cannot do without the future and without the larger temporal scheme in which the future is configured in connection to the past and the present as history.

Historical and historiographical change

These considerations finally enable an answer to the question concerning the role of the future in the claim of the previous section. Let me repeat the claim here before briefly elaborating it (this time with special attention paid to marking the accents): the ethical moment of a theory of history is a demand that *comes* from the *future*, a demand that demands *approval* in the *present* and also a demand that nevertheless is *about* the *past*.

The fact that an ethical demand for historical sense-making comes from the future means that the motivation to make a move from the non-sense of a 'doesn't look like anything to me' encounter with (remnants of) the past toward crafting sense in the shape of a written history (or any other artifact we may call historical) has to do with a vision of the future. A vision of the future does not mean of course anything like a hallucination in a feverish delirium. It means something like a present conceptual imaginary of what human (?) life and societies might look like in the future. Being a present conceptual imaginary implies that an approval of a demand deriving from this vision of the future cannot but take place in the present. Finally, as a conceptualization of the future that is carried out in the present, any vision of the future is necessarily an imagined state of human (?) affairs as already measured against the backdrop of a conceptualization of present and past states of affairs. Carrying out this measurement against the backdrop of past states of affairs is precisely what historiography does, meaning that a demand that comes from the future and demands approval in the present is still about the past.

Inasmuch as the past, the present and the envisioned different future feature together in an overall temporal scheme, this scheme implies a conception of change by which the envisioned future state of affairs may come about as relative to the present and the past. Consequentially, the claim that a motivation for getting engaged in historical sense-making comes from the future is a claim not only about the role of the future in historiographical change. It is also a claim about a conceptualization of how that future relates to the present and the past, about a configuration of change over time in human (?) affairs. Ultimately, it is about historiographical change as necessarily linked to a conception of historical change. In this sense, the final claim I wish to make goes as follows: the motivation for historical sense-making in historiography is derived from a perception of historical change taking place. Historiographical change happens when the future is perceived in a new light, that is, when the perception of future prospects as different from the present and the past results in a sense of historical change. Perceived historical novelty is thereby the condition of possibility for historiographical novelty.

Yet things are not that simple. There is another dimension to the relationship between historical and historiographical change. In the shape presented above, the claim describes the link between historical and historiographical change regardless of the particular configuration of that change. In principle, this can equally apply to the processual and developmental changes of the modern notion of history and the unprecedented changes of history as a disrupted singular. But the way in which notions of history and historiography connect may have a consequence concerning the type of change itself. If the perception of the type of historical change itself changes as historical change, the perception of historiographical change may change with it.

I believe this is precisely what happens today. In a time when historical change increasingly appears as unprecedented change, the perception of historiographical change gains corresponding qualities. In this respect, the theory of historiography as the expression ~~of~~ historical experience presented here is nothing other than the structural equivalent and correlate of the quasi-substantive philosophy of history presented in Part One of this book. Together they account for the respective senses of history in times of unprecedented change.

A summary

Arriving at this point, the theory of history (in the sense of historical writing) developed here looks both complete and incomplete. It remains incomplete in that it does not account for every single aspect of historical sense-making. Fortunately, this never was the intention of this book, hence the work is complete in that it covers what has been promised to be covered by the previous pages.

The aim of these investigations was to properly credit the non-linguistic in the overall constitution of historical work and thereby to account for historiographical change. In light of its own basic principles, narrative philosophy of history could not conceive of such a constitutive role of the non-linguistic. The last three chapters tried to remedy this situation. The remedy took the shape of a theory of history as the expression ~~of~~ historical experience, according to which historical sense-making begins in a 'doesn't look like anything to me' encounter with the external world, in an encounter with (remnants of) the past. However, this encounter remains in the realm of non-sense. For the process of historical sense-making to start there has to be a motivation in the shape of an ethical moment. A step toward expression has to be taken due to the approval of an ethical demand that derives from a vision of the future and from a corresponding conception of historical change. Finally, whatever historical sense is eventually crafted, it cannot be a straight transfer of an initial experience into language. I tried to capture this impossibility of a straight transfer that nevertheless does not exclude a constitutive relation between experience and language – between non-sense and sense – by making use of a struck-through 'of' in the theory of history as the expression ~~of~~ historical experience.

The greatest shortcoming of the theory of history as the expression ~~of~~ historical experience might be that it looks overly individualistic because it revolves around the individual historian (or anybody else invested in historical sense-making). But, again, the theory presented here does not wish to account for every possible aspect of historical sense-making. It wishes to account for those aspects that either have been neglected or could not have even been addressed within the dominant narrativist framework of the past decades of historical theory. Besides, the theory of history as the expression of historical experience does not wish to provide an explanation of how historiography functioned in Western modernity. Rather, its interest lies in the question of how historiography functions in times of unprecedented change.

What this means – beside that fact that the theory itself has a historical character – is that despite having a point of departure in the sense-making individual, nothing in the theory is incompatible with otherwise easily recognizable collective dimensions of historical work. The expression of historical experience, the entire process of historical sense-making, takes place in a web that contains all previous historical knowledge and all societal and collective pressures. These collective dimensions and societal pressures have already been discussed extensively both by narrativist and postmodern theories of history in a way that I believe is consistent with the insights centring around the sense-making individual as presented here (regardless of how the first half of the book challenged the basic premises of narrativism).

The take-home message of the explorations of Part Two of this book is threefold. The first is that, notwithstanding all those societal and collective measures that effect the final product of a crafted historical sense (be it a written history or any other historical sense), historiographical change and novelty could not emerge without a moment in which all collective measures break down, and in which you encounter a non-linguistic and non-collective non-sense. I think the acknowledgement of this moment and its constitutive role is the blind spot of historical theory as it has been practised during the entire postwar period.

The second central message is that the same is true of the motivational ethics underlying the occurrence of historiographical change and novelty: no serious theoretical attention has been paid to the question. Without approving a demand derived from a perception of historical change, without the necessary motivation it provides, there is no action taken toward achieving such historiographical novelty. Finally, the third message is closely related to the second in that a lack of a motivational ethics of historiography is due to an overall neglect of the ties that necessarily bound history as historiography to conceptions of history as the course of affairs. In that respect, the chief mistake of the past decades of theorizing about history was a general lack of attentiveness toward the fundamental role played by visions of the future both in historical writing and in any notion of history as the course of affairs.

Eventually, the three take-home messages add up to the claim that history as historical writing is contingent upon visions of the future and notions of history as the course of affairs. Neither historiography nor historical theory as a theory of such historiography is possible without (at least tacitly implying) a philosophy of history as an overall configuration of change over time. Theoretical possibility, however, does not equal practical need. Thus, as the final investigation of this book, I would like to turn to the question of whether Western societies still need history in the first place.

The Unprecedented and the Crisis of the Political: An Epilogue

An eventual historical sensibility

I opened this book with the embarrassingly simple claim that a certain historical sensibility, born around the middle of the last century in the Western world, is posing a challenge to the modern one. The chapters elaborated on this claim with respect to history understood as both the course of affairs and historical writing. In these chapters, the postwar historical sensibility of Western societies acquired a distinct eventual characteristic. The claim concerning the challenge posed by an emerging eventual historical sensibility does not wish to assert that the modern processual and developmental historical sensibility is completely abandoned. Nor does it wish to assert that the new-born sensibility now permeates every single domain of contemporary Western life. What it claims is that the domains in which this modern historical sensibility is still operative and effective is shrinking, and at the same time that inhabitants of Western societies increasingly conceive of themselves and the world along an eventual configuration of novelty and change over time that revolves around (a series of) unprecedented changes.

In this Epilogue, I wish to return to the more comprehensive societal concerns of the Prologue and attempt to enrich the rather technical work of the chapters in two major ways. First, in the hope of gaining a better understanding of the stakes of the entire endeavour, I will elaborate on the emerging eventual historical sensibility in terms of its scope, concerning the various domains of human life and human endeavours. The question of the political domain is of crucial importance here. Whereas the previous chapters considered the postwar emergence of an eventual historical sensibility as confined to the technological and ecological domains, these final remarks address the possibility of eventual and unprecedented change in the explicitly political domain.

As a second major way to enrich the work of the previous chapters, I will then pose and leave open the most troubling question of what exactly an emerging evental sensibility – and thus a configuration of change over time as (a series of) unprecedented changes – confronts us with. For despite the fact that I have constantly referred to this evental sensibility as 'historical', and despite the fact that the unprecedented promises to bring about change over time in the mundane world of human (?) affairs, it may be just as reasonable to claim that whatever is challenging the modern historical sensibility is not a rival historical sensibility but something other than history: an evental sensibility, the historical or other-than-historical character of which is disputable. Hence the most troubling question that must be asked eventually is the following: *is the evental and the unprecedented still history?*

Before venturing into the task of outlining an answer, let me offer a very brief recap in light of which the following enrichments and the most troubling question itself can become intelligible in the first place. Chapter 3 left off with the conclusion that there is a shared concern of seemingly distinct, unconnected (and sometimes even contradictory) discourses, including political theories that identify themselves as belonging to the political Left, theories of presentism, theories of presence, or Hayden White's revival of the notion of the practical past. I think the shared concern is to come to terms somehow with what Hans-Ulrich Gumbrecht (2014) calls a 'yet unnamed chronotope'. All these otherwise hardly reconcilable discourses sense that the way Western societies conceive of the relationship between past, present and future is drastically changing. Yet these efforts to conceptualize this relationship in a novel way must remain immensely crude and unrefined inasmuch as they even struggle to name the new chronotope adequately. Given that what Gumbrecht means by 'chronotope' is close to identical to what I mean by 'historical sensibility', I tried to pull together the different threads in an overall conceptualization. My suggestion – in line with the vocabulary of some of the aforementioned political theories – was to christen the new-born temporality as the temporality of the event, and to name the sense of historicity informed by this temporality as an evental historical sensibility.

The emerging evental historical sensibility underlies not only the way that we perceive change over time in human affairs but historiographical change as well. According to the arguments of Part Two of this book, the connection between the ways we conceive of historical change and historiographical change is twofold. On the one hand, a game-changing historiographical change – that is, the occurrence of genuine novelty in historiographic practice – is the result of the perception of genuine novelty in the course of affairs. On the other hand, this historiographical change exhibits the same structural features as historical change. Today, in times of unprecedented change, they both attest to a shared evental historical sensibility.

The emancipation dilemma and political change

But what exactly is such an evental historical sensibility? And how 'increasingly' does it pervade Western societies? Is there a possible limit to its extension over more and more domains? Or can an evental configuration of change over time appear as pertinent with respect to all possible human activities? In my argument, an evental temporality and historical sensibility already pertain to the ecological and technological domains due to their investment in a novel kind of future prospect as unprecedented while the political domain seems stuck without a vision of the future. Yet the closest conceptual relatives of my overall endeavour seem to be certain political theories. This is indeed an odd situation. As Chapter 3 has already mentioned, political theories of the Left are heavily engaged in redefining the possibility of politics by attributing an evental character to their desired political change. In the shape of a theory of the event, Alain Badiou does so in a distinctly comprehensive manner. In light of the preoccupation of such political theories with the question of political change, the most specific version of the questions above that has to be answered is: to what extent can political theories of the event be affiliated with the evental character of the prospect of unprecedented change in the ecological and technological domains?

The answer I wish to give begins with a fundamental difference between the approach of this book and the approach of political theories. Whereas the principal aim of my endeavour is to understand a way of making sense of the world and ourselves, many political theories try to solve a logical problem. Whereas my point of departure is the way change over time is already conceived of in certain domains of life in Western societies, political theories of the self-identified Left typically have their point of departure in a perplexing theoretical dilemma they hope to resolve.

In the last couple of decades, political theories of the Left have been engaged in an attempt to reconcile their retained commitment to emancipation with the overwhelming postwar skepticism toward the modern processual historical sensibility. Even though ideas of a directional and teleological historical process became of ill repute in the second half of the last century, the desire for emancipation survived. But inasmuch as emancipation is gradual empowerment, it is necessarily configured by a processual temporality and is thereby conditioned by the modern historical sensibility. Emancipation necessarily entails a promise of the future toward which it is directed and unfolds over time, from a non-emancipated or insufficiently emancipated past to the emancipated future. Emancipation necessitates the explicit or implicit invocation of a historical process as a condition of its possibility, and thus a deep temporal continuity within which the process of emancipation plays out.

It seems that one either retains or discards both, but in both cases one needs to make a call. And, indeed, this seems like a perplexing dilemma. For many it may even look like an equally perplexing double bind.

No wonder that political theories typically hesitate to make the call. Instead, they concentrate their efforts on the possibility of reconciliation and try to preserve the commitment to emancipation while abandoning what seems to be its condition of possibility: the modern processual historical sensibility. Theories of the event are only one instance of such an attempt at reconciliation, although most of the attempts are heavily interrelated. To mention an example that Chapter 1 has already discussed, Jean-Luc Nancy's philosophy of the always unrealizable coming-to-existence of future communities that never 'become' is a very prominent instance of the intended reconciliation of the theoretical possibility of emancipation and the theoretical impossibility of processual history.

But even Nancy's effort can best be understood by means of the structurally similar undertaking of Jacques Derrida. Generally speaking, Nancy's efforts are heavily indebted to Derrida's ideas, although not specifically to the theoretical endeavour by which Derrida tries to salvage emancipatory thought. Derrida hopes to retain the promise of emancipation 'as promise and not as onto-theological or teleo-escathological program or design' (1994: 94). The significance of retaining the promise that is nothing more than a promise comes from a twofold aim. On the one hand, Derrida wishes to execute a spirited recuperation of the Marxist inheritance without having recourse to teleology and processual directionality. On the other, he wants to achieve all this through a bitter critique of Fukuyama's 'end of history' thesis that revives the enterprise of classical philosophy of history in a not very Marxist fashion: with liberal democracy standing at the pinnacle of humanity's ideological development. Against the directional teleology of both old-school Marxist visions of history and Fukuyama's story, Derrida offers a non-directional and non-processual alternative, which comes in the shape of a revived theological vocabulary. When appealing to 'the formal structure of the promise' of emancipation common to both Marxism and Christianity, Derrida claims that:

> what remains irreducible to any deconstruction, what remains as undeconstructible as the possibility itself of deconstruction is, perhaps, a certain experience of the emancipatory promise; it is perhaps even the formality of a structural messianism, a messianism without religion, even a messianic without messianism, an idea of justice – which we distinguish from law or right and even from human rights – and an idea of democracy – which we distinguish from its current concept and from its determined predicates today. (74)

This 'messianic without messianism' – that is, this emancipatory promise without the prospect of a teleological and directional fulfilment – is what Derrida considers to be 'another opening of event-ness as historicity' (74). Accordingly, affirming the emancipatory promise as nothing more than a promise amounts to the affirmation of the prospect of the event, a singular game-changing occurrence. In other words, the singular event is the promise itself. But if this is the case, then the event must share with the promise their common defining trait: their unrealizability. For insofar as the promise is nothing more than a promise without the prospect of fulfilment and insofar as the promise is the promise of the game-changing event, the event remains unrealizable and will never actually take place.

This unrealizability brings to light two structural difficulties that theories of the self-identified Left concerning a transformative political event are prone to. I think both difficulties are inherent in the dual aim of reconciling a disbelief in a processual historical sensibility and a retained commitment to emancipation. First, a Derridean unrealizability is prone to a motivational deficit. Second, pledging commitment to emancipation as a promise amounts to pledging commitment to nothing other than the formal structure of the very processual historical sensibility Derrida otherwise wishes to overcome. The first difficulty concerns the *promise* component: its unrealizability, which entails an actual disbelief in the very taking place of an emancipatory promise (even if the promise component is evental). The second difficulty is about the *emancipation* part in a scenario when disbelief in the taking place of the promise does not pose an obstacle for action. Both structural difficulties stem from the price to be paid for the intended reconciliation: the implicit recognition of the impossibility of the actual event of the coming about of the promise and thus the implicit recognition of the impossibility of actual emancipation.

At first glance, this price may not appear too high. It may even look desirable when measured against arguments that aim to show the even higher undesirability of the implications of a historical process and its possible fulfilment. Political theories of the Left often seem willing to pay the price precisely for this reason. As Judith Butler (1993) points out in reviewing two similar reconciliation-efforts by Drucilla Cornell (1992) and Ernesto Laclau (1992), the unrealizability of the promise and thus the unrealizability of the modern idea of history and its teleological end is seen as a good thing for those who subscribe to this position. According to Butler, the reason for this is that 'the unrealizability of the end of history is precisely what guarantees futurity, for if history were to have an end, telos, and if that end were knowable in the present, then the future would be known in advance of its emergence, and the future would be always already present' (1993: 4). What this means is that it is the discontent with the idea of a realizable future along a processual historical process that makes political theories opt for unrealizability, what they consider – in the view of this book, mistakenly – as the best option there is. And the consideration is so widespread, that Butler even identifies the postulation of 'a future which is in principle unrealizable' as the general 'poststructuralist position' (with the qualification: 'if it is a position') regarding the question of history (4).

Yet it seems that the result of holding up a promise that is nothing more than a promise has the very same consequence that the 'poststructuralist position' as identified by Butler otherwise intends to avoid: the loss of futurity. As the unrealizable future never comes about, what can get realized simply does not go beyond the horizon of the present and that which is already available. When a future that is different from the past and the present cannot be realized, for actual achievement there remains only a future that is already at hand, which is no different from the past and the present. In this way, a promise that is nothing more than a promise fails to deliver the result for which it is set up: to introduce future change against the backdrop of the present condition. A future of which the only thing to be known is that it will never actually take place simply conserves the present, freezing it into a perpetual present condition in which no political action can be taken and no political change can be achieved.

No surprise that Butler relegates such reconciliation-efforts into the realm of 'logical possibility', claiming that 'this logic appears to be the site of the new dream, the dream of pure thought, pure possibility in thought', which is 'perhaps also, the transcendence of the social itself' (9). This pure logical possibility of retaining a commitment to emancipation that comes at the price of the impossibility of actually achieving emancipation points to a *motivational deficit* at the core of the supposedly retained commitment. For there is a question to ask yourself when facing the prospect of committing to a cause that you know is already lost: *if you are fully aware of the unrealizability of the promise, why on earth would you commit to it?*

Being fully aware of the unattainability of the goals of your own commitment implies an awareness of the futility of action taken in order to realize these very goals. If you are fully aware of the unattainability of your own goals, inasmuch as the promise of emancipation is nothing more than a promise, you are prone to lose your motivation to act upon a supposedly retained commitment, unless you are a main character in a Hollywood drama about fighting causes everyone knows are lost. Without a motivation to act, there is hardly any reason for retaining the commitment itself in the first place.

But even if you would be able to preserve your commitment to emancipation in the full knowledge of its unrealizability, the slightest implication to translate this commitment into action would require an evocation of the modern processual historical sensibility. For regardless of the question whether action is actually possible or not, inasmuch as action is implied by the retained promise of emancipation as a supplementary promise of action (and nothing more than a promise), you necessarily invoke a processual temporality. The promise of acting in order to bring about a 'better' future as a corollary of the promise of emancipation mobilizes the very historical sensibility you were so sceptical about in the first place. Even if the promise is of evental character, acting for the realization of the promise, acting to achieve emancipation, cannot but remain gradual empowerment. Unless there is perfect social equality and uniformity (which there is not and is not even desired by many), in a web of complex social relations, emancipatory thought can, in principle, always identify new groups of underprivileged and 'have-nots' as relative to privileged groups and groups of 'haves'. Much in the way it happens lately on the largest scale by extending intra-species emancipatory concerns over a growing perception of inter-species injustice. Such expansive, gradual, processual and developmental change lies at the very core of emancipatory thought.

It seems to me that theories such as Derrida's preserve either nothing at all (because an unrealizable promise provides no reason to save a commitment to political action and the achievement of political change) or they preserve the entire processual historical sensibility (in case you actually want to act upon your commitment to a promise). Needless to say, this conceptualization of political change significantly differs from the conceptualization of unprecedented change in domains other than the political. As discussed earlier, an unprecedented change is a change that is not a promise but an existential threat. And even when it appears as a promise (like in the self-description of transhumanism and human enhancement), the promise itself inherently contains a threat (that human enhancement results in creating non-humans rather than better humans). Moreover, the unprecedented does not imply the promise of acting in favour of the realization of an unrealizable future but calls for action in order to avoid a very much realizable and threatening future. Unlike the sudden and uncontrollable character of unprecedented change, the promise of emancipation as nothing more than a promise is either one that no one believes in because of its known unrealizablity that results in no change, or one that cannot but invoke the familiar and controlled temporality of a processual change.

The unprecedented and the crisis of the political

Does this mean that the entire political domain must fall outside the scope of the unprecedented? Is the political domain necessarily conditioned by a processual historical sensibility? No, I don't think so. Rather, the case is that the political as we know it is still mostly under the spell of the modern historical condition, and the kind of change that corresponds to it is that of emancipation as gradual empowerment. This is not how things necessarily need to be, but this is how they seem to be for now.

To elaborate on this claim let me invoke Jürgen Osterhammel, who recently described the nineteenth century – very correctly and perceptively I think – as 'a century of emancipation' (2014: 915–18). For in the first place the political domain became emancipatory only at the time when a processual and developmental historical sensibility enabled change for the better in human affairs. Emancipatory concerns could emerge when the possibility of the future betterment of the overall human condition over the course of human affairs (conceptualized as history) had already been postulated. The nineteenth century can reasonably be called 'a century of emancipation' precisely because philosophies of history – and practically every kind of endeavour relying on philosophies of history (from utopian socialists to Comte's positivism) – had already conceptualized the possibility of change over time in human affairs as history.

Under a historical condition of this kind, the function of the political domain in the modern period has been to oversee, supervise and steer this overall form of human betterment, including the innovations of the technological domain. The ability of supervising and steering overall change derived from the fact that change in other domains of human life and endeavours was perceived along the same processual and developmental temporality as political change. Throughout Western modernity, change in the scientific and technological domains was typically seen as a cumulative process, while the paradigmatic scenario for change in the ecological and biological domains was captured by the processual temporality of evolutionary thought. Having been apprehended this way, all these domains of human life and endeavours belonged to the same temporal order and were thus prone to being steered and managed by the political domain, to being appropriated and called into the service of political change.

Today, these domains no longer seem to belong to the same temporal order. In light of the earlier discussions of the relevant chapters, the situation is as follows: whereas the political domain is either deprived of a vision of change (presentism, end of ideology, end of utopia, end of history) or still relies on a processual historical sensibility in configuring change over time (emancipatory politics), change in the technological and ecological domains is being increasingly perceived as unprecedented, thereby invoking an eventful historical sensibility.

Since Western science and technology began to start natural processes on its own (cf. Arendt 1961: 60), since such human-induced changes in the technological and ecological domains began to appear as threats of a loss of human control over them, and since they began to appear as the prospect of the unprecedented, the link between these domains and the political has been loosened. Whereas the political domain struggles to uphold a feasible and credible promise of the future and/or to grant political change, whereas even political theories of the Left grapple with and take great pains to at least theorize the possibility of such political change (for instance, Laclau and Mouffe 1985; Derrida 1994; Rancière 1999; Badiou 2012; Honneth 2016), the technological and ecological domains uphold a vision of the future and a scenario for change that seem increasingly irreconcilable with the political. I believe that all of this attests to a crisis of the political domain today, by which I mean the increasing inability of the political domain to act as a reliable and competent manager of change over time in various domains and to appropriate them in service of political change.

Yet most of the abovementioned theories and philosophies of political change are still based on the premise that the political domain is the sole proper arbitrator and manager of all kinds of change that concern human life. True enough, this unquestioned assumption is not limited to theories that come from the political Left. Consider the case of Fukuyama, against whose 'end of history' thesis Derrida offered the emancipatory promise and whose book Derrida not very elegantly reproved for its supposed 'distressing primitivity' (1994: 87). To Fukuyama's credit, he has long since recognized that today's political domain has difficulties with shepherding technology and the changes technology envisions to bring about. In his book on biotechnology, Fukuyama (2002) does not only concede that there can be no end of history until science and technology promises spectacular changes but also tries to respond to the challenge all this poses to the political domain. However, Fukuyama's response sounds very familiar. It is an argument for the necessity of introducing – or rather re-establishing – political control over technology, because according to Fukuyama 'it will be the political decisions that we make in the next few years concerning our relationship to this technology that determine whether we enter into a posthuman future' (17).

With the retained emphasis on the political domain as the supervisor and governor of change in different domains of human life and human endeavours, Fukuyama, just as his colleagues of other political inclinations, seems to sidestep the problem. For if the problem is the crisis of the political itself, then advocating even more control from the political over other domains of human life and human endeavours may not be a solution. Perhaps it only deepens the problem by leaving it unrecognized.

I think the greatest merit of Hartmut Rosa's theory of social acceleration is the acknowledgement that there is a crisis of the political today. Picking up on a general theme in the work of Koselleck, Rosa (2013) considers acceleration – the acceleration of change – to be the defining feature of Western modernity. However, the focus of Rosa's theory lies not in modernity and acceleration itself, but in 'late modernity', when acceleration is no longer synchronous in all societal spheres. Simply put, what Rosa claims is that in the 'late-modern societies' of the Western world the acceleration of change in certain domains of human life and human endeavours has begun to diverge from others. Whereas technology, social change and the pace of everyday life still keep on accelerating, politics has already become a force of deceleration.

This desynchronization of the political and other domains is due to what Rosa calls 'the detemporalization of history', meaning that 'instead of being experienced as a directed, dynamic process that can be politically accelerated (or decelerated), history once again takes on the form of an almost "static" space of juxtaposed and successively unfolding histories' (2013: 270). The detemporalization Rosa talks about is nothing other than the overwhelming postwar skepticism toward the idea of a directional and unitary historical process. As I argued earlier, the political domain largely depends on this idea, as without such processual history the possibility of political change is compromised. Inasmuch as the possibility of political change is compromised, the political domain can no longer function as a manager of change, while other domains – in Rosa's view – keep on accelerating. As a result, all this leads Rosa to claim that 'the role of politics as a social pacesetter that was undisputed in classical modernity has been lost because the intrinsic temporality of the political is largely resistant to or incapable of acceleration' (262).

Despite its many merits with regard to the recognition of the crisis of the political domain, I believe that to a crucial extent the theory of social acceleration (which is far richer in details and insights than I can discuss here) misunderstands the situation. This misunderstanding seems to be due to the inadequacy of Rosa's core concept: acceleration. Although Rosa is right that the crisis of the political has certainly much to do with questions of temporality, the framework of acceleration seems largely misleading in that it attempts to comprehend the situation as a problem *internal* to a processual historical sensibility and a processual temporality associated with Western modernity. Probably the most telling indicator of this is Rosa's choice of words in the above quote. Calling the political domain a 'social pacesetter' implies that in Rosa's view what is at stake is merely the *tempo* and the *pace* of processes and not processual temporality as such. Accordingly, the crisis of the political domain must appear to Rosa as a loss of the ability of the political to set and appropriate the tempo of other processes to its own tempo. This either means that the pace of the political is completely lost and hence the domain is destined to come to a standstill (in a worst-case scenario), or that it is moving at a much slower pace (in a best-case scenario). But, in either case, in Rosa's theory the political domain changed due to the 'detemporalization of history' and not because the perceived temporality of other domains changed, as my argument suggests otherwise.

When Rosa's theory of social acceleration conceptualizes the crisis of the political as a problem that is internal to a processual historical sensibility, it suggests that the crisis lies in the divergence *of degrees of change*. But if I am right, and if the crisis of the political is rather the result of a change in the perception of the temporal configuration of change in domains other than the political, and if the new configuration poses an *external* challenge to the entire processual historical sensibility, then the crisis lies in the divergence *of kinds of change*. In my view, the changes envisioned in the technological and ecological domains are no longer perceived as future outcomes of processes that merely keep on accelerating in one tempo and pace or another. They are perceived as unprecedented changes that the political domain cannot appropriate because it is still engaged in restoring faith in a processual temporality (toward which the political domain itself is largely sceptical).

The future of the political

All this means that the crisis of the political in the Western world cuts much deeper than is commonly thought. Political theories of the Left cannot remedy it by reconciling their skepticism towards a processual historical sensibility with their commitment to emancipation; Fukuyama's assumption that the political can still re-establish control over a runaway technological domain seems more of the problem than a solution; and even Rosa's sociological theory of desynchronized acceleration struggles with adequately comprehending the situation. But if this is the case and if I am right in attributing such prominence to the challenge posed by the perceived unprecedented, does all this entail that the political domain is irremediably doomed? Does all this entail that Western societies are, in principle, incapable of conceiving change over time in the political domain as unprecedented? And does all of this entail, first of all, that the political must be in sync with the way change is conceived in other domains of human life and human endeavours?

Barring a dubious engagement in divination, I cannot give precise answers to these questions. Nor is the theory presented here of much help in this respect. Since my purpose is not to devise a normative theory about how things should be but to gain a theoretical-conceptual understanding of what the situation already is, the kind of prediction one would expect from a scientific theory does not apply here either. The most I can reasonably say concerns the sheer possibility of certain scenarios about the future of the political domain in its relation to domains of the unprecedented (in a similar way to Rosa's considerations of the possibilities that can be conceived within the framework of his theory).

I would like to begin with the scenario that political theories of any particular ideological inclination hardly wish to entertain: in principle, nothing excludes the possibility of the outright collapse of the political domain as we know it. The political domain may ultimately fail to bring about change over time in human affairs, meaning that it fails to fulfil what has been its function throughout Western modernity. If anything such as this happens, then the configuration of change over time in the technological and ecological domains and their prospect of the unprecedented might easily become considered as viable alternatives to the political domain as a whole. It most certainly would be a leap into the completely unknown and into the – by definition – unknowable. But if the political domain fails and if people still want, for whatever reason, change in the course of human affairs (or change as the replacement of human affairs with the posthuman, non-human or no-longer-human affairs), then the technological domain in particular – as the one that seems able to deliver such change and as the one that aggressively promotes itself regarding this ability – might be unleashed on its own, without any kind of control from the political domain. Of course, this does not exclude the possibility of other forms of control; it means only the end of a specifically political supervision.

At the same time, and again in principle, nothing excludes the second possibility that the political survives with a renewed investment in emancipation, and, consequentially, in a processual and developmental historical sensibility. However, for it to do so the political domain does not need to reconcile a commitment to emancipation, on the one hand, and a deep skepticism about the idea of a historical process, on the other. Rather, the survival of the political as we know it would mean the necessity to come to terms with the idea of a historical process in a pragmatic way; not as a process objectively lying out there, but as a pragmatic conceptual tool in our own hands, of which we make use in order to enable the possibility of an actual achievement of our emancipatory desires (that is, not only as a self-deceptive commitment to an unrealizable task that lacks a motivation for action).

In this second scenario, processual political change would still not be synchronous with change in other domains of human life and human endeavours that already are conceived of as having an eventual character in the shape of the unprecedented. In case of such non-synchronicity, the processual temporality of the political may serve as a means of balancing the very probable social wrongdoings and inequalities resulting from leaping into the unknown in other domains. The most illustrative example may be the prospect of social wrongdoings and inequalities between enhanced and non-enhanced humans, or between posthuman and human beings, likely to be brought about by technology. Or, alternatively, the political would not balance other domains, and all domains could just co-exist either peacefully or in a more conflictive manner. But these considerations already belong to the divinatory realm. What seems to be reasonably conceivable is only that, in any version of the survival of the political as an emancipatory force, skepticism toward the modern processual historical sensibility must be overcome and must be come to terms with as a pragmatic conceptual tool.

Finally, and still in principle, nothing excludes the possibility that the political finds a way to synchronize its configuration of change with the unprecedented of the technological and ecological domains. Nothing excludes the possibility that conceiving of political change suddenly shifts from emancipation to something like a prospect of the unprecedented. Many political theories of the Left are indeed going in this direction. As mentioned in Chapter 3, when it comes to theories and philosophies of political change, Alain Badiou's notion of the event is probably the closest to what I call unprecedented change. The central shared feature of the unprecedented and the political change Badiou conceptualizes is that both are about the birth of a previously inexistent subject. At the same time, however, the differences and conflicting elements are nonetheless sharp. Whereas the unprecedented and the subject it brings about is envisioned as a game-changer event, in Badiou's theory the new-born subject is supposed to acknowledge the event as an event only inasmuch as it already took place, by showing a post-eventual fidelity toward it. Furthermore, Badiou's event is not merely a desired political occurrence. Besides the sphere of politics, it is equally present in love, art and science (Badiou 2001: 27–8). On the other hand, this may precisely be the reason why Badiou's event is the closest to my notion of unprecedented change: because both unprecedented change and Badiou's event intend to account for a general structure of the occurrence of novelty in various (although not all) domains of human life and human endeavours.

Focusing on the question of the political, however, is focusing on the domain in which both the shortcomings of Badiou's understanding of political change and the difference between such change and the unprecedented become the clearest. First of all, Badiou's event shares certain features with Derrida's emancipatory promise, discussed earlier. The most crucial of such features is that Badiou's event in the political domain is a desired change, and in that respect it has not much to do with the inherently threatening prospect of the unprecedented. Accordingly, instead of considering action to be preventive in order to avoid the worst possible future, Badiou emphasizes the possibility of acting *for* the desired change, thereby invoking another distinctive feature of the modern processual historical sensibility. Yet the political event itself as conceptualized by Badiou seems to defy processual temporality in that political action – following an act of pledging a post-evental fidelity to the event itself in which a new subject is born – only comes in after political change (as the taking place of the event) is already conceived of as being in effect despite the need to be further facilitated.

It seems to me that Badiou's theory consists of a mixture of elements of processual and evental sensibilities. The conflation of incompatible kinds of change exposes Badiou's otherwise promising theory to a risk of inconsistency, which becomes the most apparent in the specifics of Badiou's desired political change. In a relatively recent book entitled *The Rebirth of History* (2012), the political events of the twenty-first century (political events in the everyday sense of the word), particularly the riots and revolts in Arab countries, make Badiou consider the idea that what is going on in the world today is – as the title of his book already indicates – the rebirth of 'History'. The sheer fact of capitalizing History throughout the pages of the book is already an indication of what notion of 'history' Badiou is indebted to. For what is being reborn with the rebirth of 'History' is, along the lines of Badiou's very well-known political inclination, supposed to be the 'Idea' that is 'Communism' (2012: 6).

This ideological inheritance is responsible for probably the biggest inconsistency of Badiou's endeavour. Communism, plainly put, can under no circumstances qualify as an event, not even in Badiou's own definition. The reason for this is that if you already know before the event what the event is supposed to bring about then it is anything but an event. For the event (and the subject that the event brings about) is that which does not emerge out of pre-existing structures but defies them. Or, to let Badiou speak for his own position, 'an event is signaled by the fact that an inexistent is going to attain genuine existence' (68). The event, defined this way, simply cannot be associated with the realization (or even with the rebirth) of an inherited and long-existing pattern of thought in Western culture, such as communism. Even if the 'inexistent' in Badiou's definition is a group of human beings and not ideas, their coming-to-existence as an event cannot be associated with the coming-to-existence of the already very much 'existent' communism.

It is of course possible to align with classical philosophies of history and claim that the actions of people bring about something higher than what these people themselves are aware of. A Hegelian 'cunning of reason' by which people's passions and irrational actions bring about the realization of Reason is the most famous of such schemes. Hypothetically, Badiou's birth of the 'inexistent' may be interpreted alike, as the event that brings about the Idea of Communism even without those who come to existence knowing it or caring about it in the slightest. But in this scheme, just as in classical philosophies of history, only the fulfilment of the higher purpose should matter. What matters then is anything but the event itself in which the previously inexistent come to exist; and what matters is anything but the inexistent born in the event. What matters is the Idea of Communism, which manifests itself through the birth of previously inexistent people.

Indeed, this would rather obviously entail a straightforward revival of History in its well-known form of a substantive philosophy of history. But again, there is no way in which such a substantive philosophy of history could be consistent with the theoretical notion of the event. Yet Badiou attempts to bring them together, with his efforts climaxing in the phrase: 'emancipatory event' (2012: 77). In light of the above considerations, this phrase cannot be anything other than a contradiction in terms. The event that suddenly brings about a new-born subject cannot be an improvement on the past condition of the very same subject (which must be perceived as being in an unemancipated condition), because this subject simply did not exist prior to the event. Or, conversely, if the subject is perceived as an emancipated subject, then it must have been in existence already prior to the supposed event and must have been recognized as being in a condition that calls for its future empowerment. Succinctly put, emancipation presupposes a subject that goes through a process of empowerment, which is irreconcilable with the notion of the event as the birth of a previously inexistent subject, since a subject of this kind has no prior condition of being not-yet-empowered.

All in all, Badiou's case, together with the earlier discussed efforts of the Left to reconcile emancipation and a deep skepticism toward processual history, demonstrate the difficulties and intricacies involved in the third scenario concerning the fate of the political: its synchronization with domains of the unprecedented. Such synchronization is possible only insofar as the political domain drops emancipatory concerns that still bind it to a processual temporality. Without taking sides in the question of the desirability of making such a tough call – and without even trying to predict the odds – the only thing I would like to point out is *the irreconcilability of concerns for emancipation and the unprecedented*.

Whichever way things actually play out, one thing seems to be certain: an evental historical sensibility already pervades Western societies. Even if it does not permeate all domains of human life and human endeavours, it co-exists with the processual historical sensibility that still informs emancipatory concerns. Whereas Western modernity and its historical sensibility have at least two centuries of attempts at self-understanding, unprecedented change and its evental historical sensibility are yet to come to terms with it. In doing so, the probably most troubling question to ask – and also the final question that this book attempts to settle – is whether the evental can reasonably be interpreted as historical in the first place.

Is this still history?

Throughout this book, I have constantly referred to a challenge posed to our modern historical sensibility by another sensibility that is still 'historical'. But if it really is a *challenge* that threatens to displace the modern historical sensibility, then it could equally seem plausible to interpret the new sensibility as something other than 'historical'. Besides, if what is at stake is the fate of our modern historical sensibility, and if that which threatens this modern sensibility appears not simply as its successor but also as an *alternative* to it, then it may seem plausible to claim that what I present here is actually a certain 'end of history' theory. Not one of course that would resemble the 'end of history' of Fukuyama (1992) as the final fulfilment of a process, nor one that could be linked to postmodern 'end of history' versions that put an end to the idea of history as movement (Vattimo 1987; Jenkins 1999: 1–24; Baudrillard 2000: 31–57). Instead, 'the end of history' that this book may be thought to present would be that of the end of a certain configuration of change over time in human affairs. This end would be brought about by the increasing operationality of a sensibility to conceive of ourselves and the world in terms of a new kind of change and hence a new kind of movement.

The possible interpretation of this book as an 'end of history' theory would emphasize that – unlike Fukuyama's version and unlike postmodern 'end of history' theories – history does not simply end by leaving behind a vacuum in the place where history once was. Rather, the 'end of history' this book would present puts an end to history because something other than 'history' replaces it. Against this 'end of history' interpretation, the reason why we should see the new sensibility as still being 'historical' is that the new alternative, just as our modern notion of history, still configures change over time in *the mundane world of human (and now also posthuman) affairs*. As I argued earlier, the most innovative moment in our modern history was precisely this aspect. The modern idea of history conceptualized and thereby enabled such change against the backdrop of premodern Christian thought, which reserved the prospect of change in the human condition for the promise of gaining an entry into a world other than the human world. Consequently, insofar as a sensibility concerns change over time as a matter of the mundane world of human (or now also posthuman) affairs, it seems reasonable to keep labelling it as 'historical', even if the particular configuration of change – the type and character of change – is itself prone to change.

This seems to be a fairly good reason. But however good this reason is, it is pretty much the *only* reason in favour of such an interpretation. Furthermore, even though I am not arguing for a complete replacement of the modern processual historical sensibility by an evental one in all domains of human endeavour, it can be pointed out that by calling the emerging evental sensibility 'historical' I rely on an interpretation of change over time as processual. It may be pointed out that, inasmuch as the very notion of historical sensibility appears as a subject with a retained self-identity that goes through change, I rely on a conventional processual-developmental scenario of change over time. What's more, by pointing this out, it may even be argued that, if I do not configure the birth of an evental configuration of change over time as itself being evental, I tacitly concede that 'historical' change cannot be other than processual as developmental. And if even the birth of the evental cannot be made sense of in any other than a processual and developmental way, it would seem plausible to claim that being 'historical' simply cannot have the characteristics of the evental. In this interpretation, history is by definition processual and whatever is not processual must be something other than history.

There are then good arguments in favour of both interpretations. In fact, I think that the theory presented in this book allows both. As I see the endeavour of this book, I most certainly do not recount a developmental narrative of the subject called 'historical sensibility'. I most certainly do not talk about a shift *from* a modern processual historical sensibility *to* an evental one either. Like any other 'from-to' configurations of change, that definitely would imply a developmental process. Much in line with all these considerations, by 'historical sensibility' I most certainly do not mean an identifiable subject that *goes through* stages of a historical trajectory. What I mean is, in fact, the coming about of an entirely new subject that appears *not as a continuation* of the modern historical sensibility *but as an alternative* to it, this point being probably the strongest one among those that allow for an interpretation in which the evental sensibility appears as other than historical.

Yet, for the sole but eminently strong reason mentioned above, it makes sense to me to insist on the point that what we witness in certain domains of human life and human endeavours is the birth of a sensibility that still can be called 'historical'. This emphasis is the result of the highly pragmatic consideration that meeting the general aim of providing an understanding of the challenge posed by the birth of an evental configuration of change over time to the modern Western historical sensibility is best achieved by retaining, at least to some extent, the already available components of the conceptual toolkit we are already familiar with. For the completely unfamiliar – the unprecedented and the evental – defies understanding. Accordingly, *at least for the time being*, it just seems more beneficial and appropriate to consider the birth of an evental sensibility to be 'historical'.

But this may not remain the case necessarily. The more we become familiar with a novel sense of novelty and change over time, and the more elements of a new set of conceptual tools are already forged, the easier it may be to interpret the evental sensibility as something other than 'historical'. But, again, this is not necessarily the case either. As Chapter 3 argued, neither change itself nor types of change reside in the phenomena you wish to make sense of. Things change inasmuch as you conceive of them as changing, inasmuch as you – either deliberately or (mostly) subconsciously – invoke a conceptualization of change over time in your effort to make sense of the world.

History, the modern historical sensibility, has been devised as the most refined conceptual tool to put to use in such situations. For almost two centuries, this historical sensibility has been associated with a very particular type of change over time, one that is processual and developmental. For almost two centuries, making sense of the world of human affairs has been carried out through the lens of this modern historical sensibility. If certain domains of life and endeavours (that are constitutive parts of the world of human affairs) have already been made sense of today through another lens that conceives of change as unprecedented, it is our call to decide what kind of phenomena we want to see through which lens. It is our call to decide through which lens we conceive of even the very changes that concern the ways we think about change as 'historical'. It is our call to decide whether we make sense of the birth of unprecedented change and the evental sensibility as themselves evental and unprecedented. Consequently, it is also our call to decide whether the evental and the unprecedented qualify as historical, or whether we try to conceive of it as a sensibility other than this. We decide. You decide!

Bibliography

Adler, Hans, ed. (2002), *Aesthetics and Aisthesis: New Perspectives and (Re)Discoveries*, Bern: Peter Lang.
Agamben, Giorgio (1993), *Infancy and History: The Destruction of Experience*, London: Verso.
Agar, Nicholas (2010), *Humanity's End: Why We Should Reject Radical Enhancement*, Cambridge, MA: MIT Press.
Ahlskog, Jonas (2016), 'Michael Oakeshott and Hayden White on the Practical and the Historical Past', *Rethinking History*, 20 (3): 375–94.
Allison, Graham and Niall Ferguson (2016), 'Why the U.S. President Needs a Council of Historians', *The Atlantic*, September. Available online: https://www.theatlantic.com/magazine/archive/2016/09/dont-know-much-about-history/492746/ (accessed 27 December 2018).
Andersson, Jenny and Eglė Rindzevičiūtė, eds (2015), *The Struggle for the Long-Term in Transnational Science and Politics*, London: Routledge.
Ankersmit, Frank R. (1983), *Narrative Logic: A Semantic Analysis of the Historian's Language*, The Hague: Martinus Nijhoff.
Ankersmit, Frank R. (2001), *Historical Representation*, Stanford, CA: Stanford University Press.
Ankersmit, Frank (2005), *Sublime Historical Experience*, Stanford, CA: Stanford University Press.
Ankersmit, Frank (2007), 'Manifesto for an Analytical Political History', in Keith Jenkins, Sue Morgan and Alun Munslow (eds), *Manifestos for History*, 179–96, London: Routledge.
Appleby, Joyce, Lynn Hunt and Margaret Jacob (1994), *Telling the Truth about History*, New York: W. W. Norton & Company.
Arendt, Hannah (1958), *The Human Condition*, Chicago: University of Chicago Press.
Arendt, Hannah (1961), *Between Past and Future: Six Exercises in Political Thought*, New York: The Viking Press.
Aron, Raymond ([1938] 1961), *Introduction to the Philosophy of History: An Essay on the Limits of Historical Objectivity*, trans. George J. Irwin, Boston, MA: Beacon Press.
Assmann, Aleida (2013), *Ist die Zeit aus den Fugen? Aufstieg und Fall des Zeitregimes der Moderne*, Munich: Hanser.
Bacon, Francis ([1627] 1996), 'New Atlantis', in Brian Vickers (ed.), *Francis Bacon: The Major Works*, 457–90, Oxford: Oxford University Press.
Badiou, Alain (2001), *Ethics: An Essay on the Understanding of Evil*, trans. Peter Hallward, London: Verso.
Badiou, Alain (2003), *Saint Paul: The Foundation of Universalism*, trans. Ray Brassier, Stanford, CA: Stanford University Press.
Badiou, Alain (2005), *Being and Event*, trans. Oliver Feltham, London: Continuum.
Badiou, Alain (2012), *The Rebirth of History: Times of Riots and Uprisings*, trans. Gregory Elliott, London: Verso.

Bartkowski, Frances (1989), *Feminist Utopias*, Lincoln: University of Nebraska Press.
Baudrillard, Jean (1994), *The Illusion of the End*, trans. Chris Turner, Cambridge: Polity Press.
Baudrillard, Jean (2000), *The Vital Illusion*, New York: Columbia University Press.
Bell, Daniel (1960), *The End of Ideology: On the Exhaustion of Political Ideas in the Fifties*, New York: Free Press.
Berkhofer, Robert F. Jr. (1995), *Beyond the Great Story: History as Text and Discourse*, Cambridge, MA: Harvard University Press.
Bevernage, Berber (2012), *History, Memory, and State-Sponsored Violence: Time and Justice*, London: Routledge.
Bevernage, Berber (2015), 'The Past is Evil/Evil is Past: On Retrospective Politics, Philosophy of History, and Temporal Manichaeism', *History and Theory*, 54 (3): 333–52.
Bloch, Ernst ([1954–1959] 1986), *The Principle of Hope*, 3 vols., trans. Neville Plaice, Stephen Plaice and Paul Knight, Cambridge, MA: MIT Press.
Blumenberg, Hans (1983), *The Legitimacy of the Modern Age*, Cambridge, MA: MIT Press.
Bonneuil, Christophe and Jean-Baptiste Fressoz (2016), *The Shock of the Anthropocene: The Earth, History and Us*, trans. David Fernbach, London: Verso.
Booker, M. Keith (1994), *The Dystopian Impulse in Modern Literature: Fiction as Social Criticism*, Westport, CT: Greenwood Press.
Bostrom, Nick (2003), *The Transhumanist FAQ: A General Introduction*, World Transhumanist Association. Available online: http://www.nickbostrom.com/views/transhumanist.pdf (accessed 27 December 2018).
Bostrom, Nick (2005), 'A History of Transhumanist Thought', *Journal of Evolution and Technology*, 14 (1): 1–25.
Bostrom, Nick (2008a), 'Letter from Utopia', *Studies in Ethics, Law, and Technology*, 2 (1): 1–7.
Bostrom, Nick (2008b), 'Why I Want to be a Posthuman when I Grow Up', in Bert Gordijn and Ruth Chadwick (eds), *Medical Enhancement and Posthumanity*, 107–36, Dordrecht: Springer.
Bostrom, Nick (2013), 'Existential Risk Prevention as Global Priority', *Global Policy*, 4 (1): 15–31.
Bostrom, Nick (2014), *Superintelligence: Paths, Dangers, Strategies*, Oxford: Oxford University Press.
Brady, Emily (2013), *The Sublime in Modern Philosophy: Aesthetics, Ethics, and Nature*, Cambridge: Cambridge University Press.
Braidotti, Rosi (2013a), 'Posthuman Humanities', *European Educational Research Journal*, 12 (1): 1–19.
Braidotti, Rosi (2013b), *The Posthuman*, Cambridge: Polity Press.
Breisach, Ernst (2003), *On the Future of History: The Postmodernist Challenge and its Aftermath*, Chicago: University of Chicago Press.
Brewer, John (2010), 'Microhistory and the Histories of Everyday Life', *Cultural and Social History*, 7 (1): 87–109.
Bryant, Levi, Nick Srnicek and Graham Harman, eds (2011), *The Speculative Turn: Continental Materialism and Realism*, Melbourne: re.press.
Brzechczyn, Krzysztof, ed. (2018), *Towards a Revival of Analytical Philosophy of History: Around Paul A. Roth's Vision of Historical Sciences*, Leiden: Brill.
Burdett, Michael S. (2015), *Eschatology and the Technological Future*, London: Routledge.

Butler, Judith (1993), 'Poststructuralism and Postmarxism', *Diacritics*, 23 (4): 3–11.
Cabrera, Laura Y. (2015), *Rethinking Human Enhancement: Social Enhancement and Emergent Technologies*, Basingstoke: Palgrave.
Campanella, Tommaso ([1602] 1981), *The City of the Sun: A Poetical Dialogue*, trans. Daniel J. Donno, Berkeley: University of California Press.
Carr, David (1986a), *Time, Narrative and History*, Bloomington: Indiana University Press.
Carr, David (1986b), 'Narrative and the Real World: An Argument for Continuity', *History and Theory*, 25 (2): 117–31.
Carr, David (2014), *Experience and History: Phenomenological Perspectives on the Historical World*, Oxford: Oxford University Press.
Cerutti, Simona (2004), 'Microhistory: Social Relations versus Cultural Models?' in Anna-Maija Castrén, Markku Lonkila and Matti Peltonen (eds), *Between Sociology and History: Essays on Microhistory, Collective Action, and Nation Building*, 17–40, Helsinki: SKS/Finnish Literature Society.
Chakrabarty, Dipesh (2009), 'The Climate of History: Four Theses', *Critical Inquiry*, 35 (2): 197–222.
Chakrabarty, Dipesh (2014), 'Climate and Capital: On Conjoined Histories', *Critical Inquiry*, 41 (1): 1–23.
Chakrabarty, Dipesh (2015), *The Human Condition in the Anthropocene*. The Tanner Lectures in Human Values. Delivered at Yale University, 18–19 February 2015. Available online: https://tannerlectures.utah.edu/Chakrabarty%20manuscript.pdf (accessed 27 December 2018).
Chakrabarty, Dipesh (2016), 'Humanities in the Anthropocene: The Crisis of an Enduring Kantian Fable', *New Literary History*, 47 (2–3): 377–97.
Chakrabarty, Dipesh (2018), 'Anthropocene Time', *History and Theory*, 57 (1): 5–32.
Chalmers, David J. (2010), 'The Singularity: A Philosophical Analysis', *Journal of Consciousness Studies*, 17 (9–10): 7–65.
Christian, David (2010), 'The Return of Universal History', *History and Theory*, 49 (4): 6–27.
Claeys, Gergory, ed. (2010), *The Cambridge Companion on Utopian Literature*, Cambridge: Cambridge University Press.
Clarke, Steve, Julian Savulescu, Tony Coady, Alberto Giubilini and Sagar Sanyal, eds (2016), *The Ethics of Human Enhancement: Understanding the Debate*, Oxford: Oxford University Press.
Coeckelbergh, Mark (2013), *Human Being @ Risk: Enhancement, Technology, and the Evaluation of Vulnerability Transformations*, Dordrecht: Springer.
Cohen, Tom and Claire Colebrook (2017), 'Vortices: On "Critical Climate Change" as a Project', *South Atlantic Quarterly*, 116 (1): 129–43.
Collingwood, R. G. ([1946] 1993), *The Idea of History: Revised Edition, with Lectures 1926-1928*, Oxford: Oxford University Press.
Comte, August (1896), *The Positive Philosophy of August Comte*, vol. 1, trans. Harriet Martineau, London: George Bell & Sons.
Condorcet, Marquis de (1796), *Outlines of an Historical View of the Progress of the Human Mind*, Philadelphia, PA: Lang and Ustick.
Cornell, Drucilla (1992), *The Philosophy of the Limit*, London: Routledge.
Costelloe, Timothy M. (2012), *The Sublime: From Antiquity to the Present*, Cambridge: Cambridge University Press.
Critchley, Simon (2007), *Infinitely Demanding: Ethics of Commitment, Politics of Resistance*, London: Verso.

Crutzen, Paul J. (2002), 'Geology of Mankind', *Nature*, 415: 23.
Danto, Arthur C. ([1965] 1985), *Narration and Knowledge: Including the Integral Text of Analytical Philosophy of History*, New York: Columbia University Press.
Danto, Arthur (1995), 'The Decline and Fall of the Analytical Philosophy of History', in Frank Ankersmit and Hans Kellner (eds), *A New Philosophy of History*, 70–85, London: Reaktion Books.
Darnton, Robert (1999), *The Great Cat Massacre and Other Episodes in French Cultural History*, New York: Basic Books.
Davidson, Donald (2005), *Truth, Language, and History*, Oxford: Clarendon Press.
Derrida, Jacques (1994), *Specters of Marx: The State of the Debt, the Work of Mourning and the New International*, trans. Peggy Kamuf, New York: Routledge.
Díaz-Maldonado, Rodrigo (2016), 'Historical Experience as a Mode of Comprehension', *Journal of the Philosophy of History*, published online ahead of print, 12 December 2016. doi: 10.1163/18722636-12341352.
Didi-Hubermann, Georges (2003), 'Artistic Survival: Panofsky vs. Warburg and the Exorcism of Impure Time', trans. Vivian Rehberg and Boris Belay, *Common Knowledge*, 9 (2): 273–85.
Domanska, Ewa (2009), 'Frank Ankersmit: From Narrative to Experience', *Rethinking History*, 13 (2): 175–95.
Domanska, Ewa (2010), 'Beyond Anthropocentrism in Historical Studies', *Historein*, 10: 118–30.
Domanska, Ewa (2015a), 'Hayden White and Liberation Historiography', *Rethinking History*, 19 (4): 640–50.
Domanska, Ewa (2015b), 'Ecological Humanities', *Teksty Drugie*, Special Issue: English Edition (7): 186–210.
Doran, Robert (2015), *The Theory of the Sublime from Longinus to Kant*, Cambridge: Cambridge University Press.
Epple, Angelika (2012), 'Globale Mikrogeschichte: Auf dem Weg zu einer Geschichte der Relationen', in Ewald Hiebl and Ernst Langthaler (eds), *Jahrbuch für Geschichte des ländlichen Raumes/Themenheft: Im Kleinen das Große suchen: Mikrogeschichte in Theorie und Praxis*, 37–47, Innsbruck: Studien Verlag.
Ermarth, Elizabeth Deeds (2011), *History in the Discursive Condition: Reconsidering the Tools of Thought*, London: Routledge.
Evans, Richard (1997), *In Defence of History*, London: Granta.
Ferns, Chris (1999), *Narrating Utopia: Ideology, Gender, Form in Utopian Literature*, Liverpool: Liverpool University Press.
Fillafer, Franz L. (2017), 'A World Connecting? From the Unity of History to Global History', *History and Theory*, 56 (1): 3–37.
Fludernik, Monika (1996), *Towards a 'Natural' Narratology*, London: Routledge.
Fludernik, Monika (2010), 'Experience, Experientiality, and Historical Narrative: A View from Narratology', in Thiemo Breyer and Daniel Creutz (eds), *Erfahrung und Geschichte: Historische Sinnbildung im Pränarrativen*, 40–72, Berlin: de Gruyter.
Foucault, Michel (1984), 'Nietzsche, Genealogy, History', trans. Donald F. Bouchard and Sherry Simon, in Paul Rabinow (ed.), *The Foucault Reader*, 76–100, New York: Pantheon Books.
Foucault, Michel (2002), *The Order of Things: An Archaeology of the Human Sciences*, London: Routledge.
Froeyman, Anton (2015), *History, Ethics, and the Recognition of the Other: A Levinasian View on the Writing of History*, London: Routledge.

Fukuyama, Francis (1992), *The End of History and the Last Man*, New York: The Free Press.
Fukuyama, Francis (2002), *Our Posthuman Future: Consequences of the Biotechnology Revolution*, New York: Farrar, Straus and Giroux.
Fuller, Steve and Veronika Lipinska (2014), *The Proactinary Imperative: A Foundation for Transhumanism*, Basingstoke: Palgrave.
Fussell, Paul (1975), *The Great War and Modern Memory*, New York: Oxford University Press.
Gadamer, Hans-Georg (2004), *Truth and Method*, trans. Joel Weinsheimer and Donald G. Marshall, London: Continuum.
Ghosh, Ranjan and Ethan Kleinberg, eds (2013), *Presence: Philosophy, History, and Cultural Theory for the Twenty-First Century*, Ithaca, NY: Cornell University Press.
Ginzburg, Carlo (1980), *The Cheese and the Worms: The Cosmos of a Sixteenth-Century Miller*, trans. John Tedeschi and Anne Tedeschi, Baltimore: Johns Hopkins University Press.
Ginzburg, Carlo (1992), 'Just One Witness', in Saul Friedlander (ed.), *Probing the Limits of Representation: Nazism and the Final Solution*, 82–96, Cambridge, MA: Harvard University Press.
Ginzburg, Carlo and Carlo Poni (1991), 'The Name and the Game: Unequal Exchange and the Historiographic Marketplace', in Edward Muir and Guido Ruggiero (eds), *Microhistory and the Lost People of Europe*, 1–10, Baltimore: Johns Hopkins University Press.
Goodman, Nelson (1978), *Ways of Worldmaking*, Indianapolis, IN: Hackett.
Gordijn, Bert and Ruth Chadwick, eds (2008), *Medical Enhancement and Posthumanity*, Dordrecht: Springer.
Gordin, Michael D., Helen Tilley and Gyan Prakash, eds (2010), *Utopia/Dystopia: Conditions of Historical Possibility*, Princeton, NJ: Princeton University Press.
Graham, Elaine (2016), 'Manifestations of the Posthuman in the Postsecular Imagination', in J. Benjamin Hurlbut and Hava Tirosh-Samuelson (eds), *Perfecting Human Futures: Transhuman Visions and Technological Imaginations*, 51–72, Wiesbaden: Springer VS.
Grave, Johannes (2011), 'Das Erhabene', in *Metzler Lexikon Kunstwissenschaft. Ideen, Methoden, Begriffe*, 111–17, Stuttgart: Metzler.
Grave, Johannes (2019), 'Pictorial Temporality and the Times of History: On Seeing Images and Experiencing Time', in Marek Tamm and Laurent Olivier (eds), *Rethinking Historical Time: New Approaches to Presentism*, London: Bloomsbury.
Guldi, Jo and David Armitage (2014), *The History Manifesto*, Cambridge: Cambridge University Press.
Gumbrecht, Hans Ulrich (1997), *In 1926: At the Edge of Time*, Cambridge, MA: Harvard University Press.
Gumbrecht, Hans Ulrich (2004), *The Production of Presence: What Meaning Cannot Convey*, Stanford, CA: Stanford University Press.
Gumbrecht, Hans Ulrich (2006), 'Presence Achieved in Language (With Special Attention Given to the Presence of the Past)', *History and Theory*, 45 (3): 317–27.
Gumbrecht, Hans Ulrich (2014), *Our Broad Present: Time and Contemporary Culture*, New York: Columbia University Press.
Hacking, Ian (1999), *The Social Construction of What?*, Cambridge, MA: Harvard University Press.
Hamilton, Clive (2017), *Defiant Earth: The Fate of Humans in the Anthropocene*, London: Polity.

Haraway, Donna J. (2008), *When Species Meet*, Minneapolis: University of Minnesota Press.
Harlan, David (2009), '"The Burden of History" Forty Years Later', in Frank Ankersmit, Ewa Domanska and Hans Kellner (eds), *Re-Figuring Hayden White*, 169–89, Stanford, CA: Stanford University Press.
Harman, Graham (2013), 'The Current State of Speculative Realism', *Speculations*, 4: 22–8.
Hartog, François (2015), *Regimes of Historicity: Presentism and Experiences of Time*, trans. Saskia Brown, New York: Columbia University Press.
Hauskeller, Michael (2013), *Better Humans? Understanding the Enhancement Project*, Durham, NC: Acumen.
Hauskeller, Michael (2016), *Mythologies of Transhumanism*, Cham: Palgrave.
Hayles, N. Katherine (1999), *How We Became Posthuman: Virtual Bodies in Cybernetics, Literature, and Informatics*, Chicago: University of Chicago Press.
Hegel, Georg Wilhelm Friedrich ([1837] 1975), *Lectures on the Philosophy of World History*, trans. Hugh Barr Nisbet, Cambridge: Cambridge University Press.
Hesketh, Ian (2014), 'The Story of Big History', *History of the Present*, 4 (2): 171–202.
Hölscher, Lucian, ed. (2017), *Die Zukunft des 20. Jahrhunderts: Dimensionen Einer Historischen Zukunftsforschung*, Frankfurt: Campus.
Honneth, Axel (2016), *The Idea of Socialism: Towards a Renewal*, trans. Joseph Ganahl, Cambridge: Polity.
Horkheimer, Max and Theodor W. Adorno ([1944] 2002), *Dialectic of Enlightenment: Philosophical Fragments*, trans. Edmund Jephcott, Stanford, CA: Stanford University Press.
Hughes-Warrington, Marnie (2013), *Revisionist Histories*, London: Routledge.
Hurlbut, J. Benjamin and Hava Tirosh-Samuelson, eds (2016), *Perfecting Human Futures: Transhuman Visions and Technological Imaginations*, Wiesbaden: Springer.
Husserl, Edmund (1991), *On the Phenomenology of the Consciousness of Internal Time (1893–1917)*, trans. John Barnett Brough, Dordrecht: Kluwer.
Huxley, Julian ([1957] 1968), 'Transhumanism', *Journal of Humanistic Psychology*, 8 (1): 73–6.
Icke, Peter (2012), *Frank Ankersmit's Lost Historical Cause: A Journey from Language to Experience*, London: Routledge.
Imhof, Arthur E. (1996), *Lost Worlds: How Our European Ancestors Coped with Everyday Life and Why It Is So Hard Today*, trans. Thomas Robinsheaux, Charlottesville: University Press of Virginia.
Jameson, Frederic (2005), *Archaeologies of the Future: The Desire Called Utopia and Other Science Fictions*, London: Verso.
Jasanoff, Sheila (2016), 'Perfecting the Human: Posthuman Imaginaries and Technologies of Reason', in J. Benjamin Hurlbut and Hava Tirosh-Samuelson (eds), *Perfecting Human Futures: Transhuman Visions and Technological Imaginations*, 73–95, Wiesbaden: Springer.
Jenkins, Keith (1995), *On 'What is History?' From Carr and Elton to Rorty and White*, London: Routledge.
Jenkins, Keith (1999), *Why History? Ethics and Postmodernity*, London: Routledge.
Jenkins, Keith (2003), *Re-thinking History*, London: Routledge.
Jenkins, Keith (2009), *At the Limits of History: Essays on Theory and Practice*, London: Routledge.
Jenkins, Keith (2010), 'Inventing the New from the Old – From White's "Tropics" to Vico's "Topics" (Referee's Report)', *Rethinking History*, 14 (2): 243–8.

Jordheim, Helge (2014), 'Introduction: Multiple Times and the Work of Synchronization', *History and Theory*, 53 (4): 498–518.
Kleinberg, Ethan (2017), *Haunting History: For a Deconstructive Approach to the Past*, Stanford, CA: Stanford University Press.
Koselleck, Reinhart (2002), *The Practice of Conceptual History: Timing History, Spacing Concepts*, trans. Todd Samuel Presner et al., Stanford, CA: Stanford University Press.
Koselleck, Reinhart (2004), *Futures Past: On the Semantics of Historical Time*, trans. Keith Tribe, New York: Columbia University Press.
Kuhn, Thomas ([1962] 2012), *The Structure of Scientific Revolutions*, Chicago: University of Chicago Press.
Kumar, Krishan (1987), *Utopia and Anti-Utopia in Modern Times*, Oxford: Blackwell.
Kuukkanen, Jouni-Matti (2015), *Postnarrativist Philosophy of Historiography*, Basingstoke: Palgrave.
La Greca, María Inés (2016), 'Hayden White and Joan W. Scott's Feminist History: The Practical Past, the Political Present and an Open Future', *Rethinking History*, 20 (3): 395–413.
Laclau, Ernesto (1992), 'Beyond Emancipation', *Development and Change*, 23 (3): 121–37.
Laclau, Ernesto and Chantal Mouffe (1985), *Hegemony and Socialist Strategy: Towards a Radical Democratic Politics*, London: Verso.
Le Roy Ladurie, Emmanuel (1978), *Montaillou: Cathars and Catholics in a French Village, 1294–1324*, trans. Barbara Bray, London: Scolar Press.
Lenton, Timothy M., Hermann Held, Elmar Kriegler, Jim W. Hall, Wolfgang Lucht, Stefan Rahmstorf and Hans Joachim Schellnhuber (2008), 'Tipping Elements in the Earth's Climate System', *PNAS* 105 (6): 1786–93.
Levi, Giovanni (1991), 'On Microhistory', in Peter Burke (ed.), *New Perspectives on Historical Writing*, 93–113, Cambridge: Polity.
Levitas, Ruth (1990), *The Concept of Utopia*, Oxford: Berel Lang.
Lorenz, Chris (1998), 'Can Histories be True? Narrativism, Positivism and the "Metaphorical Turn"', *History and Theory*, 37 (3): 309–29.
Lorenz, Chris (2008), 'Drawing the Line: Scientific History between Myth-making and Myth-breaking', in Stefan Berger, Linas Eriksonas and Andrew Mycock (eds), *Narrating the Nation: Representations in History, Media and the Arts*, 35–55, New York: Berghahn Books.
Lorenz, Chris (2014), 'It Takes Three to Tango: History between the "Practical" and the "Historical" Past', *Storia della Storiografia*, 65 (1): 29–46.
Lorenz, Chris and Berber Bevernage, eds (2013), *Breaking up Time: Negotiating the Borders between Present, Past and Future*, Göttingen: Vanderhoeck & Ruprecht.
Louch, A. R. (1969), 'History as Narrative', *History and Theory*, 8 (1): 54–70.
Löwith, Karl (1957), *Meaning in History: The Theological Implications of the Philosophy of History*, Chicago: University of Chicago Press.
Lyotard, Jean-François (1991), *The Inhuman: Reflections on Time*, trans. Geoffrey Bennington and Rachel Bowbly, Stanford, CA: Stanford University Press.
Lyotard, Jean-François (1994), *Lessons on the Analytic of the Sublime*, trans. Elizabeth Rottenberg, Stanford, CA: Stanford University Press.
Magnússon, Sigurður Gylfi and István M. Szijártó (2013), *What is Microhistory? Theory and Practice*, London: Routledge.
Mandelbaum, Maurice (1948), 'A Critique of Philosophies of History', *Journal of Philosophy*, 45 (14): 365–78.

Mandelbaum, Maurice (1971), *History, Man and Reason: A Study in Nineteenth-Century Thought*, Baltimore: Johns Hopkins University Press.
Mannheim, Karl ([1936] 1998), *Ideology and Utopia: An Introduction to the Sociology of Knowledge*, London: Routledge.
Manning, Patrick (2013), *Big Data in History*, Basingstoke: Palgrave.
Marx, Karl ([1888] 1978), 'Theses on Feuerbach', in Robert C. Tucker (ed.), *The Marx-Engels Reader*, 143–5, New York: W. W. Norton & Company.
Marx, Karl and Friedrich Engels ([1848] 1978), 'Manifesto of the Communist Party', in Robert C. Tucker (ed.), *The Marx-Engels Reader*, 469–500, New York: W. W. Norton & Company.
Mecklin, John, ed. (2018), 'It Is Two Minutes to Midnight: 2018 Doomsday Clock Statement', Science and Security Board, *Bulletin of the Atomic Scientists*. Available online: https://thebulletin.org/sites/default/files/2018%20Doomsday%20Clock%20Statement.pdf (accessed 27 December 2018).
Megill, Allan (2015), '"Big History" Old and New: Presuppositions, Limits, Alternatives', *Journal of the Philosophy of History*, 9 (2): 306–26.
Meillassoux, Quentin (2008), *After Finitude: An Essay on the Necessity of Contingency*, trans. Ray Brassier, London: Continuum.
Meinhof, Marius (2017), 'Colonial Temporality and Chinese National Modernization Discourses', *InterDisciplines*, 8 (1): 51–80.
Mercer, Calvin and Tracy J. Trothen, eds (2015), *Religion and Transhumanism: The Unknown Future of Human Enhancement*, Santa Barbara, CA: Praeger.
Merleau-Ponty, Maurice (1968), *The Visible and the Invisible*, trans. Alphonso Lingis, Evanston, IL: Northwestern University Press.
Merleau-Ponty, Maurice (2004), *Phenomenology of Perception*, trans. Colin Smith, London: Routledge.
Mikhail, Alan (2016), 'Enlightenment Anthropocene', *Eighteenth-Century Studies*, 49 (2): 211–31.
More, Thomas ([1516] 2002), *Utopia*, ed. George M. Logan and Robert M. Adams, Cambridge: Cambridge University Press.
Mouffe, Chantal (2005), *On the Political*, London: Routledge.
Moyn, Samuel (2010), *The Last Utopia: Human Rights in History*, Cambridge, MA: Harvard University Press.
Munslow, Alun (2007), *Narrative and History*, Basingstoke: Palgrave.
Munslow, Alun (2010), *The Future of History*, Basingstoke: Palgrave.
Musk, Elon (2017), 'Making Humans a Multi-Planetary Species', *New Space*, 5 (2): 46–61.
Nancy, Jean-Luc (1993), *The Birth to Presence*, trans. Brian Holmes et al., Stanford, CA: Stanford University Press.
Nancy, Jean-Luc (2000), *Being Singular Plural*, trans. Robert D. Richardson and Anne E. O'Byrne, Stanford, CA: Stanford University Press.
North, Michael (2013), *Novelty: A History of the New*, Chicago: University of Chicago Press.
Northcott, Michael (2015), 'Eschatology in the Anthropocene: From the Chronos of Deep Time to the Kairos of the Age of Humans', in Clive Hamilton, Christophe Bonneuil and François Gemenne (eds), *The Anthropocene and the Global Environmental Crisis: Rethinking Modernity in a New Epoch*, 100–11, London: Routledge.
Nuttall, Mark (2012), 'Tipping Points and the Human World: Living with Change and Thinking about the Future', *Ambio*, 41 (1): 96–105.

Oakeshott, Michael ([1933] 1966), *Experience and Its Modes*, Cambridge: Cambridge University Press.
Oreskes, Nancy and Erik M. Conway (2014), *The Collapse of Western Civilization: A View from the Future*, New York: Columbia University Press.
Osterhammel, Jürgen (2014), *The Transformation of the World: A Global History of the Nineteenth Century*, trans. Patrick Camiller, Princeton, NJ: Princeton University Press.
Partner, Nancy (2013), 'Foundations: Theoretical Framework for Knowledge of the Past', in Nancy Partner and Sarah Foot (eds), *The SAGE Handbook of Historical Theory*, 1–8, Los Angeles: SAGE.
Paul, Herman (2011), *Hayden White: The Historical Imagination*, Cambridge: Polity Press.
Paul, Herman (2015), 'Relations to the Past: A Research Agenda for Historical Theorists', *Rethinking History*, 19 (3): 450–8.
Pihlainen, Kalle (2012), 'What if the Past Were Accessible After All?' *Rethinking History*, 16 (3): 323–39.
Pihlainen, Kalle (2013), 'Rereading Narrative Constructivism', *Rethinking History*, 17 (4): 509–27.
Pihlainen, Kalle (2014a), 'On Historical Consciousness and Popular Pasts', *História da Historiografia*, 15 (August): 10–26.
Pihlainen, Kalle (2014b), 'The Eternal Return of Reality: On Constructivism and Current Historical Desires', *Storia della Storiografia*, 65 (1): 103–15.
Pihlainen, Kalle (2017), *The Work of History: Constructivism and a Politics of the Past*, London: Routledge.
Popper, Karl ([1945] 2013), *The Open Society and its Enemies*, Princeton, NJ: Princeton University Press.
Popper, Karl ([1957] 2002), *The Poverty of Historicism*, London: Routledge.
Radkau, Joachim (2017), *Geschichte der Zukunft: Prognosen, Visionen, Irrungen in Deutschland von 1945 bis Heute*, Munich: Hanser.
Rancière, Jacques (1999), *Disagreement: Politics and Philosophy*, trans. Julie Rose, Minneapolis: University of Minnesota Press.
Reichenbach, Hans (1938), *Experience and Prediction: An Analysis of the Foundations and the Structure of Knowledge*, Chicago: University of Chicago Press.
Rheinberger, Hans-Jörg (2010), *On Historicizing Epistemology: An Essay*, trans. David Fernbach, Stanford, CA: Stanford University Press.
Ricœur, Paul (1984–1988), *Time and Narrative*, 3 vols., trans. Kathleen McLaughlin and David Pellauer, Chicago: University of Chicago Press.
Rigney, Ann (1990), *The Rhetoric of Historical Representation: Three Narrative Histories of the French Revolution*, Cambridge: Cambridge University Press.
Rigney, Ann (2013), 'History as Text: Narrative Theory and History', in Nancy Partner and Sarah Foot (eds), *The SAGE Handbook of Historical Theory*, 183–201, Los Angeles: SAGE.
Robin, Libby (2013), 'Histories for Changing Times: Entering the Anthropocene?' *Australian Historical Studies*, 44 (3): 329–40.
Rorty, Richard (1989), *Contingency, Irony, and Solidarity*, Cambridge: Cambridge University Press.
Rosa, Hartmut (2013), *Social Acceleration: A New Theory of Modernity*, trans. Jonathan Trejo-Mathys, New York: Columbia University Press.
Rosenstone, Robert A. (1988), *Mirror in the Shrine: American Encounters with Meiji Japan*, Cambridge, MA: Harvard University Press.

Roth, Michael S. (2007), 'Ebb Tide', *History and Theory*, 46 (1): 66–73.
Runia, Eelco (2006), 'Presence', *History and Theory*, 45 (1): 1–29.
Runia, Eelco (2010), 'Reply to Jenkins', *Rethinking History*, 14 (2): 249–50.
Runia, Eelco (2014), *Moved by the Past: Discontinuity and Historical Mutation*, New York: Columbia University Press.
Rüsen, Jörn (2016), 'Post-ism: The Humanities, Displaced by their Trends', *Public History Weekly*, 4 (27). doi: 10.1515/phw-2016-6895.
Samuel, Lawrence R. (2009), *Future: A Recent History*, Austin: University of Texas Press.
Schiffman, Zachary Sayre (2011), *The Birth of the Past*, Baltimore: Johns Hopkins University Press.
Schiller, Friedrich ([1801] 2001), *On the Sublime*, trans. William F. Wertz Jr., The Schiller Institute. Available online: http://www.schillerinstitute.org/transl/trans_on_sublime.html (accessed 27 December 2018).
Schmitt, Carl (1999), 'The Buribunks: A Historico-Philosophical Meditation', in Friedrich A. Kittler, *Gramophone, Film, Typewriter*, trans. Geoffrey Winthrop-Young and Michael Wutz, 231–42, Stanford, CA: Stanford University Press.
Seven (1997), [Film] Dir. David Fincher, USA: New Line Cinema.
Shanahan, Murray (2015), *The Technological Singularity*, Cambridge, MA: MIT Press.
Sharon, Tamar (2014), *Human Nature in an Age of Biotechnology: The Case for Mediated Posthumanism*, Dordrecht: Springer.
Shklar, Judith (1957), *After Utopia: The Decline of Political Faith*, Princeton, NJ: Princeton University Press.
Shusterman, Richard and Adele Tomlin, eds (2008), *Aesthetic Experience*, London: Routledge.
Shyrock, Andrew and Daniel Lord Smail (2011), *Deep History: The Architecture of Past and Present*, Berkeley: University of California Press.
Simon, Zoltán Boldizsár (2015a), 'History Manifested: Making Sense of Unprecedented Change', *European Review of History*, 22 (5): 819–34.
Simon, Zoltán Boldizsár (2015b), 'History Set into Motion Again', *Rethinking History*, 19 (4): 651–67.
Simon, Zoltán Boldizsár (2017), 'Why the Anthropocene Has No History: Facing the Unprecedented', *The Anthropocene Review*, 4 (3): 239–45.
Simon, Zoltán Boldizsár (2018a), '(The Impossibility of) Acting upon a Story That We Can Believe', *Rethinking History*, 22 (1): 105–25.
Simon, Zoltán Boldizsár (2018b), 'History Begins in the Future', in Stefan Helgesson and Jayne Svenungsson (eds), *The Ethos of History: Time and Responsibility*, 192–209, New York: Berghahn Books.
Simon, Zoltán Boldizsár (2018c), 'The Story of Humanity and the Challenge of Posthumanity', *History of the Human Sciences*, published online ahead of print, 18 July 2018. doi: 10.1177/0952695118779519.
Simon, Zoltán Boldizsár and Jouni-Matti Kuukkanen (2015), 'Introduction: Assessing Narrativism', *History and Theory*, 54 (2): 153–61.
Skrimshire, Stefan (2014), 'Climate Change and Apocalyptic Faith', *Wiley Interdisciplinary Reviews: Climate Change*, 5 (2): 233–46.
Smail, Daniel Lord (2008), *On Deep History and the Brain*, Berkeley: University of California Press.
Spengler, Oswald ([1918–1922] 1991), *The Decline of the West. An Abridged Edition*, trans. Charles Francis Atkinson, Oxford: Oxford University Press.

Spiegel, Gabrielle M. (2013), 'Above, about and beyond the Writing of History: A Retrospective View of Hayden White's *Metahistory* on the 40th Anniversary of its Publication', *Rethinking History*, 17 (4): 492–508.
Stengers, Isabelle (2015), *In Catastrophic Times: Resisting the Coming Barbarism*, Open Humanities Press.
Svenungsson, Jayne (2016), *Divining History: Prophetism, Messianism and the Development of the Spirit*, trans. Stephen Donovan, New York: Berghahn Books.
Tamm, Marek (2015), 'Introduction: Afterlife of Events: Perspectives on Mnemohistory', in Marek Tamm (ed.), *Afterlife of Events: Perspectives on Mnemohistory*, 1–23, Basingstoke: Palgrave.
Tengelyi, László (2004), *The Wild Region in Life-History*, trans. Géza Kállay and the author, Evanston, IL: Northwestern University Press.
Tengelyi, László (2007), *Erfahrung und Ausdruck: Phänomenologie im Umbruch bei Husserl und Seinen Nachfolgern*, Dordrecht: Springer.
Terminator 2: Judgment Day (1991), [Film] Dir. James Cameron, USA: TriStar Pictures.
Thomas, Julia Adeney (2014), 'History and Biology in the Anthropocene: Problems of Scale, Problems of Value', *American Historical Review*, 119 (5): 1587–607.
Tirosh-Samuelson, Hava (2012), 'Transhumanism as a Secularist Faith', *Zygon*, 47 (4): 710–34.
Toynbee, Arnold (1934–1961), *A Study of History*, 12 vols., Oxford: Oxford University Press.
Trivellato, Francesca (2011), 'Is There a Future for Italian Microhistory in the Age of Global History?', *California Italian Studies*, 2 (1). Available online: http://www.escholarship.org/uc/item/0z94n9hq (accessed 27 December 2018).
Tucker, Aviezer (2004), *Our Knowledge of the Past: A Philosophy of Historiography*, Cambridge: Cambridge University Press.
Unger, Roberto Mangabeira (2009), *The Left Alternative*, London: Verso.
Van De Mieroop, Kenan (2016), 'On the Advantage and Disadvantage of Black History Month for Life: The Creation of the Post-Racial Era', *History and Theory*, 55 (1): 3–24.
Vattimo, Gianni (1987), 'The End of (Hi)story', *Chicago Review*, 35 (4): 20–30.
Vieira, Patrícia and Michael Marder, eds (2012), *Existential Utopia: New Perspectives on Utopian Thought*, London: Continuum.
Vinge, Vernor (1993), 'The Coming Technological Singularity: How to Survive in the Post-Human Era', in *Vision-21: Interdisciplinary Science and Engineering in the Era of Cyberspace*, 11–22, Proceedings of a symposium cosponsored by the NASA Lewis Research Center and the Ohio Aerospace Institute, Westlake, Ohio, 30–31 March 1993.
Vrielink, Jocghum (2012), 'Effort to Ban Tintin Comic Book Fails in Belgium', *The Guardian*, 14 May 2012. Available online: https://www.theguardian.com/law/2012/may/14/effort-ban-tintin-congo-fails (accessed 27 December 2018).
Weber, Max ([1930] 2001), *The Protestant Ethic and the Spirit of Capitalism*, trans. Talcott Parsons, London: Routledge.
Westworld (2016 –), [TV series] HBO, 2 October.
White, Hayden (1973), *Metahistory: The Historical Imagination in Nineteenth-Century Europe*, Baltimore: Johns Hopkins University Press.
White, Hayden (1978), *Tropics of Discourse: Essays in Cultural Criticism*, Baltimore: Johns Hopkins University Press.
White, Hayden (1987), *The Content of the Form: Narrative Discourse and Historical Representation*, Baltimore: Johns Hopkins University Press.
White, Hayden (2012), 'Politics, History, and the Practical Past', *Storia della Storiografia*, 61 (1): 127–33.

White, Hayden (2014), *The Practical Past*, Evanston, IL: Northwestern University Press.
Williams, Robert C. and Philip L. Cantelon, eds (1984), *The American Atom: A Documentary History of Nuclear Policies from the Discovery of Fission to the Present, 1939-1984*, Philadelphia: University of Pennsylvania Press.
Windschuttle, Keith (1994), *The Killing of History: How a Discipline is Being Murdered by Literary Critics and Social Theorists*, Paddington, NSW: Macleay Press.
Wolfe, Cary (2010), *What is Posthumanism?*, Minneapolis: University of Minnesota Press.
Wyschogrod, Edith (2004), 'Representation, Narrative, and the Historian's Promise', in David Carr, Thomas R. Flynn and Rudolf A. Makkreel (eds), *The Ethics of History*, 28-44, Evanston, IL: Northwestern University Press.
Žižek, Slavoj (2010), *Living in the End Times*, London: Verso.

Index

Abba 116
acceleration 8, 56
   social acceleration 181–3
action
   motivation for action 159–60, 163, 170, 184
   political 90–3, 149, 159, 178–9, 185–6
   preventive 8, 185
Adorno, Theodor 95–6
aesthetic 21, 30, 64, 116–19, 123, 127–8, 143, 145–8, 151–2
Agamben, Giorgio 98, 110
agency 81–4
ahistoricity 5, 54, 161
Alltagsgeschichte 158
Althusser, Louis 72
Anthropocene 4, 24–5, 82–5
anthropocentrism 10, 64
anthropogenic
   change in the earth system 82
   climate change 7–8, 82–3
   existential risk 82–3
   human-induced technological and ecological change 180–1
anthropos 84
Anti-Nowhere League 124
apocalypse
   apocalyptic event 93
   apocalyptic future prospects 81
   apocalyptic rhetoric 81
   biblical apocalypticism 98
   climate apocalypse 7, 83
   nuclear apocalypse 83
   technological apocalypse 82
apophatic past 29, 56, 63, 74–8
apophatic theology 56, 63
Appleby, Joyce 128
Arendt, Hannah x, 82, 86, 165
Aron, Raymond 6
artificial intelligence 4, 7, 9–10, 23, 26, 85, 96, 139
   greater-than-human intelligence 8–9, 83, 101
   superintelligence 9, 83
Assmann, Aleida 1–2

Bacon, Francis 89, 91
Badiou, Alain 98–9, 101, 175, 185–7
Baudrillard, Jean 47
becoming *vs.* coming 53–5
Bell, Daniel 50
Berlin Holocaust Memorial 153
Bevernage, Berber 72–3
big history 34–5
bioengineering 7, 10, 85
biotechnology 4, 10, 85–6, 181
Bloch, Ernst 72
Blumenberg, Hans 98, 100
Bonneuil, Christophe 84
Bostrom, Nick 9, 21, 82–3, 86
Brigadier General Farrell, Thomas F. 142, 144
Burke, Edmund 144–5
Butler, Judith 177–8

Campanella, Tommaso 89
capitalism 20, 81, 99
Carr, David 128, 133
cataclysm 80, 83, 88, 94, 97, 99
catastrophe
   catastrophic future prospects 7–9, 29, 80–3, 101
   catastrophism 23, 81
   existential catastrophe 8–9
Chakrabarty, Dipesh 84
change. *See also* anthropogenic, climate change
   change over time ix–x, 3–5, 11, 16, 24, 28, 31, 33, 35, 37, 45–6, 57, 59, 90, 93–4, 96, 99–100, 102, 105, 107–8, 159, 165–8, 171, 173–5, 180–1, 183–4, 188–90

conceptual x
historical ix–x, 3–4, 16, 31, 33–7, 41, 45, 48–9, 54, 61, 79, 105–6, 108, 159, 168–70, 174, 189
historiographical x, 30–1, 105–8, 125–7, 130, 162–4, 167–70, 174
in human affairs ix, xi, 3, 5, 8–9, 17, 24–5, 28–30, 33, 35, 39, 45–50, 57–8, 90, 93, 96, 105, 174, 180, 184, 188
large-scale 3–4, 46, 54
linguistic 109, 120, 125–6
political 99, 175, 178–82, 184–6
processual and/or developmental 5, 11, 90, 108, 168, 179
unprecedented xi, 6–13, 16, 23–30, 57, 59, 63, 68, 75, 80, 84, 87–8, 97–102, 108, 165, 168–70, 173–5, 179–81, 183–5, 187, 190
Christian, David 34
Christianity 13–14, 21, 88, 97–8, 176, 188
chronotope 2, 102, 174
collective singular 41, 56, 62
Collingwood, Robin G. 72, 114–15
coming-to-existence 53–4, 75, 176, 186
coming-to-presence 53–4, 69, 75
Communism 92, 186–7
Comte, August 44, 92, 180
Condorcet 43
constructionism 14–15
context of discovery 129–33
context of justification 129–30, 132
continuity xi, 16, 20–2, 24, 26, 29, 43, 45, 48–9, 56–8, 62, 71, 84, 86, 100, 133, 175
Cornell, Drucilla 177
Critchley, Simon 159–60

Danto, Arthur 39, 42–3, 45–6
Darnton, Robert 118–19, 140, 145
Davidson, Donald 123–4
deep history 35
demand and approval 151, 159–64
Dennis, John 144
Derrida, Jacques 12, 72, 176–7, 179, 181, 185
desire of being *vs.* desire to know 51–2
development x, 1, 3, 5–11, 14–16, 20, 22, 24–6, 28–9, 34–5, 44–6, 53, 58, 70, 72–3, 80, 86, 90, 92–7, 99–102, 107–8, 143, 165, 168, 173, 176, 179–80, 184, 189–90
developmental historical sensibility 6, 29, 102, 173, 180, 184
developmental movement 46
developmental process 1, 7–8, 80, 165
developmental view 44–5, 55, 72
historical development 92, 95
vs. progress 44
as unfolding 35, 44–5 (*see also* unfolding)
directionality viii, 28, 34–5, 37, 58, 70, 80, 93, 96–7, 165, 175–7, 182
disconnection xi, 7, 11–12, 20, 24, 26, 56–8, 102, 109, 119, 125
discontinuity 21, 48–9, 71, 100, 117–19, 144
disrupted singular 28, 41, 50, 54–8, 61–3, 68–9, 73–6, 78, 103, 168
disruption 56–7, 70
dissociation
dissociative measures 12, 61, 68, 75, 79, 94
identity-dissociation 11, 29
as relation to the past 6, 11–16, 20, 29, 48–9, 52, 56, 61–78, 101, 144
'Doesn't look like anything to me' 139–43, 145–6, 151–2, 157–9, 168–9
Dolores (character in *Westworld*) 139–41, 145
Domanska, Ewa 65
domesticating the new 20–7, 81, 84
Doomsday Clock 83
Doran, Robert 144
Double Helix History 85
dystopia
dystopian visions of the future 8, 29, 81, 83, 87
posthistorical dystopia 80, 87–8, 93–101, 103
postwar dystopianism 8, 29, 87–8, 90, 93, 96

earth system 82, 84
ecology 4–6, 9–11, 80–1, 88, 93, 96, 98–9, 173, 175, 180–1, 183–5
Eisenman, Peter 153
emancipation 25–6, 174–80, 184–5,187

Index

emancipation dilemma 175–9
emancipatory event 187
emancipatory politics 26, 92
emancipatory promise 176–7, 180–1, 185
emancipatory thinking 17, 22–3, 25, 27, 99, 176, 179–80, 187
encounter
   'doesn't look like anything to me' encounter 140–2, 145–6, 152, 157–9, 168–9
   experience as encounter 30, 116–18, 125, 127–49, 158
   encountering non-sense 149, 151, 169–70
   encountering the world and the past 30–1, 127–49, 168–9
end of history 3–5, 46–7, 50, 79, 85, 176–7, 180–1, 188
Engels, Friedrich 91–2
Enlightenment ix, 2, 6–8, 14, 33, 36, 41, 43–6, 77, 86, 95–6
epistemology 55, 117, 127–30
eschatology viii–ix, 21, 88, 97–101
ethics 76–7, 80, 90–3, 96, 99, 111, 127, 131
   ethical demand 31, 119, 122, 124
   of history 72–3, 149, 151–71
   responsibility toward the dead 162–3, 166
existential risk 82–3, 86
experience vii, ix, xi, 1–2, 22, 30–1, 40, 56–7, 61–2, 64–6, 89, 102, 109–26, 163, 169–70, 176, 182
   aesthetic 116–19, 123, 127, 143–9, 151–2
   disruptive 119, 121, 127
   duality of 121
   ethical 159–60
   everyday 61
   historical 30, 40, 109–28, 130–2, 134–5, 138, 143, 145, 149, 151–3, 156–60, 163, 169–70
   immediate 30, 109–10, 112, 117, 125, 152, 156–7
   ineffable 30, 119, 142
      Ankersmit, Frank 40, 128, 143
   initial moment of 30, 123, 133, 135, 138, 140, 143, 145–6, 151, 158
   lived 158, 163
   modes of experience 66

   mute 30, 110–11, 117, 119, 121, 123–5, 127, 157
   non-linguistic 30
   phenomenological 118
   real-life 152–4, 158
   sublime 40, 116, 143–6
   thwarting expectations 118–19, 121, 124, 141
   wordless 110
experientiality 71, 151–9, 162, 167
experimental history 131
expression 30–1, 88, 109, 112–28, 130–2, 135, 138, 145,149, 151, 153, 157–61, 163–4, 169–70
external reality 30, 133–5, 137–8, 143, 148
external world 30, 135–9, 169
extinction 7–8, 10–11, 23, 84, 86, 98, 101
event. *See also* historical sensibility, evental
   apocalyptic 93
   disruptive 54
   emancipatory 187
   encounter-event 30–1, 116, 134–5, 138–43, 145–6, 148, 151–2, 157, 159
   eruptive 80, 83, 93, 97, 101
   extinction event 86, 101
   game-changer 83, 9, 177, 185
   historical 15, 42, 165
   momentous 54
   political theories of the event 175–9, 185–7
   revolutionary 99
   singular 7, 11, 29, 80, 88, 97, 99, 101, 177
   sublime 48
   sudden 80–1, 83, 93, 101
   temporality of the event 29, 88, 101, 174
   transformative 29, 177
   traumatic 48
   unprecedented 29
evolution 47, 49, 82, 107, 180
   cultural 58

Fludernik, Monika 152, 154–5
Foucault, Michel 16
Fourier, Charles 91
Fressoz, Jean-Baptiste 84

Freud, Sigmund 48, 149
Froeyman, Anton 12, 111–12, 161–2, 164
Fukuyama, Francis 3–5, 46, 85–6, 176, 181, 183, 188
future vii–xi, 1–11, 13–16, 20–2, 24–5, 27, 29, 31, 41–7, 50–9, 62–4, 66, 69, 74–5, 77, 79–103, 136, 159–61, 164–71, 174–81, 183–5, 187
  better/desired 3, 24, 86–7, 90, 92–3, 97, 179
  catastrophic 29, 81
  expectations of the future 4–5, 9, 20, 85
  future-disorientation 80, 93
  future-orientation 2, 4, 29, 79–80, 87, 89–93, 97
  posthuman 10, 86, 181
  promise of the future 7–9, 85–7, 95, 174–9, 181, 188
  prospects/visions of the future 3–11, 13, 20–2, 27, 29, 31, 79–81, 83, 85–8, 92–4, 98, 101–2, 164, 168–9, 171, 175, 181
  threatening future 4, 8–10, 80–7, 93–4, 96–9, 179
  unprecedented 16, 79–103
  unrealizable 178–9

Gadamer, Hans-Georg 118
Geldof, Bob 160
General Groves 142
genome editing 9, 85
Ghosh, Ranjan 70
Ginzburg, Carlo 128, 166
global history 35–6
Goodman, Nelson 137–9
Grave, Johannes 65
Gumbrecht, Hans Ulrich 1–2, 69, 102, 111–12, 117, 127, 134–5, 155–8, 174

Hacking, Ian 14–15, 130
Hamilton, Clive 82
Hartog, François 1–2, 4–6, 8–9
Hegel, Georg Wilhelm Friedrich 43–4, 46, 186
historical knowledge 34, 42, 66–7, 170
  essentially contested 76–8, 132
historical past 63, 65–8, 74, 76
historical sensibility ix, xi, 2, 4–7, 15–16, 57, 61, 75, 100

eventual 29, 31, 102–3, 173–5, 180, 186–90
modern vii, x, 1, 6, 8, 14–16, 20–1, 23, 25–6, 57, 79, 86, 93, 95–7, 100–1, 173, 175–6, 178, 186, 188–90
postwar 1–2, 8, 16, 25–6, 57, 97–8, 173
processual/developmental ix, 6, 29, 102, 107, 173, 175–80, 182–7, 189–90
historical time 2, 27, 57, 61–2, 64, 69, 72–3, 75
historical writing 16–17, 19–22, 24, 27–31, 34, 49–50, 55–6, 61, 63, 67, 71–2, 74–8, 105–6, 108, 113, 121–2, 126–8, 132, 154–7, 162–3, 165, 169–71, 173
historiographical revision 105
historiography ix–xi, 13, 17–19, 23–4, 30, 34–6, 39, 42–3, 66–8, 71, 77, 105–8, 128, 130, 152–3, 155–6, 159, 162, 165–71
history from below 67, 158, 167
The History Manifesto 35
history of mentalities 158
Horkheimer, Max 95–6
human enhancement 7, 10, 23, 26, 85–6, 179
humanity 5, 7–9, 21, 33, 58, 80–4, 86, 90, 95, 100, 124, 176
Hunt, Lynn 128
Husserl, Edmund 61–2, 133

identity 11–12, 16, 29, 48–9, 51–2, 54–6, 62–3, 74, 94, 101, 116, 143. *See also* dissociation
  identity politics 12
  self-identity 15, 189
inexistent 185–7

Jackson, Michael 116
Jacob, Margaret 128
Jameson, Frederic 90
Jankélévitch, Vladimir 72
Jasanoff, Sheila 21
Jenkins, Keith 19, 47, 67, 70, 134–7, 145, 147, 164
justice and injustice 4, 72–3, 166, 176, 179

Kant, Immanuel 109–10, 115, 117, 144
Kekulé, August 129

Kellner, Hans 110–11
Kleinberg, Ethan 70
knowledge 10, 16, 29, 34, 42–3, 45, 50–3, 55, 57, 62, 66–7, 74–8, 84, 89, 92, 105, 114, 117, 123, 130, 132, 135–9, 170, 178. *See also* historical knowledge
Koselleck, Reinhart ix–xi, 28, 41, 65–7, 61–2, 87–90, 94–5, 105, 182
Kuhn, Thomas 129–30
Kumar, Krishan 89, 91

Laclau, Ernesto 177
La Greca, María Inés 67
language 30, 43, 109–16, 119–25, 134, 137, 143, 148, 152, 157, 169
    linguistic conceptualization 30, 111, 114, 118, 121, 135, 137–8, 142, 157
    non-linguistic 30, 109–11, 114–17, 120–2, 124–5, 134, 152, 169–70
Last Judgment 90, 97, 99
Latour, Bruno 130
Lord Voldemort 112
Lorenz, Chris 23, 65, 76, 128
Louch, Alfred Richard 155
Löwith, Karl viii–ix, 21, 42, 97–8, 100
Lyotard, Jean-François 143–4

makeability of history 90–2
Mandelbaum, Maurice 39, 44–5
Manhattan Project 141
Maradona, Diego 100
Marx, Karl 44, 91–2
    Marxism 41, 176
Meat Loaf 41, 61, 63
Mercier, Luois-Sébastien 89, 95
Merleau-Ponty, Maurice 120–1
Messi, Lionel 100
messianic without messianism 176–7
microhistory 35, 158, 162–3
moral anachronism 12
More, Thomas 89
motion
    history as movement 28, 40, 44–50, 53, 55, 71, 188
    motionlessness of history 46–7, 50
    suspension of history 47, 50
Moyn, Samuel 13–15
Muse 100
Musk, Elon 9

Nachleben 65
Nancy, Jean-Luc 40, 47–8, 51–4, 58, 69, 76, 176
nanotechnology 85
narrative 17, 110, 112–14, 116, 119, 120, 124, 134, 139, 148, 189
    historical narrative 17, 19, 22–3, 25, 113, 128–31, 152, 155, 157–8, 161
    metanarrative/grand narrative 6, 36
    narrative domestication 20, 22–4, 26–7
    narrative sentence 42
    narrativism 7, 17–20, 23–4, 27, 106–8, 122, 128–31, 135–6
    narrativity 154–5
    postnarrativism 128
nation-building 23, 67
Newman, Bartnett 116
Newton, Isaac 124, 129–30
non-human 10, 33, 81, 97, 139, 179, 184
North, Michael vii–viii
novelty vii–xi, 3, 9, 12–13, 20, 22, 24, 29–31, 73, 79, 81–2, 84, 87–8, 98–9, 105, 108, 111, 122–7, 131, 133, 157, 159, 162–5, 168, 170, 173–4, 185, 190
nuclear 7, 9, 25, 82, 83, 141

Oakeshott, Michael 65–6, 69–70, 74, 76
origin 14, 20, 53–4, 98
originary axiom 137
Osterhammel, Jürgen 35–6, 180
Owen, Robert 91

Partner, Nancy 34–5
Paul, Herman 64–5, 147
perfectibility 7–8, 25, 86
phenomenology 17, 61–2, 118–21, 132–3
philosophy of historiography 39, 42
philosophy of history viii–ix, 1–3, 6–7, 16–17, 20–2, 25, 27–30, 33–7, 39–59, 61, 63–5, 67–8, 70, 73, 75, 77, 92, 95–8, 102, 106, 108–10, 112–14, 126, 128–9, 132, 147, 155, 157, 169, 171, 176, 180, 186–7
    analytical 17, 41–2, 64, 113
    classical 17, 21, 28, 33–5, 41, 46, 51, 96, 176, 186–7
    critical 41
    cyclical-organicist 43–4

of the Enlightenment and German
    Idealism 41–3
linear and non-linear 43–5
Marxist 41
modern 2–3, 33, 37, 70, 97
narrative 16, 106, 108, 113, 128–9, 132, 157, 169
quasi-substantive 28–9, 39–59, 61, 68, 73, 75, 169
substantive 39–59, 46, 50, 77, 187
philosophy of science 129–30, 132
Pihlainen, Kalle 70, 135, 152–3
Plutarch 116
point of no return 7, 83
political domain 4, 17, 22, 26–7, 31, 50, 80–1, 86, 96, 98–9 173–90
    consensus politics 79
    crisis of the political 173, 179, 181–3, 185
    ethico-political 73, 80, 90–3, 96, 99
    political change 99, 175, 178–82, 184–6
    political theories of the Left 79–80, 102, 175–9, 181, 183, 185–7
    post-political 79
    sociopolitical 4–5, 26, 80–1
Popper, Karl 39
positivism 44, 92, 180
postism 13
posthuman 10–11, 13, 21, 86, 181, 184–5, 188
postmodern 6, 13, 19, 47, 67, 77, 110, 113, 131, 135, 143–4, 170, 188
poststructuralism 13, 17, 77, 110–11, 178
practical past 63, 65–70, 73–4, 76, 102, 174. *See also* White, Hayden
presence 58, 65, 69–75, 102, 134–5, 152–8, 174
    presentification 156, 162
    present past 29, 63, 65, 69–70, 72–8
presentism 1–2, 4–5, 7, 9, 50, 79–80, 102, 174, 180
prevention 96–7, 185
process vii, x, 1, 6–8, 14–15, 23, 25–6, 30, 44, 53, 89, 101, 128–33, 142, 147, 180–90
    historical process viii, x, 44–6, 54, 58, 61, 67, 77–80, 85, 90–2, 94–7, 149, 175, 177, 182, 184

process of expression 119–25, 158, 160, 164, 168
process of sense-making 30, 120, 142, 151–71
processual change/development 11, 14, 73, 84, 108, 166, 179, 190
processual historical sensibility 6, 29, 102, 107, 173, 175–80, 182–90
progress 4, 44–6, 50, 80, 92, 94

Radiohead 100
realism 30, 135–9
    irrealism 30, 137–9
    metaphysical 136–8, 157
    ontological 138
    realist irrealism 132, 138–9
    speculative 110
    transcendental 136
regime of historicity 2, 4–6
Reichenbach, Hans 129
representation
    historical representation 71, 109, 113, 119, 122, 124, 134, 147–8, 152–3, 161–2
    unrepresentable 143
Rheinberger, Hans-Jörg 130
Ricoeur, Paul 133
Rorty, Richard 124–6
Rosa, Hartmut 181–4
Rosenstone, Robert 131
Runia, Eelco xi, 21, 40–1, 48–9, 51–2, 54, 58, 69–73, 75, 111–12, 116, 127, 134–5, 152–4, 156–8
Rüsen, Jörn 13

Sattelzeit 28, 88–9
Schiffman, Zachary vii
Schiller, Friedrich 146–7, 149
Schmitt, Carl 89, 94–6
secular 63, 82, 97–9
    mundane world 9, 25, 90, 99, 174, 188
    secularized eschatology ix, 21, 97–8
sense-making 59, 128, 135, 139–40, 142–3, 145
    historical 21, 28, 37, 59, 151–71
    and non-sense 31, 143, 146–9
Seven (movie) 145
Shklar, Judith 50

space of dissociated knowledge and horizon of existence 57, 62
space of experience and horizon of expectation 56–7, 61, 66
Spengler, Oswald 41, 43–5
Stengers, Isabelle 81
#storypast (Twitter) 131
subject (of change) 5, 10–11, 14–16, 22, 33, 48, 51–5, 58, 69, 77, 90, 100
  change *of* the subject 11, 62, 100–1
  ontological 44–5, 47, 49, 54–5, 57, 77
  self-identical 16, 22, 45, 61–2, 189
  without prior existence 49, 53–4, 57, 185–7, 189
sublime 21, 31, 48–9, 52, 134, 143–9
  proto-sublime 31, 146, 148
  sublime historical experience 40, 116, 143–4
  sublimity of history 21, 146–9
substance 28, 45–7, 49, 53–4, 58, 61, 89, 100, 153
  narrative substance 129
substantive thinking and concerns 40–1, 47, 49, 53–5, 57–9
Svenungsson, Jayne 98

technological singularity 8, 83, 95
technology 4–11, 26–7, 80–3, 85–8, 93, 95–6, 98–9, 173, 175, 180–5
teleology 28, 176
temporality 11, 24–9, 42–6, 53, 56–7, 59, 62–4, 69, 72–3, 87–91, 93–6, 99, 159–61, 165–8, 179–80, 182–4, 186–7. *See also* historical time
  detemporalization of history 182–3
  developmental 29, 44–6, 96, 99, 101, 180
  disruption of time 57
  emancipatory 27, 99
  evental 29, 88, 101–3, 174–5
  processual 29, 101, 175, 179–80, 182–4, 186

temporal continuity viii, 22, 28, 80, 133, 175
temporal unity ix, 43, 57
Tengelyi, László 118–19, 121, 133
Terminator 2 (movie) 55, 141
theology 56, 63, 92, 98, 176
Toynbee, Arnold 41
transhumanism 4, 7, 10, 21, 82, 85–7, 179
trauma 48–9, 58, 125, 144–6
Trinity test 141–2, 144
truth 13, 14, 77, 124, 127–35

unfolding 15, 34, 35, 37, 44–5, 47, 53, 62, 77, 92, 182
unprecedented xi, 1, 6–13, 16, 18, 20, 22–31, 37, 57, 59, 63, 68, 75, 79–80, 82, 84, 87–8, 96–103, 108, 142, 165, 168–70, 173–5, 179–81, 183–5, 187, 189–90
utopia 6, 8, 13–14, 29, 50, 79–80, 86–8, 180
  anti-utopia/negative utopia 88, 93–7
  spatial 88–91, 93
  temporal 88–97
utopian socialism 8, 80, 91–2, 180

Vattimo, Gianni 47
Vinge, Vernor 83
Voltaire 116

Weber, Max 20
Western modernity viii, 8, 21–2, 25, 29, 56, 62, 68, 88, 94, 105, 165, 170, 180, 182, 184, 187
Westworld (series) 139–41, 145
White, Hayden 17–19, 21–4, 63, 65–70, 74, 76–7, 102, 106–8, 110, 113, 128–9, 131, 146–9, 174
Wyschogrod, Edith 161–2, 164

Žižek, Slavoj 81, 98–9

www.ingramcontent.com/pod-product-compliance
Lightning Source LLC
Chambersburg PA
CBHW052041300426
44117CB00012B/1916